# Breaking Digital Gridlock

# Breaking Digital Gridlock

## IMPROVING YOUR BANK'S DIGITAL FUTURE
## BY MAKING TECHNOLOGY CHANGES NOW

John Best

WILEY

*Library of Congress Cataloging-in-Publication Data:*
Names: Best, John, 1970– author.
Title: Breaking digital gridlock : improving your bank's digital future by making technology changes now / by John Best.
Description: Hoboken, New Jersey : John Wiley & Sons, Inc., [2018] | Includes bibliographical references and index. |
Identifiers: LCCN 2017060722 (print) | LCCN 2018000084 (ebook) | ISBN 9781119421993 (pdf) | ISBN 9781119421924 (epub) | ISBN 9781119421955 (cloth)
Subjects: LCSH: Banks and banking—Technological innovations. | Banks and banking—Information technology. | Bank management. | Information technology—Management.
Classification: LCC HG1709 (ebook) | LCC HG1709 .B48 2018 (print) | DDC 332.10285—dc23
LC record available at https://lccn.loc.gov/2017060722

# Contents

# Foreword

### Brett King

*International Bestselling Author of* Augmented: Life in the Smart Lane *and* Bank 4.0

Whenever you have a book that rounds out with a chapter entitled "Big Data and the Zombie Apocalypse," you know you're in for an unconventional ride, and yet I have to say the conclusions behind John Best's debut tome are undeniable and sound.

In a world where almost every industry on the planet is being transformed in some way by digital technologies, the question always seems to be can the incumbents do enough to survive? In the case of music, books, retail, transportation and video, we've seen enormous disruption through the emergence of pure-play digital competitors. Initially, this was through so-called e-commerce players during the dot com, and in 2007 it started all over again with the emergence of the iPhone and its App ecosystem. Today we're talking blockchain, artificial intelligence, robotics, energy transformation and gene therapy, but the pattern is the same. It's been the same since the luddites smashed up the steam machines, the first US transcontinental telegraph line killed off the pony express, and automobiles disrupted horses.

Faced with potential disruption many organizations delay a response, hoping upon hope that they'll be "different", and when the inevitability of change is evident, the organization is simply unable to adapt fast enough. Best tackles this from a practitioner's point of view, of someone who has been in the trenches trying to enable such transformation. He starts with the classic psychological myths that inhibit a reasoned response in the early days of the digital threat, and then details the building blocks of resistance and how to circumvent those processes, legacy behavior, thinking and systems.

I've seen many of the organizational symptoms Best identifies over and over again. Even today when we're seeing the emergence of so called "unicorns" in financial services such as Ant Financial, Stripe, Klarna, Credit Karma, Transfer Wise, Ripple, SoFi, LuFax and many more that could end up dominating in their categories, and where they've mostly already overtaken incumbent contemporaries – there's still uniform denial that there's any "threat".

*Breaking Digital Gridlock*, however, is about just that. It's about how you truly transform your organization. We hear a lot about digital transformation in the current day and age, but if you were to ask me (and I get asked this constantly) which banks or financial institutions were the best examples of true transformation, I'd struggle to identify a handful. Why? Because if you want to compete against the FinTechs and Technology (or TechFin) companies gunning for you, competing as a traditional player is like having both hands tied behind your back and your shoelaces tied together in a 100-meter world championship sprint final. If you're going to try to win or just survive in the digital world – you have to think and act differently.

From simple innovations like remote check deposit, through to cloud, AI, Blockchain and Crypto, Best meticulously explains what the evolutionary or revolutionary technology impact is, why you should be worried as an incumbent player, and what your options are. Later in the book when explaining API banking and PSD2, Best uses the analogy of the McDonald's brothers faced with the possibility of the franchising model and dismissing it as impossible or potentially that it would undermine their core business. Banks and FIs have some choices in this disruptive landscape, but culture, leadership, skill sets and approaches must all be revamped. It takes enormous will to embark on such a transformation.

In the final section around strategy, Best asks the fundamental question that all incumbents will need to ask themselves over the next 5–7 years in order to survive. *Are you a Technology Company that delivers Financial Services? Or are you a Financial Services Company that delivers via Technology?* Best argues that many FIs in the midst of *digital transformation* get stuck in the middle. They're certainly not technology companies because they don't have the experience, pedigree, people and technology to honestly stake that claim. But if you're going to compete against Unicorns who are born of tech, you can't do it as a part-time, conflicted technology wannabee. You need to step up your game – bigly.

The conclusions of Breaking Digital Gridlock are pretty clear. If you want to survive you're going to have to break as many of the typical gridlock barriers as possible, and you're only going to be able to do that through strong leadership, culture and capabilities that don't exist in your organization today. Best probably made the case for me that most organizations talking about transformation today are only just starting on a very long journey, and many of them simply are not capable of making enough changes quickly enough to be ultimately successful. However, what Best shows in his book, is that success is possible if you're willing to commit to a truly transformational approach.

As a teen that started his career essentially coding on a VIC-20, Best has seen the revolution of the internet, mobile, AI, cloud and blockchain through the eyes of a technologist. Today he represents a guild of experts and specialists that you will need to rely on every-day if you're financial institution is going to make it. It's for that reason alone that at the boardroom *Breaking Digital Gridlock* should be required reading. It will give you a nice, neat shopping list of projects you need to embark on to survive. If you don't, you'll miss the party.

My guess is if you're a CxO reading this you'll say, of course we want to survive the fintech revolution. Ok, then. Time to get started. Read on . . . .

Brett King

# Preface

grid·lock
ˈɡridˌläk
*noun*
noun: **gridlock**; plural noun: **gridlocks**
1. a traffic jam affecting a whole network of intersecting streets.

**H**ave you ever been in serious gridlock? When I was working in California, I would often have to drive from Pasadena to Yorba Linda. The 40-mile trip often took me three to four hours. Many days I would find myself on a freeway at a dead stop, sometimes for hours. It's a helpless feeling to sit there in your car, not moving. You are stuck and have no idea when it will clear up. Perhaps most unnerving is that you don't always know what is causing the gridlock.

While you settle in for the long wait, you start to look around. You get familiar with the people in other cars. Sometimes there is a weird moment where you catch them looking at you, and then you quickly look away (after all, it's not good gridlock etiquette to stare). The smell of the exhaust forces you to recirculate the air in your car. As you inch along the route, you suddenly find yourself reading every street sign and examining all of the details of the freeway that you wouldn't normally notice. Every now and then, you get just a glimpse of hope because the brake lights in front of you disappear and you move forward 10 or 15 feet and you think, "This is it! We are moving again!" Sometimes you even get up to 15 or 20 miles an hour and you begin to celebrate with your gridlock mates, remote high-fiving and smiling, mouthing the words, "We're moving!"—only to have the brake lights ahead glow red. You're stuck again. The small celebration you were just having with the guy in the BMW two lanes away is suddenly over. Meanwhile, someone somewhere is waiting for you to arrive, and there is nothing you can do to get there any faster.

To me, that's the same feeling as working in an environment where you can't seem to move forward. Every time you get enough steam to move ahead, something or someone thwarts it and you are back to being stuck in traffic.

## What Is Digital Gridlock?

Digital gridlock is made up of several different kinds of paralysis that, when combined, cause a slowdown or a dead stop in your organization. There are six organizational areas where paralysis can emerge:

1. Processes: Systems and workflows must keep up with technological advances to prevent digital gridlock.
2. Technology: As technology advances, it does more than affect processes; it also fundamentally changes the way people do business.
3. Security: A lack of preparation for security breaches can leave an organization vulnerable to attacks. This can not only put customers at risk but also lead to legal and financial liability and a damaged reputation.
4. People: The right people must be in the right positions for an organization to succeed.
5. Culture: Poor communication and lack of trust are two major symptoms of cultural paralysis. This prevents organizations from making the changes they need to.
6. Strategy: Governance, planning, and execution are at the heart of strategy. They will keep your organization moving forward.

This book is broken into six parts, each one corresponding to a particular area where organizational troubles can arise.

## Riskphobia

Riskphobic leaders have a default response to every new idea put on the table: *No!* This is interesting because measuring and deducing risk is a key competency for those of us working at financial institutions. It's how we make loans and investments and even determine the advice we give our customers. Yet, when it comes to technology, the financial sector is so afraid of regulations or creating waves that many have stopped progressing. Ironically, their fear of risk poses its own risk.

I believe riskphobia stems from a lack of data analysis. We have all of the data we need to make smart decisions, but we are afraid to implement it. We know more about our customers than any online retailer, search engine, or blog. We know what our customers buy, we know when they buy it, we know when they go on vacation or travel. The kind of data financial institutions possess is most valuable; Google, Amazon, or Apple would pay for it. Despite this, we're afraid to use it, even when it is in service of making our customers' lives better. Our customers will feel violated and that the institution will lose their trust. We live in fear that we will be called Big Brother or that we will unknowingly violate some obscure regulation and be fined by the Consumer Financial Protection Bureau (CFPB). No one wants to be on the 10 o'clock news. This paralysis of riskphobic leadership teaches your organization to be very skeptical of new technologies and to avoid new features, products, services, or business paradigms until they have been thoroughly worked out by someone else. While this may seem like a logical plan, this leads gridlocked businesses to stay on the stagnant highway instead of getting off at a promising exit to take a chance and circumvent the blockage. The belief is that it's less risky to stay on the road you are on than to try a new way to get there.

You can think of your customers as the people waiting on you to get to your destination. Your customers are waiting on you to roll out new features and their expectations of digital services are influenced based on their experiences with companies like Facebook, Amazon, Google, Netflix, and Apple. They expect a seamless experience and continuous improvement. They will be patient as long as they see progress, but if they sense that you are gridlocked they will look elsewhere for these services.

The next paralysis that causes gridlock is cultural paralysis. It happens like this: You've got a lot of folks working in your bank or your credit union, and some of the best employees are at the lower levels in the organization. They're the people who are interacting with the members every day. Coincidentally, they are also the lowest-paid

people on your staff. Frontline employees have tremendous opportunities to assess what customers want and what they don't like
about your business offerings, especially the digital services because
chances are if they are having to do a transaction manually its
because the transaction wasn't available in your digital banking
platform. These employees don't need a survey to find out how
customers feel and react to your services; they can see it and sense it
when they interact with customers. Unfortunately, most of the time
we don't give these employees a platform to share their firsthand
knowledge. As a result, there is no way for organizations to use
data from direct customer interactions and synthesize it to improve
business, products, and services. In most organizations, lower-level
employees are not empowered to fix issues and, as a result, they, too,
are stuck in paralysis.

I once did a presentation and I asked how many people had some
sort of innovation suggestion box. To my surprise, there were even
fewer than I thought. When I dug deeper, I found out that one of
them had an *anonymous* suggestion box. When I asked why it was
anonymous, the person couldn't answer. The only reason I can think
for a suggestion box to be anonymous is because people are afraid
to share their ideas. That says something serious about an organization's culture. I asked someone with a normal suggestion box how
they used the suggestions. They said they vet them and then talk to
the people who submitted the ideas that were deemed good. I asked
what they did with the suggestions they didn't use and they stated
they just set them aside, I asked if they reached out to the employee
to thank them for their submission and found that they did not. This
was fascinating to me, because I think every suggestion should be
followed up on. How would it feel to be an employee who takes the
risk of putting an idea on paper and submitting to leadership only
to never be acknowledged? Certainly demoralizing. If you were this
employee, would you be willing to submit another idea? The paralysis
of culture goes hand in hand with the paralysis of communication.

Digital gridlock occurs when all of these elements come together
and prevent an organization from moving forward. It is what makes
us feel helpless, stuck in a meeting for a project that is six months
behind schedule with no end in sight. We don't know if there is an
accident up ahead or if the road is permanently closed. The only way
out is to get a higher perspective to see how all of these elements are
interacting and identify the sticking points.

This book is a manual on how to break that gridlock. I will share with you how my teams and I have gotten things done and how other great organizations have been able to overcome stagnation. This book will help you defeat paralysis with proven management methods and technological approaches. These tools will help to align your organization in a way that promotes candid communication, rewards risk (when approached in the right way), and fosters innovation. Your financial institution will learn how to become data driven and how to drive results from that data. How to try and fail and still be okay and fail again and fail again after that, and do all of this without being on the 10 o'clock news. This book will help you get up to 80 miles an hour on that highway and feel the wind in your hair.

# Acknowledgments

There are so many people to thank for this book that it could've been another chapter. However here is a list (in no particular order, other than my family first).

My family, Christie, Ryan, Abby, Don, Lynn, Tracy and Melissa – You have all supported my craziness over the years and with out you I would never have been able to accomplish this.

Ed Gonzalez, Tom Stacy, Elliot Cotto and the rest of Best Innovation Group, thank you for not killing me while I was writing this.

Kevin and Susan Johnson – Thank you both for your support over the years in this industry, your insight and leadership was a big part of the inspiration for this book.

Kevin and Irene Sarber – Thank you for your support and enthusiasm for all my projects!

Suncoast, GTE, Wescom and all of the other organizations I have been a part of over the years, this includes every person I worked with and the members of each of these storied institutions. Each of the organizations shaped me.

The crew from WRG for all of the hours we spent in the trenches.

Paul Ablack and OnApproach, Paul and his group have helped shape the collaborative landscape of data analytics and I am deeply thankful for their support.

Kirk Kordelski – Thank you for your wisdom and guidance.

CUNA – The Credit Union National Association, Julie Esser, Eric Gelly, and Cheryl Sorenson who once said "you should write a book..."

My Podcast network. John Jancleas, Glen Sarvady, Anne Legg, Laura Wiese and all of the listeners.

Christina Verigan – The poor lady who was assigned to turn my giant mess of thinking into a book!

James Burke Frazier – The king of "what if we did this boss?" and one of the most creative people I have ever met.

Kirk Drake, Paul Fiore and Chris Otey- Who taught me how to be an entrepreneur and not give everything away.

Brett King – for inspiring me to follow in his footsteps (even if his shoes are too big to fill).

There are a million more people to thank and I have no doubt missed more than a few for this I apologize, there are only so many chapters in a book.

# Introduction

## Five Myths about Going Digital

Before an organization can break its digital gridlock, it is necessary to dispel the myths that prevent it from moving forward. In the past 20 years I have visited hundreds of credit unions and spoken to hundreds of executives and board members. Based on this experience, I have identified the top five myths that prevent that bank executives, board members, and staff from believing in digital. The first step in moving forward with digital transformation is to realize the truth.

### Myth 1: We Are Too Small for Digital

This is my favorite myth, and it's the easiest one to dispel. In terms of digital transformation, being small is actually a huge advantage. If you don't believe me, consider this for a moment: Why did the *Titanic* sink? Most people believe it is because the ship hit an iceberg.

Nope, I say. The *Titanic*'s crew saw the iceberg and may have had just enough time to correct their course.[1] I argue that the real reason the *Titanic* sank is because it couldn't turn in time. It's hard to turn a large ship, and large organizations face the same difficulties. The more people, branches, and assets an organization has, the longer it takes to retrain, revamp, and retool the people, places, and things required to support digital transformation. Smaller institutions have the advantage because they are more nimble. In fact, the biggest challenge for the smaller institution is not turning too quickly and throwing people overboard.

## Myth 2: Our Customers Are Too Old

Another classic myth: People are too old for technology. I hope someone tells my mom, who is 71 and the queen of social media, that she's too old for tech. I am not saying that there isn't some truth to this myth, but we shouldn't paint every elderly person with the same brush. Seniornet.org shows that since 2012, seniors have steadily been flocking to Facebook. It actually makes perfect sense. Seniors have time, they enjoy seeing pictures of their grandkids, and they really enjoy connecting with their old friends. Facebook is the perfect tool for this type of interaction.

I was recently on a flight and I watched a senior citizen break out her iPad, log in to in-flight Wi-Fi, and start checking her email and her Facebook account. Meanwhile, the 30-something woman next to me asked me for help to get her laptop on the Wi-Fi system. If you have ever tried to connect to an airline's in-flight Wi-Fi system, you know it isn't always a cakewalk, but the senior citizen made it look easy. Simple fact: Not all seniors are techno-phobes.

## Myth 3: Our Board Won't Get on Board

I often do board sessions with CEOs to help everyone understand what is going on in the tech space. I am always excited to meet

**Behold, I have discovered digital!**

members of the board and executive leadership. In the case of credit unions, the board is made up of volunteers that usually represent each of the employee segments that credit unions serve.

What I have discovered from these sessions is that board members are passionate about their institutions and, when they are presented with facts and figures regarding the digital shift, they easily get on board. Of course, sometimes I see gridlock at the board level or meet obstructionist board members. In most cases, these people aren't opposed to adopting new technology; they just want to see data to support the move. This is something that many institutions cannot provide, in large part because they haven't done their research.

### Myth 4: Digital Is Too Expensive

This is an easy myth to dispel. The truth is that not going digital will be *more* expensive than doing it. Consider that most mid-sized institutions are woefully behind in implementing analytics. Their lack of analytics is driving up their costs, while the bigger financial institutions are finding more efficient and effective ways to market products, provide services, and determine where and when to deliver their services. Analytics is a game changer for the industry. A key differentiator for financial institutions will be their ability to use data to become prescriptive for customers. Those without analytics will fall further and further behind. Having analytics is like discovering fire. Suddenly, you don't have to be afraid of the dark; the fire will illuminate your path.

## Myth 5: Digital Leads to Layoffs and Branch Closures

I am not a proponent of closing branches, but I am proponent of changing how the branch network functions. I am also a proponent of proportionate spending between digital and physical branches that is commensurate with the number of customers each channel serves and the profit they provide. No matter what, closing all of your branches isn't good idea. New branching will consist of more sales and fewer transactional services. Take, for instance, Financial Partners Credit Union, which just recently renovated all of its branches by adding personal teller machines. I interviewed the CEO, who said that they closed no branches and the Full time employee (FTE) is the same, but the credit union's production is higher. This is an important concept: it is the responsibility of the leadership to plan for transition. This is often overlooked as organizations transition to digital processes. If the displacement is known ahead of time, then people can be retrained to provide even more value to the business.

The other reality is that if you don't look at digital, you may be forced to lay off parts of your workforce due to marketplace pressure. At least with digital transformation there is room for a thoughtful transition as it relates to your employees.

## John's Story

I would like to introduce myself before we get in to the deep, dark places that digital transformation will inevitably take us to. I grew up as a military brat, and a lazy one at that. I spent most of my life traveling around the world with my father, usually coming up with Tom Sawyer–like ways to get out of work. When I was nine years old, my dad retired from the army and we moved to Stuttgart, Germany. This is where I did most of my growing up. My dad was some sort of engineer who worked with computers on a military base. I attended American schools on base and, when I was 11, I built an ASCII emulator for the school science fair. It was a breadboard with dip switches that represented binary positions, and when you flipped them in the right order you could make a letter appear on the digital screen. I got an ASCII Char 70 (otherwise known as a capital F) for a grade on that project. The teacher said my dad helped me too much. I guess she didn't believe I could solder wires or understand binary. I was especially discouraged because my dad was away for work much of the time, so he wasn't able to help me very much. I drowned my sorrows by spending hours on his VIC-20 typing in programs from a magazine called *Compute*.

Yes, there was a time when, if you wanted to play a game, you had to spend hours typing code in line by line and save your work to a cassette tape. As we all know, this wouldn't work today, because computer games are millions and millions of lines of code. My dad eventually upgraded our home computer to a Commodore-64 and floppy disks, and at that point I started programming my own games. Since I was in Germany during the 1980s, I didn't get out much because it wasn't always safe to wander around by yourself, so I had tons of time to play with computers and my dad's electronics. I would dismantle Atari games, Sony personal stereos (apparently, Sony disapproves of calling them Walkmen), and basically anything electronic I could I get my hands on. I didn't know it, but I was preparing for my future.

Fast forward to 1996: I was a year married to my amazing wife and had my second child on the way. I was trying to make a living as a teacher or quasi teacher in the Hillsborough County School System in Florida. Some forward-thinking schools had decided to bring in technology specialists to teach the kids during the school day, and I was lucky enough to have gotten one of these jobs. It was the best job I ever had. I loved hanging out with the kids because they didn't live by any preconceived notions about what could or couldn't be done. This fit right in with my own philosophy that nothing is impossible. As a matter of fact, this was a family philosophy. If you ever said to my dad, "That's impossible," he would quickly respond, "Nothing's impossible." To these kids, anything was possible because their spirit hadn't been broken by life yet, and I would feed off their energy daily. As much as I loved this job, I couldn't stay because I needed to make more money to support our second child. I decided to leverage my natural computer skills and I applied for a job at the information technology department at Suncoast Schools Federal Credit Union (as it was known then). I was a member of Suncoast long before I became an employee, thanks to my job in the school system, and as a result, I knew a little bit about the credit union.

I successfully landed the job of technology monkey boy. (Honestly, I don't even remember my title, but I was happy to have the job.) I was hired by Kevin Johnson, who at the time was one of two people working in the IT department. Today he is the CEO of the credit union and, I am proud to say, still a good friend. You might find us crawling under desks to re-pin RS232 cables, in the ceiling running cables, or hauling a giant printer across the campus in the Florida sun. I discovered quickly that PCs, or personal computers, weren't commonplace in the institution. A few select departments might have one personal computer, but most people worked on dumb terminals connected to a large Unisys A series mainframe. It was a great job, and I was thankful for the work. I enjoyed the people I worked with and I started to get to know what each of the different department's functions were.

One day, I was working in an area near a lady in the ATM department who I would often see early in the morning working at her desk. I was there early to rewire some desks before the regular employees came in so we wouldn't interrupt their work. She was working on one of the few PCs in the department and I watched her print out a long report on the dot matrix printer, sat it next to her desk and began retyping the report into the computer. One thing you should understand is that I am super lazy, and super lazy people always look for shortcuts. Upon seeing her retyping data from a report that so clearly had come from the very PC she was typing on, my super-lazy senses kicked in and I couldn't help but ask her the following question. "Excuse me, you know that stuff was already in the PC, right?" to which she responded, "Yes, but it is in a different program, so each day I print this report from this program, and then I type it back into this program." As you might imagine, I was confused. Long ago I had mastered the art of cutting and pasting, even in Windows 3.1, which was the operating system we were working on. I asked her if I could look at the program. An hour later, I had written a quick .bat file to bring the data automatically into one program from the other. The lady was amazed. She told me that I had just recovered two hours of her day. I learned two important lessons that day. First, I learned that non-super-lazy people, when they recover time, don't use it to play video games or wander around looking for free office snacks. Instead, they will take that two hours and do something that they had been wishing they had the time to do to benefit the company. I also learned that when you help people, they feed you and appreciate you—two things I really like.

Word soon spread of my good deed and others approached me with similar problems. After that, I spent time creating complicated .bat files to import files from Payroll into ACH. I found myself writing macros in Lotus and doing merges in WordPerfect. Slowly but surely, I helped a lot of people who had very monotonous jobs recover their time and move on to more important tasks. I also gained a lot of weight thanks to all the cookies and treats each department would feed me for helping them.

I was promoted, and I don't even remember what the new position was. I did get a raise and I got to work on our networks and our ATMs. One day I was out at the ATM during my lunch break and I noticed that the line for the ATM was really long. So long, in fact, the Credit Union had put in side-by-side ATMs to accommodate the large number of people using the machines. When I reached the front of the line and it was my turn to use the ATM, I noticed how long it took to perform a transaction, which was over three minutes. I thought to myself, "What if this process could go faster?" At the time, I was working with Motorola to replace our old dial network with a frame relay network, and I had a fantastic mentor named Tom Bennett who enjoyed my crazy ideas. I said to him, I think we could speed up these transactions considerably by changing some parameters in the system. His response was, "Sure, let's do it."

Tom loved innovation and was always supportive. He was famous for drawing on walls, and at this point we were in the elevator, he quickly whipped out his pencil and drew a diagram on the elevator wall (I had gotten use to this behavior at this point), and we agreed the design should work. We made the changes and we tested it. What used to take three minutes now took less than a minute. I had no idea what the impact of this would be; I had no idea that for each foreign transaction that came through the ATM network, the credit union made money. I only knew that there were long lines and short lunch breaks. I also didn't think about the fact that if I sped up the transactions, the ATMs could do more transactions a day, which translated into more income from the ATM network. The ATM network almost tripled its income the first month after our little adjustment. Once again, my super laziness and impatience paid off.

After this, I was given the task to convert the entire ATM network from one vendor to another. It was one of my first big projects, and it was vastly complex and difficult. That much I knew at the start. What I didn't realize was how dangerous this project could be to my career. I was working directly with the ATM department. As usual, I worked my way through the project, asking questions and learning along the way.

We finally finished the project and I was at home having dinner with my family when what I call "the voice from above" announced that I needed to check in. The "voice from above" was my Nextel cell phone. Those of you old enough to remember them know that they worked a lot like old walkie-talkies and had a distinctive beep before the voice would start speaking. To this day, I still twitch if I hear the Nextel beep. The voice said that something was wrong with the debit card network and that people's debit payments were being declined at alarming levels.

Now in the late 1990s, if you were declined when trying to process a payment at the grocery store, you would be very embarrassed. It would feel like the entire store stopped and everyone was staring at you with their hand over their mouth in surprise and pity. At this point, more than 50 percent of the incoming transactions were being declined, and the worst part was that these people had plenty of money in their accounts. It was not good, not good at all. This was my first brush with adversity. I wasn't yet 30 and I had just broken the payment systems for tens of thousands of people. However, by the time I got in to the office (no VPNs back then), everything would mysteriously have fixed itself. Then around 5 p.m. the next day, it would happen again. I toiled over the problem for a few days, until finally I was asked to come and explain the problem personally to the CEO, Tom Dorety, a legend in the credit union industry. I had met Tom many times before then but I had never had to deal with him with regard to an issue of this magnitude. Before I went to the CEO's office, Tom Bennett told me, "Don't go in there until you have some idea of a solution," so I started working more frantically to figure this out.

I had discovered that at the end of the day, around 5 p.m., Visa would send what is called a "force post" of transactions down the line to be processed. These transactions would come very quickly and overwhelm our communication lines. I asked if they could run these transactions later than 5 p.m. (a peak transaction time) and I was told that wasn't possible. I was at wit's end, sitting on a curb in the parking lot late at night, watching an amazing lightning storm, and it gave me an idea. When we designed the new network, we had created a backup line in case we lost connectivity on the main line. This was common in Florida, where massive thunderstorms frequently caused outages. So I called my friend at Visa and we fired up the backup line and split the transactions (odds and evens) between the two lines. It solved the problem. I could go to the CEO and tell him I had screwed up by not anticipating the force posts causing line issues, but at least I had fixed it. I learned two things that day. First, I learned that when you play with fire every day, you are going to be burned more often than folks who rarely play with fire. I also learned that being calm in the face of an emergency is far better than freaking out. After that, many more *fiery* projects would come my way.

In the years to come, we converted the whole organization from one computer system to another, bought personal computers for the entire staff, implemented the organization's first email system, got the credit union on the internet, set up firewalls, and established one of the very first home banking systems to run on the internet. I remember replacing our dial-up home banking system with an internet-based system. A few management higher-ups told me the internet was a fad and the project wasn't worthwhile. Things have certainly changed.

All in all, the job was an amazing opportunity. My co-workers took the time to teach me how things worked, and for this effort I would reward them by finding ways to use my knowledge and computer skills to make things easier for them whenever I could. I had the free-dom and trust to explore every corner of a well-respected financial institution and learn all aspects of financial systems.

After that, I left to become a vice president at another credit union across town. I was very excited because this credit union wanted to pursue even my craziest ideas. That was where I started working in a process that would eventually become known as agile development. My team and I were tasked with creating a loan interface that linked to the American Automobile Association (AAA). It would allow our credit union to provide auto loans to AAA customers. We locked ourselves in a room and, fueled by snack food and Mountain Dew, spent almost three months working on the lending project. We had two projectors running, and if team members needed help or wanted to get some code reviewed, they would plug in their laptop and display their screen on the wall for everyone to see. Three or four times a day, a representative of the loan group would show up and we would put what we had on the wall for review so we could get instant feedback while we were working. It was electric when we first turned on the system and the loans started rolling in from AAA. The early results were overwhelmingly good. When I joined GTEFCU, it was a $750 million credit union. In two short years we almost doubled our asset size to $1.4 billion. I was very proud and thought I was in heaven, but I still had an itch.

I accepted a job offer to be chief technology officer at a new credit union service organization (CUSO), WRG. At GTEFCU, my team and I had spent a fair amount of time writing our own home banking product and, in the process, I began to think that some of the systems we were purchasing from vendors could be custom-built in-house cheaper and better. Usually, these proposals were rejected; however, Rob Guilford, who hired me at WRG, had been interested in this same approach for quite a long time. In Rob, I found someone who believed as I did, that in-house products were going to be the future. At WRG we built a team that would go on to build and implement a digital suite of products that now serves over 200 credit unions across the United States. Along the way, we caught the mobile wave and were very early to the Apple App Store with our own in-house product, and we were the first credit union to have an application on the Android platform.

Today, I spend my time with my team at Best Innovation Group, dreaming up new solutions and implementing new products using the latest in technology. My team has been with me for over 30 years, and together we have experienced all the ups and downs of creating systems, developing products, and supporting financial institutions. We have taken this experience and shared what we know with our partners, and we have helped many credit unions navigate the murky waters of the new digital world. We innovate and create, we teach and share, and most importantly, we care about what we do and who we do it for.

If you aren't too scared, read on and find more stories like the ones above and more solutions, and hopefully start to form your ideas and solutions to your challenges. Seize the opportunities that are in front of your organization. Today's world is more connected, more engaged, and has more opportunities for a financial institution to differentiate itself than ever before. We live in a peanut butter and chocolate world, and the best part about that is, you don't have to make the peanut butter or chocolate, you just need the vision to put them together.

## NOTE

1. Jasper Copping, "The 30 Seconds that Sank the Titanic—Fatal Delay in Order to Change Course Doomed Liner," *The Telegraph* (October 25, 2017), http://www.telegraph.co.uk/news/uknews/8933109/The-30 -seconds-that-sank-the-Titanic-fatal-delay-in-order-to-change-course -doomed-liner.html.

# PART

# I

# Processes

# 1

# How to Improve Internal Processes

**C**ontinual internal process improvement is often the greatest threat to any organization. It's never more apparent than when an organization commits to changing a computer system. When a new system is chosen, it will result in the need for process improvement. You may wonder why there would be a chapter on processes in a digital transformation book, and the reason is simple. Eventually, every process in your organization will be digitized, and as a result, your digital processes will reflect your analog processes. For instance, if there are 71 steps in your current loan application process, there will likely be 71 steps in your digitized process. However, a digitized process should *reduce* steps, improve speed, and improve efficacy. For example, solid processes can—and should—transform a 71-step loan application process into a 3- or 4-step process. Unfortunately, our human instinct to avoid change kicks in. Our instincts are to avoid the unknown and resist things that force us to change, and as a result, getting the process down to a few digital steps will prove to be an uphill battle for even the most seasoned executives.

## Regulatory Gridlock

The fear of the unknown is normal for everyone. We know that the existing 71-step process works, so why would we change it? There may even be obvious improvements in the process, and the staff may even acknowledge these initially. Eventually, though, they begin to worry that that outcome of the process will slow them down or put their jobs in jeopardy. This is when we encounter another kind of gridlock. I call it *regulatory gridlock*. Regulatory gridlock is when subject

3

matter experts (SMEs) on a certain process decide that they don't like whatever is being proposed. Because they are the experts in the process, they invoke a regulation or some other rule that forces the organization to abide by their process.

To understand how irrational and unproductive this is, consider this nonbusiness example. I have a friend whose wife is devoutly religious. Whenever they have an argument or there is contention about something, she will say that God has told her that she is right. As you might imagine, it is difficult to counter the rule of God. It's also difficult to counter an SME's subjective interpretation of a regulation. Sadly, I have seen this tactic work many times, usually because the SME is well regarded in the organization or has overseen a process for many years.

The SME usually believes in what he or she is doing because of what I will call *the 1 percent rule*. Here is how it works: The SME is a tenured staff member, and as such has seen every permutation of a process. Somewhere along the line, there was a trauma during the process and, as a result, a step was added to the process to resolve this issue. The trauma was real, but in the scheme of things, the chances of it happening again are slim. So now the process has a step in it that covers something that rarely happens or may never happen again.

To be fair to the SME, when the problem does happen, it's not fun. But is it necessary to force everyone through an additional step to avoid something that hasn't happened in 10 years? For the SME, it feels like the issue occurred yesterday. I use the analogy of a *wound* and a *vow*. The SMEs and their staff were *wounded* by the fallout of the trauma and they *vowed* to never let it happen again. Now you are amid an opportunity to rework this process, and they are blocking the effort. No one wants to challenge the SME because of fear of retribution or, worse yet, a regulatory beat down. To counter this, use analytics to determine the likelihood of the issue happening again.

### Regulatory Gridlock in Action

Here's an example of gridlock: An organization that once had an issue with its passwords added a PIN. To log in, you had to have an account number or username, password, and PIN. As you are no doubt aware, the standard for logging in has become username and password, and the organization's customers thought it seemed odd to have an extra step. Where it really became an issue is when the company introduced mobile. It was very expensive to add the PIN to an existing product because it was not standard—the mobile systems were set up to use only username and password.

This particular organization wound up implementing the PIN in the mobile application at a great cost. Many years later, the organization wanted to remove the PIN from the process but it was met with many challenges. This is because of organizational trauma that caused a freak-out when it was revealed that management was considering removing the PIN. Some in the organization remembered the earlier password problem and were worried that they might have to experience the same trauma again—even though nearly every other financial institution had implemented a process that was easier and more secure using only a username and password. Now they had a reverse problem: If they were to unwind the change, the organization's current membership, who had become accustomed to the PIN-and-password process, would have to be retrained. As you might imagine, retraining hundreds of thousands of users who have been logging in a certain way for many years would be difficult. In addition, some will see the change as a step down in security and complain.

### The Risk Spectrum

Inability to reduce or reengineer processes due to organizational muscle memory is a common theme in financial institutions. The main reason is that there is a high price attached to failure, and as a result, processes are often engineered for the 1 percent because in the employee's experience, failure is not an option. In this regard, it is important that the organizational leadership put the right perspective on failure. Failure, when it happens, shouldn't be a taboo subject; it should be talked about and shared. One thing that might help to put failure in perspective is to look at failure by industry.

By evaluating the two extreme ends of the spectrum, one can gain insight into the playing field. At one end is the entertainment company Pixar, where employees are encouraged to fail, and fail fast. The price for failure at Pixar is missing a date on a movie or losing money due to failure. At the other end of the spectrum is an airline company, Boeing. The consequence of failure in this industry could be loss of life (Figure 1.1).

**Figure 1.1    The risk spectrum**

Where does the financial industry fit in this continuum? By using the failure outcome as a litmus test, we can try to put some perspective on where we are on the risk continuum. We can start by saying that no one is going to die from a failure at a financial institution, so we don't belong at the end with Boeing. We can also rule out the other end of the spectrum, as there is the potential for a financial loss and there is a big reputational risk to the organization, particularly with a digital risk that could lead to a security breach. So, on this spectrum we are somewhere in the middle—people won't die, but there is a lot at risk for the organization and for that organization's customers.

The first thing to do is find your place on the risk spectrum and devise a process to evaluate risk for new processes as well as to reevaluate risk in current processes. Here are some things that should be included as part of any process risk review:

- *How often is this process performed?* If the process is rarely performed—such as, for instance, a reverse mortgage, perhaps it is not even worth having the product that the process is attached to. Or conversely, if the process is excessively used by the entire organization, then it needs to be on a list of critical processes that are continuously evaluated for improvement.
- *How much of the organization is affected by this process?* Is the process specific to a department? Processes that are cross-departmental, such as a loan application, need to be evaluated differently than an internal department process like collections.

On the website, you will find a template for evaluating the risk within processes, products, and new features. The risk review should be scored and shared with senior management as well as any process governance groups within the organization. If the process needs to be changed, the risk review should be performed again. For a process, the risk review should cover each of the steps of the process. The process review should provide data definitions and justification for each step of process.

## Flawed Bank Processes

It is not necessary to evaluate every process within the average bank to discover the major flaws in our processes. Instead let's take a look at a very common process and point out improvements that can be applied to other similar processes. One simple process with potential complications is an address change. Here is the scenario: A customer calls the call center, goes to the branch in person, emails, or visits the website to change an address. Seems simple, right? Shouldn't it just be going to a screen somewhere and changing the address? Simple processes are often the most deceptive. The address process has several complexities to consider:

- *In most large organizations, customer addresses can exist in several systems.* For instance, if the organization outsources its credit card processing or mortgage servicing, the address would need to be changed in each system.
- *There can be more than one address.* Many organizations allow their customers to have a primary address and a secondary address for, say, a business account. Changing the wrong one can be catastrophic. I once worked with an organization that had not identified the primary and secondary address, and when it changed the process, it accidentally copied the primary account address into the secondary address. While this might not seem like a big deal, it is to the customer who doesn't want someone at the primary address to know about his or her other account (especially if it is conveniently named DIVORCE ACCT, as this one was). As you might imagine, the organization had a few upset customers. This oversight created a liability for its organization related to privacy.
- *The address might be associated with more than one account holder.* For example, there might be a joint or beneficiary but the

customer might not remember to tell you. How do you update them all? Do you update them all?

- *Address changes can be subject to fraud.* As a result, it would be necessary to notify a customer out of band when there are changes on their accounts such as phone numbers or addresses. How do you notify them? Email, snail mail? All the above? Do you do this in all situations? What if, for instance, members come in person to the branch and verify their identity?
- *Digital address validation is now possible, using online services such as the national change of address repository.* However, I have found in many organizations that the practice of validating addresses is spotty. Meaning that if a customer calls the call center, the address gets changed with no validation but if the customer uses the home banking platform, the validation happens.
- *There are many types of addresses to consider.* These include foreign or military addresses, which require different fields and different validation.
- *Addresses also have to be run through the OFAC process.* This is necessary to make sure that they are not associated with terrorism.

As you can see, this process is far more complex than it seems on the surface. So how can this process be improved using simple process improvement practices? Using the process review form from the website, one could score the risk related to each step, and based on that risk either remove, improve, or add steps. Second, since the review for this process revealed the process is cross-departmental as well as self-service, it would benefit from process centralization. A general rule of thumb is that if a process is either a candidate for self-service or currently self-service, there is a good chance it can be centralized by exposing the *same customer self-service platform to the staff.*

Confused? Don't worry; let me explain. In 2003, when my team and I were developing an in-house home banking solution, we frequently had to go into the staff portal (these are the green screens that the employees use) to validate that the home banking product was working properly. During the continuous back and forth between the home banking application and the staff portal, something occurred to me: Why can't the staff just use the home banking interface we were developing? My reasoning was that we were creating a financial portal for millions of customers and we expected them to use this platform with little to no training. This meant that the interface had to be intuitive and couldn't depend on the customers remembering codes or the steps of a process.

For instance, if a staff member needed to tell customers what the balance was on their mortgage, the staff member would have to open up a new program, sign into a different system, and type several codes to see the current balance. However, in the home banking platform, we collected these data on behalf of the consumer via electronic means and conveniently displayed it for them on the accounts screen alongside all of the other balances from the various systems the bank used to process their data. I realized that if the staff had access to this screen, they could reduce the process of getting a mortgage balance for a customer by several steps. I immediately started working on what it would take to allow staff access to the home banking platform and presented this to the management as a new feature.

Now let's consider the address change process in this context: If your organization has digitized this process for the customers, then this should be reused for the staff, and focusing on the customer version of the process would produce a more efficient transaction. In the situation I mentioned above, we had already built an address change process that addressed all the complexities just mentioned. Moreover, the digitized version, when used by the staff, would ensure that each step of the process was followed, regardless of which channel the request was received on. Since the process was centralized, it greatly reduced the work to integrate the other systems such as credit cards or mortgages. Rather than integrating three or four different processes, we could integrate one, which reduced technical debt. Finally, this allowed the statistics of the process to be accurately recorded.

The trick here is to understand the difference between a customer using the product and a staff member and consider this during your development and implementation phases. For instance, the address change that is done by a staff member must include the proper audit mechanisms, whereas the customer will likely have a different set of rules. How many processes could be improved by exposing the digital process that you have created for your customers to your staff?

## Continual Improvement

Now let's take the address process and apply the practice of continual improvement to it. *Continual improvement* is the practice of improving a product, process, or feature in small increments on a regular basis. One challenge I see in banks is the lack of continual improvement. Once a project or process is done, the organization moves on to the next project and only returns to the project in a crisis such as a regulatory mandate to update it, or if a loss was incurred due to an unforeseen risk. In these situations, the process is reviewed, but usually it is only updated to deal with the issues at hand. In a continual improvement environment, the process would be reviewed regularly by a different group than the group that originally implemented the process whose purpose is to continually improve the process.

Analytics and innovation would play a strong role in this process. If analytics for the address change revealed a rise in mismatched zip codes, perhaps the continuous improvement group would add a zip code validation process to the field that collects zip codes, or perhaps your team identified an opportunity to innovate and to make address updates easier, by adding a way for a customer to use their smartphone to take a picture of their new address on their license, or any other document, and use the evolving object character recognition engines (OCR) to input the address on behalf of the member. The group responsible for process improvement would release new updates at scheduled intervals and continuously and aggressively solicit candid feedback from the process stakeholders. The group would also continually review the process at other organizations looking for improvements.

## Project Management

Project management is a process within the organization. It's a very important process, but in most financial organizations it is broken because of the way financial institutions have evolved—especially when compared to fintechs.

### Waterfall

In many financial organizations, their first brush with project management was related to building branches. I have had the good fortune to be involved in the process of building a branch, a headquarters, a kiosk, and pretty much every other kind of a structure a financial organization might need to build. In the case of physical buildings, the project management approach is called *waterfall*.

A waterfall process is a way of managing process by sequencing tasks with a very rigid schedule. Each resource is planned based on the outcome of the previous resource. The tasks for the project are grouped into milestones, and it is not necessary to frequently consult subject matter experts during the project. In the case of the branch, it is not likely that that the branch manager will be involved in the laying of the foundation or purchasing the land.

The waterfall approach is sequenced because many tasks are dependent on other processes to finish. For example, there is no need to have the painters on site until the walls are up, and because of this, they are sequenced behind the drywaller installers. This form of project management works very well for building something physical that has well-defined requirements. However, as bank processes, features, and products become increasingly digital, the waterfall approach to project management impedes the organization's ability to deliver digital projects on time. This is because the waterfall process creates a separation between the end users and the feature or service they are using.

Imagine that as you built a branch, each day you would invite hundreds of your customers that plan on using that branch to review each step of the process. They could check the foundation and give their opinions on where the bathrooms should be, and pick colors. This would cause chaos in branch design, because the physical building is a static object that cannot be changed without incurring large expenses (like digging up the foundation after it is poured). However, a digital asset, such as the address process in the previous example, can be changed easily. Applying the waterfall methodology to software results in unhappy end users. This is because software, unlike a building, is hard to quantify upfront, and when the company or software development group waits until the end to unveil its work, it is often met with criticism. There are two reasons for this: the developer's inability to understand the process it is trying to automate and the end users' inability to articulate their precise needs in a way that the developers can work with.

## Agile

The answer to this problem is a project management process called *agile,* which can be applied to any project (even building a new branch, although it wouldn't be the best use of it). Agile is the process of building a project in incremental steps. At regular intervals, feedback is solicited from the end users. Each task or change is collected and then organized into work queues called *sprints*. At the end of each sprint, the work in progress is presented in what is called a *stand-up meeting* to the end user to get their opinions (because everyone is standing, the meetings are short). The end-user feedback is then incorporated into the next sprint. Since the end users or project stakeholders never go more than a week or so without seeing the product, they are intimately involved in the design and can help the developers change course before they move on. If the developers aren't understanding the requirements or if the requirements are not working out, this will be clear to the end user during the stand-up meetings.

Admittedly, agile is far from a perfect process. One weakness is that there must be controls put in place to keep end users from endlessly polishing the diamond and to keep the programmers from doing the same. In the software development arena, the result of a product or project built using agile is a much faster way of developing code, implementing new features, and if the sprints are continued, a way of continuously improving the asset when completed. This process also creates a tighter bond between the developers and the end users. The end users slowly discover the capabilities of the vendors or the development department and the developers better understand the needs of the staff. John Janclaes, CEO of Partners, recently started his organization down a path of agility. Here is an excerpt from his communication to his staff and board.

> Agility! So many leaders are talking about this subject with so many viewing points about what agility is and is not. I suggest it has little to do with lean or agile training for our PMOs or DevOps teams, it's about organizational agility....
>
> I think we need to look more broadly by understanding the entire organization, the entire operating eco-systems, need to operate with greater agility—effortless, effort. When thinking of eco-systems, I can't help but look to biology or physiology for clues. In these sciences agility requires full muscle recruitment of fast twitch muscles (agile) and slow-twitch muscles (waterfall) to achieve peak performance. How can we harmonize fast and slow processes, fast and slow economic engines, and teams to realize our full potential for our organizations?

John is clarifying for his audience (in this case the staff and the board) that he envisions two types of processes in the organization, fast and slow. Each of them has a place—the trick is knowing which one to use, and when.

## When to Use Agile versus Waterfall

Figure 1.2 depicts a quick flowchart to help you decide when to use agile and when to use waterfall:

1. Are the requirements fully known and documented?
2. What is the availability of the stakeholders?
3. Are the stakeholders familiar with the agile process?
4. What will it cost if there needs to be changes made?
5. Can the project be phased?
6. Will the project be completed by in-house resources or out-sourced?

John also correctly points out that agile must be taught to the entire organization. There is a tendency for organizations to only train the information technology employees and project management in agile. This will not work. It's a little like putting a Ferrari engine in a Volkswagen—it's great that the engine is new and fast, but if the frame, tires, and other parts of the car can't handle it, it will fall apart quickly. I had one CEO liken it to having a rowboat where one side of rowers is far stronger than the other side, and as a result, the boat just goes in circles. Agility is important to the entire organization, and if staff members are not trained and do not buy into the concept of agile project management, the result can be catastrophic. Other untrained departments will view all the stand-up meetings and constant involvement of their staff as unnecessary overhead, and because they haven't experienced the end result, they will likely not fully participate, which will sour the group on the agile approach from the start. Half measures always avail us nothing.

## In-house Staff and Outside Vendors

I can hear you saying, "But John, I am not in control of my products; we don't have a development department." Good news! Most of your digital vendors have likely adopted the agile methodology of software development and are usually happy to have some end-user

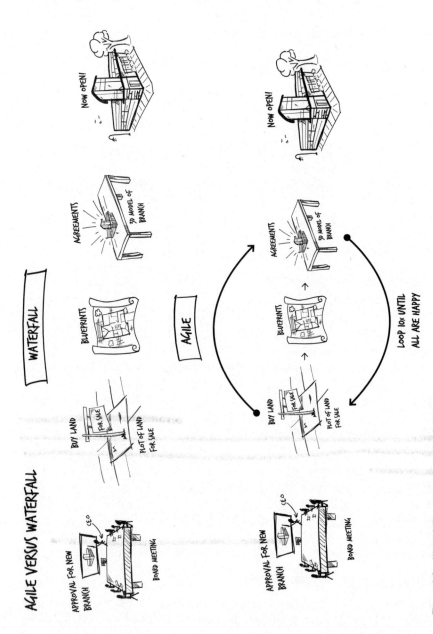

**Figure 1.2   Waterfall versus agile > Branch Issues**

participation. This prevents them from releasing software that doesn't meet the needs of their customers. Often, these vendors will have advisory groups or user groups that are specifically designed to collect, document, and evaluate processes (often referred to as user stories) for their continuous improvement process. Key staff members should be encouraged to participate in these communities on behalf of your organization. This will help you influence the future of your software packages as well as share and learn best practice from other organizations. Push to be part of their agile process and see if you can attend their stand-up meetings for software packages that are key to your critical processes. Even implementation of a vendor's product can be executed using an agile project plan. This is an important distinction—that you can replace development with implementation in the agile process model in cases where your organization is not in control of development.

This same process can also be applied when using a consultant group to do your development. In fact, this process is likely the only way to achieve success when dealing with a offshore consultancy, as the agile process allows the organization to overcome the culture challenges that are often present when working with offshore development groups. Learning to work with consulting groups will be an important part of every financial institution's digital future. The resource challenge is real for financial institutions, especially the push and pull between new projects and keeping the lights on in the organization. One way to combat that is to develop in-house expertise at working with outside consulting teams.

Developing leadership inside the organization will pay huge dividends, especially if those leaders can expand their influence beyond the four walls of the institution. A project leader or technical project leader might work with several outside firms at once to create a single platform, feature, or process within the organization. The leaders' most important task is to determine what should be outsourced and what work should stay in house. For instance, if there is a massive amount of business logic that is not formally documented in a project, then it may be necessary to have the in-house resources build the business logic services because they have a better understanding of the business processes and more access to the subject matter experts, since they are onsite with them. If there is a front end that consists of building screens to collect data and send it to the business processes and it is a documented experience, then that would be a good use of the outside development group since they don't need to understand the complex business logic involved in the process. If the outside development group has technical domain expertise beyond what is in house (like designing mobile applications), then the leader may decide to farm out entire projects to the outside firm, relying on an agile process to keep the project in scope.

Let's use building a mobile loan application as an example project. I have added a few major tasks in the process (Table 1.1). Note the location of the working group for each task. Would you make the same choices in your organization?

The idea is to make the best use of your local resources who have special knowledge and, as a result, are more valuable to the organization, and augment them with cheaper outside resources who work on less complex tasks. The value in this approach is increased speed and agility, as well as reduced cost.

Interdepartmental processes are also a challenge inside of financial institutions. An online loan application, for instance, might start in the e-business department, transition to a branch, then go through the call center, and finally to a closing agent. How do you maintain continuity and communication, both with the user and the staff, when a process traverses many departments?

## Process Management

The first thing is to standardize the entire organization on a single tool for process management. The majority of the time, the organization will be looking to digitize an existing process and as a result, most process enhancements usually include a website or

**Table 1.1    Mobile loan application tasks and workgroups**

| Task | Workgroup |
| --- | --- |
| Development of lending decision process | In-house development |
| User experience | In-house development |
| Create screens and workflow on IOS based on user experience documentation and wireframes | Outsource |
| Create screens and workflow for Android based on user experience documentation and wireframes | Outsource |
| Documentation | Outsource |
| Writing test scripts | In-house |
| Testing based on test scripts | Outsource |
| Security review | Outsource |
| Code review | Outsource |

digital forms. However, if accounting has its own accounts payable process built on proprietary software, then it will be difficult to automate certain stretches of the process because they are not on the same system. This is where the digital governance group comes in to play, as they are responsible for ensuring that all systems introduced to the organization are open and compatible with the other platforms. A digital process platform is often referred to as *workflow* platform. There are many tools available to financial institutions in this space.

Microsoft Workflow is a product that integrates with the Microsoft office suite of products and allows for automation of processes and tasks. If you are a heavy Microsoft shop, then this could be a great tool to use to start digitizing processes and creating efficiencies. There are also many cloud-based tools that are evolving. Process Street (www.process.st) is an example of a workflow product entirely hosted in the cloud. The platform is designed to automate tasks and processes, and track the progress. Another very popular tool is Kissflow (KiSSFLOW.com). Kissflow is a tile-based system that presents a user with a list of tiles (known as apps in the system) that can be done on the system (start a new loan, request a check copy, etc.). When accessed, the application walks them through the task with intuitive screens (Figure 1.3).

## Team Organization: Centers of Excellence

The next step is to organize your teams into centers of excellence (CoE) around your major functions. A simple breakdown might look like this:

1. Lending
2. Enterprise
3. Member contact (Branches Call Center)
4. Digital services

Figure 1.3    Kissflow tiles

Once you have organized your groups, it is far easier to assign tasks while designing a process. For instance, a lending process might cross each of the groups (as described in the example above). In the old model, call center representatives might have been forced to specialize in lending, or lending experts would deal only with application origination. Neither of these is an effective use of the resources' time. In the new model, the call center representatives would be based in lending and work directly with member contact as part of their charter. This reduces the risk of dysfunction between the call center and the lending group by organizing the resources into a structure that shares common work threads.

When all processes are mixed together without regard for function, there is no accumulation of domain knowledge as these processes evolve. This happens because no one feels specifically responsible for the process. The lack of ownership or accountability is especially common in cross-functional processes. This is precisely because the process is cross-department, and as a result, no one wants to take ownership because they feel that they don't have total control. It is valuable to implement workstreams or processes that are aligned with the centers of excellence. When the processes are aligned with functional areas, the owners will be more comfortable that they can be managed without having to deal with departments that they have no control over. Each process will have a defined owner, and as a result, the process will be more aligned with its discipline as opposed to its delivery channel.

## Cultural Considerations

When I am reviewing organizations, I often hear from middle managers that they feel understaffed. When I interview the manager, I usually find that there aren't any steps being taken to work smarter. The group is always very willing and passionate about working hard to complete each task as part of a process, but they lack the ability or authority to review a task or process and try to find a tool, product, or service that could reduce the workload. This is a cultural issue; the employees don't feel empowered to present ideas to improve a process that they work on every day. As you might imagine, it is demoralizing to work passionately on a process each day and then not be consulted when there is a process change. This is a fatal organizational mistake, because those closest to the process need to be heard the most. They are the ones who are most likely to have a great idea on how to improve the process, or they can scuttle a process change to protect their turf. For more on how culture contributes to gridlock, see Part III.

Regularly reviewing your processes and looking for incremental improvements by implementing digital assets, reducing complexity, or centralizing the process is necessary to achieve digital transformation. *A bad process, digitized, is still a bad process.*

---

### Chapter Review

- Technology should simplify processes. If your tech-based workflow has the same number of steps as your analog workflow, you're doing something wrong.

- Regulatory gridlock is when experts on a certain process don't like what is being proposed and try to stop it.

- Digital governance is responsible for ensuring that all systems introduced to the organization are open and compatible with the other platforms. This is critical to understand when developing processes.

- Establish centers of excellence around your business's major functions. This simplifies task assignments and organization.

- It is necessary to regularly review processes to find ways to improve.

# PART

# II

# Technology

# 2

# Tech Evolution versus Tech Revolution

**B**efore we begin the technology section of this book, I feel it is necessary to define the types of technology. In my career, I have found that tech always seems to come in two flavors, evolution or revolution.

Evolution is gradual change; it's something that takes time. In technology, it usually means that someone has taken an idea and adapted it to work better, or taken an idea and figured out how to scale it. Revolution occurs when technology fundamentally changes the way an industry does business. Revolutionary technologies are typically new, or present drastically new ways of doing business.

Successful technology platforms really revolve around two things, utility and scale. Utility is key because it is the reason the users come to the system. Scale is important because it implies to the users that the system works (otherwise, why would so many people use it?). Scale also means funding, and funding means that the platform will continually improve.

Let's talk about evolutionary technology.

## Evolutionary Technology

I think one of the most successful evolutionary companies in the world is Apple. Now, many people think of Apple as the disruptor, the great revolutionary company, but if you think about it, mobile phones had been around for a long time when Apple came out with the iPhone. Apple evolved it. Nextel, Blackberry, and different kinds of phones were out there for a long time. They even had email—that's what initially made Blackberries different in the marketplace. It was a new idea that you could get your email on a device hooked to your belt (if you were cool, like I was). Blackberries could play music and take pictures. Blackberries even had little games that you could play. I still remember playing Bejeweled and some sort of poker game on my Blackberry Pearl. So what did Apple do different? If all of these features were part of the Blackberry platform, why did Apple disrupt them?

Apple waited around, they watched what happened, and took note of the things that consumers didn't like. One challenge with the Blackberry was downloading applications. Most of the time, to get an app on your phone you had to connect it to your laptop and, as any former Blackberry user knows, connecting your Blackberry to your laptop can often be the kiss of death. I once connected my Blackberry to my laptop to update it before a trip, and it loaded a new operating system. This would've been fine if I had known that it was going to delete all my settings. I spent the rest of the trip configuring the device in my spare time. Apple took note of the fact that it wasn't easy to download applications, that the voicemail function was difficult and clunky, and that Research in Motion (RIM), Blackberry's parent company, needed to continually update devices because of the form factors they choose. Apple resolved each of these issues with innovation.

Visual voicemail, the ability to access voice messages from a visual interface rather than dialing in, was a necessity for Steve Jobs when he envisioned the iPhone. He worked with every carrier until he found one that would support his vision for visual voicemail, and now this feature is a table stake for mobile devices.

To solve the form factor problem, Apple put in the touchscreen, so the device only had one button. This was unheard of before Apple released the iPhone. Finally, the big game changer was introducing the App Store, which was more than just a place to download apps; it was a platform designed to attract developers that would create applications for the device and increase its functionality beyond what the engineers at Apple could envision. Now, one could argue that the App Store was revolutionary, and I could agree with that, but overall, the iPhone platform was an evolutionary process.

Apple disrupted the phone industry like it had done to the personal music industry years earlier. Before there were ever iPods, there were MP3 players. But yet again Apple swooped in with a new strategy, they knew that they were going to create a music service to go with their MP3 players to solve the ever-evolving music pirating issues that was plaguing the music industry. Long before iTunes, there was Napster, a music-sharing service that allowed its users to share any music that they could get their hands on whether they owned it or not. It could be said that Apple was revolutionary in convincing the music business to sell music as singles and implementing the iTunes platform. But I would argue that this was just a natural evolution of the illegal things that were going on with Napster, and that Steve Jobs saw an opportunity to take music in a new direction.

## Evolution in Banking

If we look at this opportunity in banking, let's look at the things that have really been evolutionary, that we thought might be revolutionary. I think a good example is personal financial management. In the mid-2000s, personal financial management, or budgeting software, was going to be the next financial holy grail. Every vendor or consultant was talking about implementing a digital way of presenting a consolidated view of a customer's entire book of business no matter which financial institution they banked with on a single screen. The goal was to take all your customer's different accounts, no matter where they reside, and provide a consolidated view where they could see all their financial assets in one place. Mint, Yodlee, and Mvelopes are great examples of this type of technology. These sites are also referred to as aggregators because they aggregate financial information on behalf of a consumer.

Each of these platforms allows a customer to set up each of their financial institution relationships by choosing the financial provider from a list and providing the site with their user name and password for that FI's home banking platform. The aggregator then uses screen-scraping technology to retrieve account balances, history, and other data from the FI's site and display it in an aggregated way. The concern was that if your customers suddenly started flocking to these third-party sites you would lose your opportunity to market your products and services because the aggregators would not be displaying your targeted marketing inside of their site. In fact, most of the aggregators would instead be using the data to cross-market other national credit cards and financial instruments that compete with the FIs that unknowingly provided the data.

Many FIs spent time incorporating a version of this aggregation feature into their own digital offerings to head this trend off at the pass. Over time, though, the FIs that implemented this feature realized that it wasn't widely adopted by the users. The reasons were varied. In some cases, the screen-scraping technology used to provide the balances was unreliable; in other cases, the FI didn't take the time to fully integrate the feature into its entire platform, and because it wasn't front and center on the main page, many customers either couldn't find the feature or decided it was too much work to set up, and as a result, we saw that personal financial management *wasn't* revolutionary.

Personal financial management never turned into the boom it was supposed to be. To this day, in most organizations that I see using it, about a third of their membership use the personal financial management software. Billpay is a product that suffered a similar fate. Billpay was supposed to be the great game changer. It is often referred to as a *sticky product,* meaning that if someone goes in and sets up these payees by painstakingly typing in all the information for each of their billers, they are not likely to want to spend time setting up the same information somewhere else, and as a result, they will pay their bills from the FI's DDA account, thus making the FI the primary financial institution for that person. This line of thinking certainly makes sense; however, I haven't seen a lot of organizations that have evolved their bill-paying penetration beyond about a third of their customers.

In both cases, PFM and Billpay, it has taken a long time to achieve a large user base in the financial institutions community. As a matter of fact, Billpay is a great example of an ever-evolving platform. The product providers have added overnight payments, same-day payments, and the ability to do direct payments to billers. Even though there have been many additions to these platforms, they are fundamentally still the same—you put in a biller's address, you say when and how much money you want taken out of your account, the organization or financial institution does that, and the bill is paid.

This service has been disrupted in large part by the billers wanting to have the consumers come to their own sites to pay bills so that they can cross-sell the users on new features or up-sell their service. The billers often encourage the users to pay the bills from their sites instead, using ACH as opposed to paying the bill from the FI's home banking site. This tension often results in the users being confused about the best way to pay their bills.

## True Revolution

Now let's examine some examples of revolutionary technology. Revolution comes from the Latin word *revolutio*, meaning "to turn around." If something is revolutionary, it changes fundamentally how you think about that thing, how you approach it, and how you go about it. Revolutionary technology is often used as a synonym for disruptive technology. The first name that comes to mind for me when I think of disruptive revolutionary technology is Netflix. I wish I could've been a fly on the wall in the Blockbuster boardroom when it reviewed threats and it was someone's job to update the board on this new competitor, Netflix. I'm sure that the chairman looked at everyone else in the room and said, "OK, what do we know about these Netflix guys?" and an SVP said, "Well, they have a slightly different business model than us." The chairman replied, "Well what is it?" Feeling a bit silly the SVP stated, "Well sir, they mail DVDs to the customers."

As he said this, snickers could be heard in the room all around. After a good laugh, the chairman asks the SVP, "What kind of

guarantee do they have that they are going to get them back, and how much are they charging for late fees?" To which the nervous SVP replied, "They don't seem to care, sir; they just send you the DVD, and you can send it back whenever you'd like." This response elicited an even bigger round of laughter than the first round, and they dismissed this silly organization as another of the many weird startups that had been popping up all over the internet and trying to challenge their business model.

We now know the end of this story: In 2000, the CEO of Blockbuster was offered the chance to buy Netflix for $50 million, but Blockbuster passed on the deal, and Netflix eventually killed Blockbuster. Blockbuster didn't see that Netflix wasn't content to just mail DVDs. Its organization recognized that the future of the internet was going to be households having greater and greater bandwidth, and with this development they envisioned a streaming service that would instantly provide access to movies and other digital content in any household. They also recognized that people want to watch videos everywhere—at the airport, at the library, while eating lunch, and they proceeded to work with all the major device providers to make their application available no matter what device you have.

Today, Netflix comes automatically loaded on over 25 different platforms including set-top boxes, televisions, gaming consoles, mobile devices, and major operating systems. Its bet on the future was spot on. Today, there are many services such as iTunes, Xbox, Playstation, and Roku where you can buy a movie that was recently released in theaters, from the comfort of your couch, in your own home and watch it in 4K, full-digital 3D (if you have a TV that can handle it). You can also keep that movie forever by either storing it locally or storing it in the cloud without taking up any physical space in your home. The real key to Netflix being a revolutionary company is that it never stops innovating.

In 2013, Netflix moved on to providing its own custom content, which was also disruptive. Until Netflix started releasing quality shows like *Stranger Things* and *Orange Is the New Black,* internet content sites were only known for replaying content from the major networks and movie studios. This was also incredibly revolutionary and disruptive to the networks, the movie industry, and other digital media providers. Consider the fact that Netflix now has major awards from the Emmys and Golden Globes. Apple has not embraced the custom content with its own platforms like iTunes and Apple TV, but based on its history, I would expect Apple to do so soon and to have a different take on it—perhaps interactive television shows where the audience participates in the story.

When Netflix started out by sending DVDs to people's homes, it wasn't even sure that it would get the DVDs back. But Netflix pivoted to delivering a world-class technology platform, compelling content, winning Emmys, and pushing the limits of the internet itself. Netflix had other lesser-known revolutionary moments as well. For instance, it operates its entire platform out of the Amazon Web Services cloud. So if you could go back in time and you knew what Netflix would become, what could your organization have done to take advantage of its success? Would you have approached Netflix while it was still small about payment services? Allowed it to directly debit from your customers' accounts? Maybe you could have started a campaign to encourage your customers to put your credit or debit card into Netflix as their preferred form of payment, or maybe struck a deal with Netflix to advertise its product in return for reduced fees for your customers.

*Time Travel Challenge:* If you could go back in time and visit your own organization, knowing what you know now, what technologies would you bet on that you didn't before? How would you organize your company to be ready for today? Don't focus on the obvious things, like home banking and mobile, as those are pretty easy. Focus instead on payments, and the things you wouldn't have done. What positions would you hire earlier? What systems would you replace? What products would you discontinue? When you finish, compare these to your organization.

## The Financial Revolution

So, what is a revolutionary tech, or what does it look like in financial business? The most revolutionary technology that I can think of that fundamentally changed the way we do business is remote deposit capture. Remote deposit capture, as many know, is the act of taking a picture of a check with your smartphone, flipping that check over and taking a picture of the backside, and then sending the images to the financial institution to be processed in a Check 21 format. The FI would then instantly deposit the funds to your account. Introduced by USAA, this feature quickly became popular and was duplicated throughout the industry. But what's more amazing to me is the fact that my then-65-year-old mother, not exactly a tech-savvy maven, saw this technology and said, "Woo hoo, I'm never going to the bank in the snow again," and through a sheer force of will, she learned how to use this feature.

She learned how to take her social security and VA checks and process them using the Check 21 feature. More importantly, not having mobile deposit became a deal breaker for many consumers. For a while, they waited for their financial institution to get the feature, but when it didn't deliver, they began the process of switching to a financial institution that offered the feature.

Getting this feature up and running became a challenge for all but the largest institutions. Many financial institutions had to wait to install this solution because of the magnitude of this service's success. Vendors who provided technology services, specifically mobile banking providers, were besieged with requests to implement this feature. This created a backlog of implementations because they didn't foresee this coming, and since mobile programmers were in high demand and other projects were already in flight, many FIs had to wait for a long time before providing their customers with this service. Over that time, how many consumers walked away? How many customers kept their account with the bank but started doing most of their banking elsewhere, so they could take advantage of this feature? This revolution was not spotted soon enough, and as a result, business was lost for institutions at the back of the implementations line.

How do you spot revolutionary technology? How do you handle evolutionary technology? The first thing is when you are looking at revolutionary or what I call innovative tech, right away, if it is not displacing something in your world but it is adding something new, you can at least say its innovative, and if it scales quickly, then it is likely to be revolutionary. If you're replacing your home banking or going to another bill-paying platform, that's not revolutionary. One great example of a revolution that is ongoing right now is the success of the Amazon Echo and the Amazon Alexa platform, the voice-based platform that Amazon has been pushing out into the world.

It's become a normal thing to see in people's homes. It scaled quickly; it was easy to put out there. It was not something I already had in my house. I did not have a talking black piece of plastic that I could ask about the weather or when movies were on or have it turn off and on my lights. I did not have anything like that. That was a great example of revolutionary tech that was not displacing something in my home. It wasn't a new form of my TV, it wasn't a different form factor on my computer—it was something radically different that I had to interact with in a different way.

By contrast, evolution involves scaling or building on a current idea. Electronic bill paying evolved from risk-based versus good funds models. Personal financial management evolved into setting goals for consumers and implementing safe-to-spend models. The mobile phone evolved into an MP3 player plus a mobile phone. It then evolved to include a camera. The mobile phone continued to absorb things that we carried around daily until we got it into a smaller, more compact offering that we can keep in our pocket. But that was ever evolving. If you think about it, scaling that was hard. We had to wait for cell towers to get into place. We had to wait for them to support LTE. We had to wait for them to support 4G. As a matter of fact, there was a time in this country that if two people were on different cell providers such as Verizon or T-Mobile, those two people could not text each other. That may seem crazy looking back now, and I believe we will look back at our payment methods in much the same way. It will seem crazy to our grandkids that we ever carried around a plastic card that we could lose or break. The trick to technology is how to spot things and see them as they come around the curve. To help you learn to identify revolutionary technology, in the next paragraph I am going to share with you some examples of things that I believe are going to be revolutionary technologies. The first one is artificial intelligence, or personal assistants. I mentioned it earlier; I mentioned Alexa. There is a whole new group, such as Siri—another artificial intelligence personal assistant. I think that in the future, you're not going to talk about what kind of cell phone you have. You are going to talk about who your personal assistant is, and how well that personal assistant is connected into your world. We are going to see these personal assistants grow in intelligence, they are also going to grow in their ability to connect to your world. They are going to connect to your email. They are going to connect to your task platforms. They are going to connect to your phone. They are going to read your voice mails. They are going to be able to read to your emails and respond to your emails. They are going to connect to your websites where you do your planning. They are going to be able to go in and make changes to your accounts, all by speaking to them. The next one is distributive ledger technology, also known as *blockchain*. It is a decentralized network that allows entities to directly interact without a entity in the middle. Understanding this technology is going to be particularly important for the financial institutions of the world. Distributive ledger solves a great many problems that financial institutions face when doing business with other organizations, moving money around, making payments, as well as selling and tracking assets. Blockchain technology, the underlying elegant technology that was invented to support the Bitcoin platform, will turn out to be a game changer in the financial space—and I am going to devote a whole chapter to that later, so hold on to that thought.

Finally, the other evolving technology is sovereign identity. Today, we have a password crisis. We all have too many passwords; we have too many usernames, and it has created fraud, it has created extra work for the call centers of the world, it's frustrating, and now we are going to see that identity is going to become like currency. The impact of this new technology will be felt worldwide, and again I am going to devote a whole chapter to sovereign identity.

What should you do when you identify one of these technologies? The simple answer is to dabble—this helps your organization to gain experience with whatever the technology has to offer. I have drawers full of stuff that I will never use again but I don't consider any of these devices to be a waste of money because I learned something from each one.

Apple Pay, Google Wallet, and Samsung Pay have all recently evolved into the marketplace, and yet none of them has started the payment revolution that everyone predicted. Instead, these platforms are considered just another layer in the ever-evolving payments ecosystem. Each of these systems were built on top of the very old payment rails that exist in the world today because none of them were willing to take the risk to create a new network.

Consider that Samsung bought a company called Loop. Loop had what I would call revolutionary technology that allowed people to translate their credit cards into magnetic communication that could be used at any store that has a magnetic point of sale device (POS) (if the POS doesn't need to have the physical card in it to operate). Thanks to my curiosity and identifying this technology before it was mainstream, I could experiment with the Loop technology long before Samsung purchased it. Understanding how this technology worked helped inform my perspective on its place in the payments world, which, in turn, helped my clients understand how to prioritize it in their project plans.

There are times you must go all in on these things, and there are times that you can just dabble. Dabbling is almost always a safe bet, as it usually isn't expensive to evaluate emerging consumer technology. It's valuable to have organizational knowledge about new technology. If you oversee your financial institution's innovative destiny, then it needs to be on your horizon to look at things like artificial intelligence, virtual reality, and drones. All too often, we tend to dismiss things that we just do not believe are going to have any direct effect on us, and that's really something that we must resist the urge to do.

You might dismiss cars that drive themselves because there's no use case for financial institutions. However, you must also consider the social impact that new technology can have on your business. How will self-driving cars change the way FIs do auto loans? How do you evaluate the impact it may have on the economy? How has a platform like AirBnB impacted your mortgage business? Could a case be made that less people are defaulting on their loans because they have a new source of income? Are new homebuyers considering AirBnB in their purchase plans? How many of the vehicles that your customers have financed are being used for Uber every day? What could your organization do to embrace these trends? Are these trends a threat? Those are the kinds of thinking exercises that executives need to continually be having with their boards and senior management. Just having the skill to recognize whether a technology is revolutionary or evolutionary is not enough. Your organization must also have the courage to capitalize on these insights.

As we go through the technology portion of this book, we're going to point out things that are evolutionary, point out things that are revolutionary, and more importantly, continue to try to help everyone put together a plan to identify the difference.

Here are some things to think about when evaluating a new technology:

1. Would customers be willing to leave your organization if you didn't have it?
2. Does it scale quickly and easily?
3. How hard is it to set up?
4. What kind of utility does it provide, and how often is this utility needed?
5. How much does it cost?
6. Does it replace anything? (If not, it's additive.)

## Chapter Review

- Evolutionary technology changes or scales an existing process or way of doing things.
- Revolutionary technology changes the fundamental way of doing something.
- Key revolution in the banking industry will come from the cloud, artificial intelligence, blockchain, and sovereign identity.

CHAPTER

3

# The Cloud

**Run! The cloud has become self aware!**

Unless you have been living under a rock, you probably have heard someone somewhere mention the cloud. Usually in the context of "that freaking cloud," in reference to trying continuously to delete a file only to have it mysteriously reappear, or, "The cloud is the greatest thing ever," uttered by a data center engineer who can now set up an entire system in minutes instead of weeks or months. Whatever the context was, I am sure that you recognized this was an upcoming technology and took note of it or asked a few questions to gain knowledge about it. From there, you likely made some snap decisions about the cloud based on your years of experience with services that have been run outside the four walls of your organization.

The cloud concept isn't exactly new, and in the financial business it's been around for a while. I know many organizations that outsource their ATMs or credit-card processing to what could be considered a cloud in today's terms. I have also seen many organizations move these services in house because of service issues, or a perceived lack of control of the service. I believe that by and large, these experiences have shaped the financial industries' overall fear of cloud-based services. Unfortunately, things can change, and sometimes we need to reexamine things before depending on our past experience to make a decision. The cloud fits into the category of things that we need to look at with a new pair of eyes. Let's start by defining what it is today. What exactly is the cloud? Maybe you have heard of Apple's iCloud, or maybe you saw an advertisement about a personal cloud. In terms of the financial business, what is the cloud?

## The Financial Cloud

The easiest definition of the cloud is that the software you run and the files you access are no longer tied to your computer or workstation; instead, they exist somewhere that is very accessible via the internet. In the corporate context, the cloud often refers to moving infrastructure and services from the corporate data center to an internet accessible data center like Microsoft Azure, Google Compute, or Amazon Web Services. For instance, think about the email on your local desktop. For a long time (and maybe even it's still true at some organizations), email was housed in a company-owned data center. The emails would come in through the internet and then be stored on a server somewhere within the company. Someone in the IT group would be responsible for backing up this server or making sure it had the appropriate protection against email viruses. They would also be responsible for setting up new users, planning upgrades, and general maintenance of the email server. Finally, financial institutions would make sure the server complied with Sarbanes–Oxley and any other regulations that the industry needs to implement.

The software a person uses to access email is located on their local computer, and it communicates to the email server in their data center to get your email and to send your newly composed emails or replies. The situation I just described is the opposite of the cloud. Everything is contained within the four walls of the organization.

Here is what a cloud version of email would look like: Email is stored on some hardware somewhere, but company employees wouldn't need to know where, or be concerned about how it gets there. In fact, their email could be stored on servers in a data center in Seattle on Monday but on Tuesday it could be stored on a data center in Kentucky. Wherever it is, the users don't have to worry about it. All they need to know is that their email works. The company hired to provide cloud email service would be responsible for knowing where the email is and making sure it gets to the right desktop. The same company would also be responsible for maintenance of the systems that are collecting and storing the email, complying with regulations, backups, and anything else that must be done to maintain your email service. Instead of accessing email via software stored on a local PC, employees would likely access their email by executing software over the internet.

Why would a company do this? Why would it outsource its email to some other service? After all, email has become a critical component of all business. (Don't believe me? Unplug your email server and watch what happens.) It seems crazy to lose control of it to a service with people you don't know. The answer to this daunting question lies in scale, aggregation, and efficiency.

Wow, I didn't think anyone was still using email...

The cloud-based email service provider can scale very easily. The email service has likely built out a very flexible infrastructure that allows them to do things like add storage or bandwidth on the fly. They can also easily expand the number of servers supporting the organization during busy times and then remove the excess servers during periods of low activity. If the servers were kept in house, the company would be forced to architect its email service to the greatest demand, even though that demand was only for a short period of time. Since the cloud bills are based on server usage, you only pay for what you use.

The cloud is also based on aggregation. In the case of email, a company is likely sharing servers, bandwidth, and support personnel with hundreds of other organizations. A medium-sized organization might have 2,000 email accounts on its server. While this might seem like a lot, the reality is that supporting 2,000 or 200,000 accounts is very similar in terms of the amount of work it takes for an email administration person. So, by sharing this person with other groups, companies are reducing their full-time employee count and, therefore, their overall ongoing cost to support email.

I would guess that an IT person reading this would think, "There you go. Best is talking about getting rid of <insert name of highly valued employees here> and replacing them with some idiots that I have no control over." Think again. I would actually say that the best thing to do with your highly valued employees is to retrain them so that they can manage your cloud service—but with the time they recovered, they can be of use in some of the new technologies that are going to be at the forefront of banking soon, such as chat servers or Skype communication. Their experience will be valuable for these new channels, and without email to weigh them down, they will be free to leverage what they know to help make new channels a success.

Efficiency is also a great motivator to move to cloud services—let's say an organization is going to upgrade its entire email platform over a weekend. If they haven't been through this process before, it can be very stressful. Often, new hardware is purchased and the emails need to be migrated from one server to another, which can take hours. When everything is done and the new platform is in place, then there is the need to test the platform and make sure everything is working properly, including things like secure email, virus protection, work-flow, and other critical features of the email system that employees depend on, day in and day out. However, in a cloud platform, one can easily provision new hardware, run the necessary updates and conversions, and then sit back and let the operators at the cloud service deal with the rest. Consider if they needed a new email server for a new division to test inbound sales emails with Salesforce. In the non-cloud situation, they would be responsible for building and deploying this system, but in the cloud they can provision a new system, test, and then simply turn it off when the team is done. One of the biggest slowdowns in new projects is often acquiring and setting new servers in a new environment. The cloud removes this issue from the equation by having infrastructure available on demand.

During my time at WRG and BIG, we have worked with both organizations that are all in house for their data processing and organizations that have embraced the cloud. The organizations that have embraced the cloud would finish a project almost two months earlier than the ones that were in house. This is because the in-house organizations had to purchase servers, have them shipped, then unbox them and get them on the network. After all of that was done, they had to be configured with the correct software and finally opened up to the implementation engineers via the internet so that custom home banking software could be installed. This could sometimes take months, whereas a cloud-based organization would go to their cloud console, click some buttons, answer some questions, configure security, and in less than an hour, they could make three to five servers available to our engineers for installation purposes. Any time you can turn months into hours, you need to pay attention to however it is being done. That said, the first time I experienced this, I immediately made it a point to reach out to the CTO of that organization and ask some questions.

## What Are You Afraid Of?

Like everyone, I had fear of the cloud. Here are my fears, in order of magnitude.

### It Is Hard to Control

Many organizations worry that they will have no control over their cloud-based processes and systems. Even worse, they worry that, as part of a huge cloud ecosystem, their concerns won't be important to the people who can effect change. What does control really mean in terms of a data center? For me, control meant being able to physically turn off a computer by pressing the power button if I wanted to, or unplugging the ethernet from a port if I wanted to or login in locally. Control also meant that I had someone who was accountable for these servers—a person who I trusted and who, if necessary, I could reprimand if there was a mistake. How do these things translate in the modern version of cloud software? Turns out, the modern cloud has many answers to this. First, you can actually "power off a system" or "unplug it from a hub," and second, you can also work with service providers that will provide management of these systems effectively, giving you accountability.

### It Is Insecure

Security is a huge consideration in the financial industry, and many people worry that the cloud can put sensitive data at risk. After all, companies might not know very much about the cloud provider's services, and they can't see the firewalls that are protecting them. This makes them doubtful that such security measures are even in place.

Even I have encountered this. Security was a huge concern because I was running data systems for a large financial network. What changed my mind was when both Amazon Web Services and Microsoft Azure became C2 certified, and offered a government ramp. Having some background in what it takes to meet these criteria from my security days helped me understand the protections that each of these groups had put in place. This by no means exonerates an organization from putting in all of the protections necessary and conducting the necessary penetration tests to ensure that their security is functioning. Also, this doesn't help if a company is writing applications that have inherent security flaws. In that situation, no amount of firewalls or other protections will save anyone from trouble.

I also discovered that organizations can deploy their own firewall systems in each of these cloud services, which was valuable information. Finally, how could I compete with Amazon or Microsoft in terms of the amount of security that they are able to afford versus my own organizations budget?

### Data Will Be Shared with Others

This isn't one of my actual fears, but I do encounter questions about it quite a bit. One concept of the cloud is that an organization doesn't need to provision an entire server. It can share the computing resources with others in order to reduce cost. Many people have concluded that if you are sharing a server with other organizations and an application on that server is hacked (even if it isn't yours), then the hacker would gain access to everything on that server. Fortunately, the smart people at Amazon, Microsoft, VMware, and other companies that provide this sort of technology accounted for this and created systems that are walled off from each other even though they are sharing computing resources. The data itself are never intermingled in that all processes are executed in their own space, and all data are stored in their own secure data areas, without intermingling. I can see why people would think this, because before true virtualization existed, many web-hosting providers would share a server or resource in a way that did expose the other applications if someone could gain access to any of the applications on that server; however, this technology is not in use in the major service providers.

### It's Unreliable

The number-one reason that people built their own data centers was because they had been involved in an outage while participating in a shared data center or some other service and the resulting loss of service cost money so as a result, they concluded the only way to ensure service availability at the level they could live with was to own the data center themselves. Once again, the big players like Microsoft, Amazon, and Google have thought of this. Each of them has spent enormous amounts of money building data centers around the world. In the new world of the cloud, a company can instantly transfer its entire service or server from, say, a data center in West Virginia to a data center on the West Coast. Even better, they could easily run their service in both places. This is something that would be very costly for a single organization to do by itself. As a result of these services, the cloud services have become very reliable.

### It's Super Expensive

This is one I actually will agree with to some extent. However, it's not super expensive if you factor in building a data center, maintaining it and paying for electricity, as well as air conditioning and all of the other critical systems that are needed to run a financial data center. Nevertheless, I have found that when an organization first discovers the cloud, its people go a little crazy when they realize how easy it is to set up networks and systems—things start exploding in what I call *SharePoint effect*.

Anyone who knows me knows I am not a fan of SharePoint, but it's not SharePoint's fault; it's my own fault. One day, my team discovered Microsoft SharePoint and we decided to implement it. The next thing I knew, at every meeting someone would say, "I put it on SharePoint," referring to a document or spreadsheet, and someone else would ask, "Which Sharepoint?"

The reason this happened is because I failed to see that a utility that was as easy to implement as SharePoint needed governance. I just saw it as a simple website that could help make things better. What I hadn't thought of was that it was so easy to set up that anyone, and I do mean anyone, would request one, and magically, it would appear. It got so bad, I had to ask them to color code the SharePoint services. This didn't seem like a big deal to the local users because they only used the one SharePoint site, but for cross-functional teams like accounting, or the executive group, it was a nightmare to even figure out what SharePoint site you were on. At one point, I actually caught myself saying, "Well, what we need is a SharePoint site to track SharePoint sites."

It was like trying to put out a fire using more fire. The same thing happens with the cloud—a new server can pop up in no time, instead of taking hours to set up a network or getting approval to set up a new server. So, yes, the cloud can be expensive if you don't put some governance around it. You must treat it like buying a server or any other service, and make sure that your team understands how to use it. This includes setting up the ability to turn it off during off hours, or sensing use and having it grow during busy times. I believe that at the end of the day, the cloud can be cheaper, but only if properly governed.

### There Will Be Staff Cuts

I have a theory about cutting people in IT. The theory is: Don't do it. If you manage to achieve a cost-saving factor, cutting heads isn't the best idea. Information technology is not like the call center, or a teller line where these folks have a single job. The information technology team is often well versed in the processes of other departments, and as such, they can be very valuable in the new and upcoming technology, I would suggest retraining them, learning distributed ledgers, implementing cloud-based programming (turning off and on servers to save money), or training them in artificial intelligence systems. These employees' inherent knowledge is valuable. Many times, they have many years of experience in your organization, so you must be very cautious about throwing this experience away. It might be easier to train them in a new technology rather than training an expert in new technology about your organization. They can also be transitioned to run outsourcing groups capitalizing on their experience and relationships within the organization to implement new services.

### The Internet Could Go Down

There is some truth to this one. Organizations using cloud services are dependent on the internet. However, let's face it, this is a truth even if you don't use the cloud. If you don't believe me, go ahead and unplug the internet now and see what happens. The reality is that while the cloud does add to the dependence on the internet, I would argue that you are no more at risk than you are today. I would also argue that due to the redundancies mentioned above, in the event of a major outage, the cloud providers have a better chance of surviving a event like this than you do on your own and as a result your customers will at least be able to access your digital services.

### It Is a Direct Expense

Keeping your storage services or servers in house can deceive the average CFO who is used to depreciating the hardware, software, storage, and network services associated with a project over three to five years, which, on paper, is seemingly favorable compared to the paying monthly fees for cloud services.

The biggest difference is the amount of overhead needed to maintain the infrastructure. This is often not factored into the "move to the cloud" equation. Also, I find it is unusual for an organization to factor in the disaster recovery or business continuity planning that was handled much more elegantly in a cloud services situation. Fully loaded costs will show that moving to the cloud is either a wash or cheaper.

A quote for Kirk Kordeleski former CEO of BethPage Credit Union in Long Island:

> Total cost of operations can be difficult to assess but if you go through the exercise we think you will find, like so many leading edge companies have found, it is far less expensive to operate in the cloud. As the cloud is the very definition of operating in the economies of scale. Economies of scale always prevails in commoditized business models (server storage is commoditized).

### What about Our Data Center?

Here is the bad news: If a financial institution is running a system on a mainframe, it will likely still need its data center in order to run core processing or main general ledger processing. However, what I have seen in some industries is a concept I will call AirDC. It's sort of like AirBnB but using data centers instead. An organization with a data center could share it with other organizations that use the same processing systems or other platforms. This could reduce costs. However, it's likely that an organization will continue to need its data center, but it can reduce power consumption and licensing costs.

### The Cloud Won't Conform to Regulatory Needs

I have heard the concern that the cloud doesn't provide enough control over where data are stored, and as a result, it may be stored in a geographic area that would make a financial services firm liable in the jurisdictions where we do business.

While this was once true, it is now possible to choose where data will be stored. Organizations have control over where their data are stored and processed. It's also important to note that custody of data can be directly related to where the data are decrypted.

### The Cloud Kills Baby Seals

OK, this isn't true, but there are people who believe that cloud computing's carbon footprint will increase global warming and kill baby seals. Through my research, I have discovered that that the main players are all working very diligently to use clean energy for their data centers. Google data centers have solar panels on the roofs of their data centers. Microsoft and Amazon both have clean-energy initiatives. The reality is that it's more likely that a non-cloud data center is killing baby seals. The big cloud players are likely cleaner.

## Types of Cloud Services

Now that we have talked through the main concerns, I would like to put a little more definition around the cloud to help you understand how you can use it. There are (at this moment) three main definitions of cloud services.

### Infrastructure as a Service (IaaS)

IaaS, or infrastructure as a service, is defined as providing computing and network services over the internet. Here is an example: Let's say that an organization has a new fintech lending organization that it wants to work with, and you need to set up a *sandbox* for them to work in. A sandbox is a network of servers that has access to development versions of your internal platforms like your lending platform so that the fintech dudes can do their thing.

If companies use their local data center, they might have a virtualization server from VMWARE and would provision the servers and create a network for the fintech folks to use. They would still need to have the fintech providers log in to the local data center, probably using a VPN. This requires approval from an internal security group and then building a private network to keep them out of anything else. In the cloud model, you would be able to provision the server, the network, the firewall, and the VPN all as a service and then make the sandbox available to the fintech players over the internet.

The internal setup could take a few weeks; the cloud setup might take a few days or hours. The other important concept here is that the fintech providers are in India or the United Kingdom and, as a result, their time zones are very different. They are not working during the same hours as your support staff, and with this in mind, your IT team can program the IaaS to shut down the sandbox when it is not in use, thereby saving money and reducing security concerns (every hour the servers are turned off is a hour the server cannot be hacked). IaaS dashboards are quickly becoming the norm in the fintech industry.

### Software as a Service (SaaS)

The best example of software as a service (SaaS) is Salesforce.com. Salesforce provides your sales team a database in the cloud. If an organization wanted to set up a customer relationship management (CRM) platform instead of buying or licensing the software, it would need to purchase the servers and have its IT team set it up. You would go to Salesforce.com and set up your organization with Salesforce.com. Your sales team would then use the web browser on their local PC or their smartphones to access the salesforce system and perform their duties. The beauty of this is that your information technology team is not responsible for upgrading or maintaining Salesforce; they are only responsible for making sure that the systems and devices the sales team uses to access the Salesforce.com website comply with the standards that Salesforce has set forth in their agreement. What this means is that the sales team can't be using Windows 95 running Internet Explorer 5. They will likely need to be on the latest operating systems and the latest browser technology to get the full benefit of the Salesforce product.

### Platform as a Service (PaaS)

Platform as a service (PaaS) is the third and final category of cloud services that is offered. Here is my example of platform as a service: Let's say that a company is organizing itself around the technology services organization, and as a result the team has decided to develop its loan application process in house. The team has chosen to use the Microsoft Net software as their programming system and as a result, the software they design will need to run in a Microsoft environment. This means that the developers will need to have software to develop on. In Microsoft, this is called Visual Studio. They will also need a place to store their code, which can be done using Team Services.

Finally, when the software is done, the team will need to have a place to deploy it, and the licensing to support the number of people that will access their new loan application. This would be an application called Microsoft Server, which can also cost money. So at the end of the day, all in to support the Microsoft development your team is doing, it could be hundreds of thousands of dollars. This doesn't include the hardware and firewalls associated with the application.

Nor will it include the environments that are needed to support the ongoing new application. By this I mean production, testing, and development, which are all distinct copies of each other meant for different purposes.

What is the answer to all of this? Microsoft sells all the afore-mentioned software as a platform services. This means a company's developers can use the platform to develop and it is automatically connected to their team services as well as their in-house environments. This frees the team to focus on the end result, which is the application. I could tell the same story using Amazon Web Services, Linux, and Java. Why is this important? One reason is because in the brave new world of development and innovation, sometimes projects will fail to produce the desired results and then when it is necessary to shut it down, companies are stuck with all the setup costs depreciating away on the books. The second reason is time to market, when your marketing, analytics, or sales team identifies an opportunity and your development team designs a solution to capitalize on it, you need to be able to move fast, build up, tear down, and make it happen. Waiting on servers and licensing can add months to a project. The final reason is that this allows your team to effectively outsource; this is going to be important in the new digital world of finances that is coming.

## Major Players in the Cloud

There are many players evolving in the cloud market—too many to cover in this book—but I did want to talk about some of the major ones.

### Amazon Web Services

OK, right off the bat you are probably thinking, Amazon? The same Amazon that sends me my dog food? Yes, that Amazon. Amazon had a problem to solve. Its internal projects that were supposed to finish in four months were taking twice as long as they should. Amazon realized that its network engineers were spending far too much time with its application engineers trying to coordinate infrastructure and other details. So Amazon decided to build a framework that could be used for all of its projects. After the framework was designed, Amazon realized that others could use it. So it started Amazon Web Services in 2006. As of this writing, Amazon Web Services provides a platform for hundreds of thousands of businesses in 190 countries around the world. Amazon has data center locations in the United States, Europe, Brazil, Singapore, Japan, and Australia.

### Microsoft Azure

Microsoft Azure was announced in 2008 and released in 2010, mainly in response to Amazon's offering. It was originally called Windows Azure, and eventually became Microsoft Azure. Azure provides a console application that allows administrators to easily setup environments, implement network changes, and take advantage of Microsoft services such as the business intelligence platform or artificial intelligence platforms.

### Google Compute Engine

Google Compute Engine (GCE) was introduced to the world in 2012 and is considered an IaaS solution. Similar to its competitors, it provides the ability to virtualize and run operating systems such as Linux, Microsoft, and BSD. GCE provides access to Google services such as its search engine, Gmail, YouTube, and their AI services via its cloud offerings.

### Commonalities between Each of These Platforms

Each service has similarities. They all support multiple operating systems, and billing for all three is reduced to a number that represents the compilation of computer resources (power, hardware, storage) that are called units.

Each platform also sells and supports its distinctive tools. For instance, in AWS, storage is powered by its proprietary storage platform called S3. Google has baked in some of its products to make it easier for developers and fintech providers to use its platform.

All three have multiple certifications such as SOC 3 (Service Organization Controls), PCI (Payment Card Industry), DSS (Data Security Standards), and DOD (Department of Defense) impact level 5 provisional authorization.

### How to Choose?

Much of the decision is going to depend the prevalent architecture and internal expertise within your organization. For instance, if your organization uses Microsoft products for both development and to service the front-line employees, then your obvious choice is Azure. Conversely, if your organization runs on open source Linux software and your internal expertise is in the Linux platform, then Google Compute Engine or AWS are probably a better choice for your cloud. You can also use both platforms (which is as a hybrid cloud), but don't expect them to easily communicate with each other. The current cloud environment is very competitive, and as a result, there isn't a huge incentive for Amazon to make it easy to connect your AWS cloud to your Microsoft Azure cloud.

## Capital One in the Cloud

So, have any major banks moved to the cloud and talked about publicly?

Yes, Capital One publicly stated in 2015 that it intended to move most of its data processing services to Amazon Web Services:

> "Technology is going to play a central role in the future of banking as we move toward an experience that is real-time, digital-first, and that anticipates customer needs. The AWS Cloud enables fast, efficient development and deployment of software and allows our teams to focus on what we do best— building great software and delivering innovative experiences to our customers," said Rob Alexander, CIO, Capital One. "We're taking a cloud-first approach to development with AWS as our predominant cloud infrastructure provider."[1]

Capital One has made it clear that this is not an experiment, it's a conscious strategy based around the reasoning that the winners in the banking industry will be the strongest technology players.

## Strategies for Moving to the Cloud

I find that the cloud is a very black-and-white subject with in financial organizations. FIs either find the cloud to be abhorrent or embrace it. I believe there is middle ground. Some things can be safely moved right now to the cloud that would improve security as well as your ability to execute. I call this approach to cloud migration the *hybrid cloud* approach. The hybrid approach involves only moving nonproduction platforms to the cloud. One example would be a development or test environment. It also includes connecting the cloud to your local infrastructure.

Regardless of whether you develop software in house or purchase software from vendors, your organization will have a place for these entities to test out their new releases or to do their initial installations. Having been on the other side of the process for many years, I know that just getting connected to a financial institution test or development environment can be an incredibly painstaking process. Some organizations will demand a VPN be used, and so all users must have VPN software installed on their employee's equipment. In fact that's what vendors talk about when you aren't around. They say things like, "OMG, dude, did you have to give blood to get connected to such and such?" and, "It took us six months just to get the test environment up." Some organizations insist that all development be done on virtual environments, and these environments must be set up inside of the organization. Another issue is that if the environment doesn't exist—say, in the case of a new application—then the FI will often order new equipment, and that can add months to the project. The cloud is a perfect place to put this sort of environment. The test systems shouldn't contain any actual real customer data that should overcome any security objections, and since the cloud isn't connected to the organization's backbone, it effectively creates a walled garden for the vendor. This should reduce the security requirements to access the environment. It is far easier for the IT staff to provision servers and other services (like a mail service or phone service) in the cloud since it is not connected to any production systems. Finally, a nonproduction system doesn't need to be on 24/7 and can be scheduled to shut down during off hours, which will also reduce cost. This approach increases security, reduces cost, and increases time to market. In general, every production system has a mirror-image test system and development system somewhere in your infrastructure. Identifying each of the systems and moving them to the cloud could prove to be the perfect first move for an organization considering using the cloud.

There is also an evolving new option that would allow you to take advantage of some of the services of the cloud inside your own data center. Microsoft has announced azure services that can be run inside the four walls of any data center, or data centers. This allows the advantages of instant provisioning, scheduling resources, sharing resources, and migrating between data centers instantly. There are some limits to this approach; your options for data centers will be limited to your own data centers. However, this approach can also be synchronized with Microsoft Azure Cloud, allowing your data center to be integrated with the cloud. I would imagine that organizations that are resistant to the cloud will avoid this feature; however, for those who embrace it and have a significant investment in a data center, this could extend the life of that investment.

Here are the primary reasons for a financial institution to consider moving to the cloud:

- Leverage cloud services to minimize replacement costs of current IT infrastructure.
- Refocus the technology team in supporting the front-line and back-office staff and business-focused projects.
- Assign the day-to-day administration and management of network and server equipment to a third-party provider.
- Implement a redundant, fault-tolerant, highly available data center and eliminate single points of failure on networks, server farms, communications systems, core platform, and enterprise storage.
- Provide capability to have quicker flexibility in our IT infrastructure.
- Enforce best-practice perimeter and internal information security systems to preserve confidentiality, integrity, and accuracy of assets.
- Effectively support business continuity and survivability of corporate facility and all remote branch offices.

## Chapter Review

- The easiest definition of the cloud is that the software you run and the files you access are no longer tied to your computer or workstation. Instead, they exist somewhere that is accessible via the internet.

(continued)

(*Continued*)

- The three primary types of cloud service are infrastructure as a service (IaaS), software as a service (SaaS), and platform as a service (PaaS).
- The hybrid approach involves moving only nonproduction platforms to the cloud.

## NOTE

1. Casey Coombs, "Big Amazon Web Services Deal Ups the Stakes in Cloud Battle with Microsoft," https://www.bizjournals.com/seattle/news/2016/11/30/big-amazon-web-services-deal-ups-the-stakes-in.html.

# CHAPTER 4

# Artificial Intelligence

Let's get one thing out of the way quickly: This chapter will NOT be about fictional artificial intelligence (AI) systems gone rogue. There's no Skynet here. What it will be about is how this technology is going to change financial institutions and services as we know it soon. This promise that artificial intelligence will change everything has been made many times, but we are very close now. One reason for the recent boom in artificial intelligence applications is the amount of data that are available. This thinking is kind of counter-intuitive, right? Most people think that artificial intelligence is being driven by Moore's law, which originally stated that the processing power of computers would double every year, and as of 2015, Intel a leading maker of processors, has stated that the cadence is closer to two and half years. However, the real driver of the AI revolution is the amount of data now available. To understand why the data revolution is driving the AI boom, it is necessary to understand a bit of how AI works under the covers.

## Computers Will Be Trainable

I was in an airport and I bought a *Wired* magazine to read on the plane. It contained an article titled "Soon We Won't Program Computers. We'll Train Them Like Dogs."[1] As I read the article, I pondered what that really means from a financial institution's perspective.

If you're doing any research at all on artificial intelligence, you'll see that the concept of training is a recurring theme. The *Wired* article used the concept training a computer to recognize a cat. Jason Tanz points out the logical place to start is to teach the computer how to look for whiskers, ears, and fur. However, thanks to the evolution of artificial intelligence platforms and the ability to analyze pictures, the best approach is to feed it pictures of cats. In fact, the more pictures of cats you feed it, the smarter it gets and the more likely it is to be able to identify a cat from a group of photos.

There are limits to this approach. For instance, it may eventually start misclassifying foxes as cats, as they are similar. The answer to solve this problem is to send the AI engine pictures of foxes as well. A great example of this technology is Google's TenserFlow, which is the backbone of Google Photos. If you haven't used Google's Photos, it's a great example of what artificial intelligence looks like in practice. It categorizes your photos based on who is in them, where they were taken, when they were taken, and even what is in them. For example, of you searched for the term *elephant* and you had taken a picture of an elephant or many pictures of elephants, it would return a list of these pictures. It will even find a picture of an elephant on a TV that is in a picture. A highly used feature of Google Photos is its ability to automatically create a video with music from your vacation photos to share with your family. Recently, Google added the ability to create videos about your pets. It can recognize your pets (yes, it will discern your dog from other dogs) and create a video about your dog's day, or a trip you took with your dog—and let's be real, you know you want an instant video of your dog pictures. How can you resist?

## Machine Learning: Familiar Names

For more context, let's look at an example such as Siri. Siri is Apple's personal assistant software that has been in place on all iPhones released since 2010. Siri will take notes, give you directions, send texts, make calls, take pictures, and look up information for you. Recently, I was having dinner with a friend and he was sharing a story where he and his friend were trying to decide how old Charlton Heston was when he made *The Ten Commandments*. My friend, as a joke, picked up his phone and asked Siri, "How old was Charlton Heston when he made *The Ten Commandments*?" thinking that there was no way that Siri could handle this request. Without missing a beat, Siri replied "Charlton Heston was 33 when he filmed

*The Ten Commandments*." My friend was astonished; he didn't think there was any way that Siri would answer this question. However, if you consider the training concept above, it is not surprising at all. According to Siri herself, Siri answers more than 1 billion questions a week. Here is how it works: A person asks Siri a question like, "What time is it in Rome?" Siri answers, "In Rome, Italy, the time is 7:30 a.m." However, the requestor wanted the time for Rome, Georgia. The challenge here is the ambiguity of the request. The user will likely realize the mistake and ask again, "Siri what time is it in Rome, Georgia?" and Siri would respond correctly.

The interesting part here is that these data would be analyzed by Apple, and the system would notice a trend where people were having to qualify their requests to get the information they were really looking for. So how would they disambiguate this data? Siri could ask which Rome the user wants the time for, but there are many cities in the world named Rome. Siri could also look at past requests to determine context. If the user had recently asked Siri to "Show me flights to Rome, Italy," then Siri could assume the time request is also about Italy based on the inference from the previous question. This is a more complex example; here is an easier example. Let's use our Charlton Heston request as an example. Since Siri processes over 1 billion requests as week, it is highly likely that someone asked a similar question at some point. When this question was asked, Siri didn't understand how to respond, and the user that asked simply moved on. However, his failed request was recorded, and somewhere deep in the bowels of Apple's Siri department, there is a team of people reviewing failed requests. If there are enough of them, they will train Siri to answer the question, and the next time someone asks a similar question, Siri will respond. This learning mechanism didn't require a software upgrade to the Apple device, nor did it require a hardware upgrade. Siri simply learned a new trick, like a dog.

Understanding that artificial intelligence needs to learn should lead you to the logical conclusion that the quality of an artificial intelligence application is dependent on the quantity and quality of the data it is trained with. If this is the case, then to be successful with AI, your institution's data must be in order.

It is also dependent on the number of users and the different types of requests it is exposed to. This is of concern for financial institutions, because it is not likely that even the most robust financial intelligence application will generate 1 billion request a week, especially for small to medium-size institutions. What this means is that unless you are Bank of America or some other large institution, there is a need for cooperation or collaboration for this technology to be valuable for financial institutions. If each institution goes about training individually, there will not be enough requests and peer data to increase the intelligence of the application to keep up with other AI applications. If a customer asks the FI's AI application a question like, "What is the available balance of my checking account?" and for one reason or another the AI didn't understand the request, the good news is that the FI can "teach" the AI what the customer wanted. However, that will only be for that FI. If another FI is using the same engine but it is not connected in terms of learning, the second FI will derive no benefit from the teachings of the other FI. This means that each FI will learn at an inconsistent rate, and furthermore, each FI will take twice as long to get to the same intelligence state as if they combined their requests so that each could learn from each other's requests.

## Artificial Intelligence versus Intelligent Augmentation

So far, we have been discussing artificial intelligence as the primary form of this technology. However, many computer scientists believe that the real future of AI is related to creating intelligence that incorporates human interaction into the learning mechanism. Consider the process I described in the previous paragraph, where a human is reviewing the things that people are saying that the computer didn't understand. This is an example of augmenting the human intelligence. The computer handles everything that it can understand, and what it cannot it sends on to its human operator for review.

I believe that this approach will be the most common form of intelligence that is incorporated into the financial services platform. So, while there has been many predictions that systems using some sort of AI will replace humans in jobs, I believe that humans will still be integral and that these technologies will boost the humans' ability to perform in the workplace and instead of replacing jobs, it will slow down job growth by allowing the current workforce to handle more requests than previously thought possible. Intuitive services will anticipate the needs of the customers that a staff member or system is serving, and as a result, transacting business will be quicker and more efficient and will foster new engagements.

*Machine learning* is the most commonly used term to describe the science that is behind the most popular AI engines. Machine learning is also closely related to statistical computations, and, as mentioned before, it relies heavily on data analytics.

One of the most popular emerging AI platforms is Amazon's ECHO product. Released in 2015, in a little less than two years Amazon has now sold over 11 million units. The ECHO platform and its underlying natural language processor (NLP) Alexa have been opened up to developers to create what Amazon refers to as *skills*. Skills are similar to apps in the Apple app store, but these skills extend the ability of the Alexa platform. Many banks and credit unions have released skills for Alexa that allow customers to use the Alexa platform as their own personal teller.

USAA recently released its Alexa skill; it was the first skill to use something other than the Alexa NLP. USAA worked with a company called Clinc. The Clinc platform can engage in conversational commerce without needing to have a trained rule set. The Clinc brain processes all requests to the USAA platform and provides the response. It also allows it to understand complex questions such as, "How much money did I spend on my recent vacation?" or "Can you compare how much money I spent at Starbucks this year versus last year?" This is contextual and represents a significant leap in the AI space as it relates to financial services.

Facebook announced that it was opening up its messenger system to allow organizations to utilize the popular communication platform to communicate with their customers. At the FaceBook F8 developer conference in 2016, Bank of America announced its intention to release a chatbot and work with FaceBook, and in October of that same year, it released its chatbot Erica. Erica will update you on your FICO score, send you alerts, and help you pay your bills.

JPMorgan Chase introduced an artificial intelligence product called COIN, which is short for *contract intelligence,* whose purpose was to review complex contracts and reduce the need for humans to review commercial loan agreements. JPMorgan reports that the service is doing work that once required more than 360,000 man hours per year.

These kind of wins represent a significant advantage for the larger players and widens the gap between the largest financial services companies and their smaller competitors.[2]

What if AI solutions evolve to write their own code?

Siri co-founder Dag Kittlaus debuted his new artificial intelligence assistant called VIV.AI at the New York Disrupt in 2016 that does just that. In addition, he introduced the term *conversational commerce*. Following is an excerpt from his speech and incredible demonstration:

> I'm going to take another bigger leap to sort of a question you might not ask actually, just to show you a little more of the power. Will it be warmer than seventy degrees near the Golden Gate Bridge after five PM the day after tomorrow? . . . Okay. So this is a pretty sophisticated query. Very few assistants in the world do stuff like this, but this is where VIV can be trained up by developers. . . .
>
> So, looks fairly straightforward here but there's actually something pretty extraordinary going on. The first thing that we do is we have our friends from Nuance, who we're using for our speech recognition today, turn the sounds into words. Then you can see we have a very sophisticated natural language understanding and that generates something called an intent. But then here's where the magic comes in. So we've got a new technology that we've been working on patenting, and it's a computer science breakthrough called Dynamic Program Generation. So when it understood the intent of the user, it generated this program. So, this is software that's writing itself. . . .
>
> It's hard coded, but that doesn't scale. This is a dynamic program that in ten milliseconds it writes itself, that creates an execution program that goes out and ties the pieces of the services that you need.[3]

After he demonstrated his new platform's amazing feats, he moves on to demonstrate "conversational commerce" by demonstrating VIV's integration to the popular person-to-person payments platform Venmo. He simply says, "Send Adam $20 for the drinks last night," and VIV automatically finds the payee and finalizes the payment. This integration should be especially eye-opening to financial institutions, as it is moving an experience that has been traditionally executed inside the financial institutions digital platform to an experience that is not controlled by the FI. This should serve as a wakeup call for FIs that are not exploring AI solutions.

VIV will continue to learn, and not just learn from your conversation or your members or customers conversations, but everyone in the world's conversations. As it goes along, it will create custom programs on the fly to accommodate its incoming requests. Now imagine this same solution with full access to your transaction history. How could it adapt a request like, "How much did I pay my homeowners' association last year?" What kind of program could it write with access to your bill pay history? Could it redistribute your funds for maximum profit based on monitoring the stock market? The possibilities are endless.

However, AI doesn't stop at just voice or text solutions. For instance, what can we do with image recognition in the financial space? How about using image recognition to instantly recognize people adding skimmers to your ATMs by training an AI system to monitor the ATM camera and alert you when a person has put on a skimmer? Similar technology could be used to monitor cash room workers for fraud.

The use cases for AI in the financial sector are piling up. In the next two years, I believe that the most innovative solutions in banking will involve artificial intelligence.

## A Conversation with Brett King

I recently had the pleasure of interviewing world-renowned speaker and *New York Times* best-selling author of *Bank 3.0* and *Augmented* Brett King on my podcast. It wasn't very long before we started discussing AI solutions, here is an excerpt from that podcast.

Brett      The personal impact of this technology [AI] is what really interests me. So things like wearing a sensor on your wrist or in your clothing that can predict that you're going to have a heart attack. And so maybe you have a wristwatch or smart watch where you have embedded sensors in your shirt that you're wearing, and it can read your heart rate. And over time, we build up these sample data of people's heart rate around the world and we can see when people get into cardiac distress and when it leads to declining heart health and so forth.

And we can start to track that now using AI. And so, within about a year from now we'll start to see this sort of

*(continued)*

(*Continued*)

algorithm-based technology be able to predict maybe a few days out or a few weeks out that you're going to have a heart attack. This now prevents the cost of a $90,000 cardiac event because we can get you to a health care professional well before the heart attack occurs. But in a few years as that technology matures, then we'll be able to tell two years out that you're going to have a problem with your heart. And we'll be able to now instead of rushing you off to the hospital, we ought to put you on a nutrition program. Or get you to a dietitian that can, or get you to a fitness trainer that can deal with the problem in a different way.

. . .

Now when you apply that to, say, banking, and you start thinking of automation of advice as you do the snowplow or the truck driving or the heart analysis, the medical. But then what's interesting here is that the sort of advice that the banks have sold us that we need, we actually will find that we probably don't need that. I'll tell you why, right now today if you go to a bank and you're thinking about buying a home, then what advice do you get from the bank? What you don't get is, you don't get advice as to whether you should buy a home. What you get advice on is [whether] you can take this mortgage or that mortgage, you get product advice. When you go to a bank and you get investment advice, you don't really get investment advice about how you should save more money, how you should plan for your retirement. You need to go to a financial planner or a money coach for that.

When you go to a bank, you need this asset class or that asset class. Again, it's product-based advice. So the advice that we're going to get from AI built into the world around us with banking is going to be more personalized around you and your financial health. So, a simple answer to a simple question like, hey, Siri, can I afford to go out to dinner tonight? This is the type of advice that will be embedded in the ecosystem around you. Surfacing bank utility in a way that's more personalized.

You suddenly have all these machines executing comments on our behalf, and that's not that different from the online ordering systems we have today right now, where you initiate the transaction. Right, you initiate the transaction, but in the future your agent will do that for you. But what's really different is that product design will have to change, because now a product like a restaurant is fairly—or a service like a restaurant—is fairly simple, it's not going to change that significantly. But in banking, if you think about payment for example, a 16-digit credit card that has attached to it airline miles that relies on you increasing the frequency of use of that specific piece of plastic to get airline miles, just doesn't fit in that world anymore. Right? It's of no benefit. You're not going to stop halfway through the Alexa transaction for reserving the restaurant, say, "Hang on Alexa let me give you this other credit card number because I'm going to get more airline miles on it." Now, you might set up two or three different payment mechanisms and you might say, "Hey Alexa, pay using my corporate account."

|  |  |
|---|---|
| John | Right, you might have Alexa have access to both of those accounts. And she would go, "Yeah, if I buy this on this one I'll get more value out of the return proposition from the organization than I would if I bought it here. And also, then I could get a free Uber to the place for him by doing that." And that's where the super intelligence is coming in. And this concept of "agency" that you just tossed out there, I have been putting a lot of thought into this concept and what these agents are going to look like. How do we prevent this dysfunction around these agents over time? And I think that there's no way around it. It's just going to be a disruptive force. . . . But let me throw something else at you that I've been working on quite a bit. . . . We've been working on our FIVE (financial interactive voice experience) platform which runs Alexa. It now runs Google Home, Cortana, and Facebook chat all together. . . . If I said to you, "Brett, let's have dinner while I'm out in New York in a couple weeks." And I didn't say anything else, what would you say? |
| Brett | I'd say that I've got to check my calendar. |
| John | . . . We agree to follow back up on it after you check. So that's something we're building into Alexa. If you get in the middle of something, and you don't have what you need you can just say, "Hey, put a pin in it. Or hang on to that." And later on, it will remind you. But that's where these more human concepts . . . combine with this idea of agency to bring in like |

(*continued*)

*(Continued)*

| | |
|---|---|
| | you said just amazing stuff. Like that future that you just said right there, I just don't think it's that far away. I mean, how long would you say before you can get to the dim sum Chinese Alexa order? |
| Brett | Well yeah, exactly. We're just not that far away from being able to execute this. . . . And the idea is to embed it into our life and capture as much of your comments in day-to-day life as possible. Because that's what the stickiness to the platform is. Not apps on your phone anymore. It's now which voice assistant you use. |
| John | Right, and so here's the concept that I also have been looking at for our FIVE platform. So let's say that I build Movin, a platform, which you already have a great one. And I get on it and I say, "John wants to know his balance." Alexa doesn't quite understand that. But I would actually get to go in and see that there was this response that Alexa didn't understand. And then I could train it. So this concept of training an AI is really important. It's a mechanism of time. And so, I've been telling a lot of folks in the banking industry that every day that goes by that you're not training an AI, you're losing a month. |
| | So one of the things we did with FIVE is we put it all together. So let's say Movin's on the platform, but a different institution is on that same platform and I say that weird thing. Once I teach [one AI assistant], now Movin also knows that, too. And so, I'd like you to comment on this little AI training thing. Because here's the thing, how long is it going to take before that AI understands Brett's behaviors? And what kind of training does it take? And do we have those facilities today, which is basically an element of having data? |
| Brett | The speed with which these AIs learn and learn our behaviors is going to be incredible—just going to blow our minds in terms of how quickly these machines can learn and come up to speed. I think it's going to happen much faster then everyone expects. |
| | In terms of the jobs around this, MIT actually did some really interesting research and it classified the jobs that it created by AI into three broad categories into learners, explainers, and |

sustainers. So, in terms of the sort of role that you could have working with an AI, the trainers or the learners, that's pretty straightforward. . . .

It's a set of creative [people] figuring out how to make AI acceptable from a psychology perspective. When is the right time for an AI to pop up? How do you have a relationship with that AI and communicate with it? And on a sustained basis, how do you continue to keep it relevant? So there's a lot of really interesting potential in this space.

The key really is that what AIs are going to be doing is, it will be—it will be taking out all of the friction that we have around the current system, whereas today humans are perceived as adding value because they remove the friction. . . . Half the time you go to a bank branch . . . is [because] you've come up against a point where you can no longer solve this problem yourself. And you need to go to someone to get advice. And particularly with a bank, you might even have a situation where the bank creates this problem, this artificial problem: Now you must come in and present an ID before we will do this transaction like a wire transfer. And so they force you into that scenario. Or you've got to sign this piece of paper. And so those elements where today you go and see a human, you know all that's going to be gone because it adds zero value to your experience today. If anything, it just creates frustration and more friction.

So we're attacking that friction with AI initially, but then after that then the opportunity is to say, "Well what has an AI learned about me that we can leverage off?" And how does that present itself in ways that a bank couldn't do? For example, I can't ask my bank today, "Can I afford to go out for dinner?" But that's going to be a pretty simple task for an AI that's linked to your various bank accounts. That's going to be a pretty simple. So that's an example of where—actually, that's probably far more valuable to you than which type of mortgage you should get for buying a home. Because ultimately, it's those sort of day-to-day decisions, financial decisions where if you've got assistance and advice on that would have far more impact to your ability to save and your ability to manage your financial health well.

*(continued)*

(*Continued*)

John    So that would be your sustainer, right? So your learners are your classifiers, which is kind of AI speak for the learning piece of it. The explainers are sort of the contextual implementation of it, like, where does it fit in the process, and how is it valuable? And then the sustainers are taking the knowledge from those transactions and making it smarter. And then also pushing it into other areas and growing it. Is that kind of what those three things kind of come together as?

Brett   Yeah, absolutely.

John    Interesting. Because I've been looking at this neat site. The point of the site is that somebody's realized that we're all doing this training, but we're all doing it separately, right? . . . And those classifiers or those routines are going to be fundamentally valuable. But the challenge is they're not going to be portable. . . . This year I started work on something for myself, I call it winston.net. . . . I hooked it into my calendar. I hooked it into my Wunderlist. I hooked it into my bank accounts. And I hooked it into my email. And just that alone, having access to all four of those things, it allowed it to really go crazy.

And for me that kind of leads to this idea of banking where we're always trying to sort of be everything to a customer or a member. We're trying to be their email, we're trying to be their calendar, we're trying to be all these things and its sort of a captured business model. AI is going to require that we set that information free, right? AI is going to require that your bill pay payees need to be moved to me. But the thing is, I don't think the banks are going to give up on that captured business model until they're forced to. Which is going to be by consumers, sort of a revolution type thing. Consumers going, 'Yeah, I'm not doing that anymore.' Am I way off here?

Brett   Well, this is why we have fintechs—this is why we have fintechs. Because the fintechs aren't married to those old business models and ideas. And are rapidly trying to embrace those abilities to create value. What's really interesting is *Bank 4.0,* my new book, I talk about how the future of financial services is emerging.

In 20 or 30 years' time, what banking will be like, then if you want to look at what is a good model to see where banking is going, then . . . the best examples of this are actually from developing economies. . . . You look at Elon Musk with SpaceX and with Tesla. The super-charging network is an example of first principles design of how we think about energy for a vehicle. The design of the vehicle itself is a lot of first principles thinking.

We've gone down from a million parts to a few hundred parts. So that's a pretty big shift. But in the process of using first principles design philosophy with SpaceX, Musk's been able to get to a point where now we're looking at about $300 per kilogram to orbit. Compared with the space shuttle days, which was $6,000. So you're talking about a 95 percent reduction because of rethinking that design methodology. If you were going to start from scratch today, would you build a rocket the same way as the Germans built the V2 rocket in WW2 and the answer is no. You use 3D printing, you use different manufacturing techniques, different materials, different fuel sources—the whole thing you model is on a computer. The whole thing's very different, right?

Now if you apply the same to banking, if you ask that simple question: If I was going to start from scratch today and redesign banking to work better in people's lives, would it look anything like banking today? And the answer is an emphatic shout-it-from-the-rooftops *no*. Frankly, you're not going to say, "I'm going to build this building, and I want you to come along to this building and sign a piece of paper. And then I'm going to give you a booklet of paper that you can tear off a page in that book and send it to someone that represents money. Or I'm going to give you this plastic card." You just wouldn't do that. If you were starting from scratch today, that is not how you design banking.

So, if you look at examples of first principles design in banking you see Alipay in China, you see Tencent WeChat with financial services embedded in it. You see M-Pesa in Kenya, you see Paytm in India. And what you observe in those countries is the fastest ever shift in financial inclusion ever. Not as a result of bank branches or bank products or bank charters or bank licenses, but as a result of the mobile phone. As a result of technology.

*(continued)*

*(Continued)*

... You see a product that in eight months raised $90 billion in baseline deposits, that put 40 percent of deposits at risk from traditional banks because of this new technology on mobile. And it proved instantly overnight that the mobile phone was a much, much better deposit vehicle than the branch had ever been. I could name a hundred of these examples. So you look at first principles design philosophy and you say banking has to be different. Now, that presents a problem for incumbents. Because now you're looking at Venmo, which is going to issue their own debit card, and Apple Pay, which has got their own wallet now. They're essentially bank accounts. Starbucks has its own bank account. Xbox has its own bank account with your credits and so forth. And between Xbox and Starbucks, you know how much those guys manage in deposits? We're talking about $60 billion of deposits that they have.

John    Oh, yeah, I've actually been doing a ton of research on that for our SetitCredit product. Being top of app is the new future.

...

Brett    Now if you look at what is the requirement of a bank? Or the banking architecture that we have in place. What do you need from that as an individual? And it's very simple. You need a safe place to store your money. You need a value store. And if that value store can appreciate even better, right? So you need a value store. Then you need the ability to move money, to pay people, to send money. To send money to a friend or pay a service provider, or pay for goods and services. Payment capability, right?

And then the last thing you need is, you need access to credit from time to time at various occasions. Whether that's emergency cash to buy your groceries, or whether it's buying an iPhone you can't afford to buy out of cash today or whatever. Right? So you need access to credit. But this is the core pieces of utility for banking that we need. So what is the reusable rocket in banking? The reusable rocket in banking is access to that utility experientially. So it's contextual credit. The ability to just move money and save money without having to worry about physically going to a branch opening a savings account. Or all of those things that can just happen seamlessly. So it's access to that utility.

It's not access to bank rails, it's not access to bank products, it's not even being banked. Because we talk about Kenya, prior to Empasa, a quarter of the Kenya et al. population had access to a bank account. Effectively today, 100 percent of the adult population has access to a quasi-bank account as a value store on their SIM card on their phone. Now for that 75 percent of adults who've come into the financial system over the last 10 years, they don't necessarily think of Empasa as a bank. But they do know that their money is on their phone, and it's secure. Right, so and that is able to provide the utility for that.

Empasa doesn't need a banking license to do that. Then if you start thinking about those other pieces of utility, you probably don't need a bank to do much of that stuff, either. So, as we shift away from bank products, a savings account, a checking account, a credit card, a car loan, to now just embedded utility of a bank. The ability, hey, I've got money on my phone, I can pay for this. I can send you money, I can buy this, I can walk into a store and get credit for an iPhone, whatever it is. As that utility becomes embedded through AI and agency and so forth, you now have the utility of banking, you don't have the products and channels of banking that you used to have. You just don't need those anymore. You don't need a plastic credit card. You don't need to sign a physical application form to open a savings account anymore. That's really the first principles redesign is thinking about where that utility of banking fits logically in people's lives on a day-to-day basis.

## The AI Threat

Not everyone is excited about this upcoming technology. Elon Musk the entrepreneur and driving force behind SpaceX and Tesla, two of the most innovative companies in the world, is very afraid of artificial intelligence technology and stated this many times publicly. Elon Musk has made it very clear that he believes that AI is, in his words, "humanity's biggest existential threat." In fact, he is so concerned that he has invested in many AI technologies with the purpose of influencing the decisions made in regards to the development of these threats. So how could this concern come to life in the financial world? I believe that due to the lack of financial education for our future generations, that they will come to rely on a financial AI of sorts, so much so that some will give it complete control of their money and allow it to prevent them from making purchases, or forcing savings on their behalf. In this situation, the customer might tell the AI "not to allow me to purchase anything even if I tell you to," or they will give the ability to shut it down to someone else they trust in order to prevent themselves from overspending. This sort of AI would impose discipline around savings. I could see this sort of arrangement resulting in some interesting situations for users of this technology. I call it the Pink Panther effect. In the *Pink Panther* movies, the Peter Sellers character, the hapless Inspector Clouseau, instructs his sidekick Cato to continuously attack him in order to keep him vigilant for his job on the police force. He also instructs him **NOT** to stop, even if he is asked to, or even begged to. The results are many hilarious moments through the movies where Clouseau is surprised by Cato, hiding in different places and trying to kill him. Sadly, Inspector Clousaeu didn't think about the times he would rather not be attacked, and since he told Cato not to listen to him, there is no way to stop Cato from attacking. An intelligent financial application that has been told to help you save might not release your funds for an emergency room visit or for a taxi or Uber to get home. If the AI application is told to act on your behalf, it may be difficult to get it to stop (however this is easily solved with some forethought; this is just an example). The most popular fear is centered on the idea of the AI reaching a level intelligence often referred to as *the singularity*. The singularity refers to a time when supercomputers running artificial intelligence solutions become so intelligent that they transcend their human creators and, as a result, humankind experiences exponential technology growth that may or may not be detrimental to humanity (depending on how our new AI overlords view us).

More recently, Elon Musk, Alphabet's (formerly Google) Mustafa Suleyman, and 116 other specialists from 26 other countries, called on the United Nations to ban the development of autonomous weapons.

"Once developed, lethal autonomous weapons will permit armed warfare to be fought a scale greater than ever, and at timescales faster than humans can comprehend."

The experts fear that while AI weapons would make warfare safer for soldiers, it would also increase the loss of human life exponentially. Elon Musk has said, "Sometimes what will happen is a scientist will get so engrossed in their work that they don't really realize the ramifications of what they're doing."[4]

AI represents the most significant threat to financial institutions. Just like an autonomous weapon is capable of waging war in timescales faster than humans can comprehend, autonomous banking could create a significant gap between smaller financial institutions and the largest banks. This gap will be revolutionary, and by my definition, it will lead to services and features that customers will be willing to leave your bank or credit union to have access to. This is technology that also lends itself to a collaborative approach. Since the largest banks can create the scale (as discussed earlier in this chapter), the medium and smaller banks will need to find a way to achieve scale. The logical solution is to collaborate. Even larger banks will be forced to collaborate, thanks to technologies like distributed ledger and sovereign identity. Institutions that embrace collaboration for technologies like AI, sooner rather than later, will survive the upcoming revolutions that this technology will bring.[5]

## Chapter Review

- Machine learning is the most commonly used term to describe the science that is behind the most popular AI engines. Machine learning is also closely related to statistical computations and, as mentioned before, it relies heavily on data analytics.

- Artificial intelligence will most likely be used in the financial services platform to augment human intelligence. The computer handles everything that it can understand and what it cannot it sends on to its human operator for review.

- Autonomous banking could create a significant gap between smaller financial institutions and the largest banks.

## NOTES

1. Jason Tanz, "Soon We Won't Program Computers. We'll Train Them Like Dogs," *Wired* (May 17, 2016), https://www.wired.com/2016/05/the-end-of-code/.
2. Debra Cassens Weiss, "JPMorgan Chase Uses Tech to Save 360,000 Hours of Annual Work by Lawyers and Loan Officers," *ABA Journal* (March 2, 2017), http://www.abajournal.com/news/article/jpmorgan_chase_uses_tech_to_save_360000_hours_of_annual_work_by_lawyers_and.
3. TechCrunch, "The Team Behind Siri Debuts Its Next-Gen AI 'VIV,'" at Disrupt NY 2016 (May 9, 2016), https://www.youtube.com/watch?v=MI07aeZqeco&t=322slater.
4. Maureen Dowd, "Elon Musk's Billion-Dollar Crusade to Stop the A.I. Apocalypse," *Vanity Fair* (March 26, 2017), https://www.vanityfair.com/news/2017/03/elon-musk-billion-dollar-crusade-to-stop-ai-space-x.
5. Samuel Gibbs, "Elon Musk Leads 116 Experts Calling for Outright Ban of Killer Robots," *The Guardian* (August 20, 2017), https://www.theguardian.com/technology/2017/aug/20/elon-musk-killer-robots-experts-outright-ban-lethal-autonomous-weapons-war.

CHAPTER

# 5

# Application Programming Interface (API)

## Why Create an API?

What does digital banking look like in the 2025, and what does it mean to be a true digital bank versus just another bank with an Application Programming Interface (API)? How do banks keep from being disintermediated in this new world? After all, if financial institutions are forced to open up their systems to literally anyone, how do they retain relationships? How do they keep from becoming nothing more than an engine that processes account information, while leaving the digital experience to fintech players and other new entrants to the market who don't live under the regulatory scrutiny that financial institutions live with?

To be fair, I totally understand the resistance to making a banking system accessible in this manner. However, it's important to understand that this is already happening in our industry every day. Products like Mint, Yodlee, and Quicken may log in to members' accounts each day to harvest information—despite not having a relationship to the FI. They simply mimic a member logging in through the home banking platform and then harvest the information on behalf of the member. In this process, the financial institution is getting the short end of the stick in terms of the value exchange. The harvester gets their customers' valuable data. The harvester gets the transaction history of the customers, including what they bought and where. The harvester also collects the account balances and credit card rates and terms so they can cross-sell another credit card to the bank's customers. Meanwhile, the FI loses the ability to the market to this customer without paying to have banner advertisements inside Mint, Yodlee, and others. The FI also gives valuable information to competitors who use the credit balances and other data to make offers to the customer to move their accounts to their FI. So, if this is happening already, then why bother creating an API? Answer: Because if you don't do it, someone else will.

---

**Handy Tip**

Never give anything away for free. This especially applies to your customers' data.

---

**A Conversation with Florian Moser**

I like to keep an eye on what goes on overseas because trends and technologies have a way of migrating. One day, while researching application programming interfaces, I discovered a German bank that I hadn't seen before. I was working with my team at BIG to connect Amazon's Alexa platform to a financial system and I wanted to see if there were any sample banking APIs out there that I could download. I had hoped to find a piece of software that would emulate a banking interface to save time on the development work I was doing. During my searches, I discovered Fidor, a European bank with headquarters in Munich, that had an online open API that connected to a test version of the platform. Literally anyone could connect to it. I was floored. I immediately signed up and started reviewing the API. In less than a few days, our team was able to connect the Amazon Alexa prototype to the Fidor banking system and test all of the features that we had in mind. Intrigued, I found a friend who knew someone at Fidor, and he introduced me to Florian Moser, head of products and marketing at the time. We chatted online and he invited me to Munich to see their shop. While there, I interviewed Florian for my podcast and I asked him about Fidor's strategy of opening its banking platform to the world. This is our conversation:

John        I've been fascinated by Fidor's rise, and what I want my listeners to understand is that [while] we think a lot about America from a credit union perspective—and I have a lot of folks who are European and listen to this from a credit union space, as well—is that there are other people doing really exciting things out there.

I discovered Fidor when I was speaking to a big bank in Kansas City. One of the folks there brought up Fidor. Then I was speaking somewhere else and your name came up again. After that, I dug in, and I was just fascinated by what I found. So, before I get into my fascination, why don't you give us a little background on yourself and Fidor?

| Florian | I am personally a customer at Fidor [and have been] for five years now. I joined Fidor as an employee in 2014, so almost two years ago. I am responsible for product development and all of our business relationships and partnerships. We have a very open approach. We definitely have our own products and we open up our account to various parties. We have a lot of partnerships, too. |
|---|---|
| | Fidor Bank is a fully regulated, 100 percent digital bank in Germany. We have currently about 300,000 people in the community and about 110,000 bank customers. We were founded as a financial community in 2008, meaning at this time the founders started a financial community, which is a place for people to talk about money in a transparent way due to the financial crisis and to speak about how a bank should look in the future. The community was able to speak transparently about the financial issues. |
| | Just imagine going into a banking branch and asking the person in front of you, "Are you new here? What products are you buying? How do you like the branch? How do you like the bank?" |
| John | That doesn't happen, yeah. |
| Florian | That is exactly what we want to do. So, building a bank around the customers, we ourselves understand that it is 100 percent customer centric. One hundred percent customer centric means living the way the customer lives. That means being 100 percent digital. So, everything that we need or want to do needs to be 100 percent straight through processes. What we offer customers is current account with a credit card, with savings or loans, anything you need. The nice thing is that we open our technology in order to integrate a lot of third parties, as well. We don't always have the best product out on our own but we include, for example, partners that enable fixed trading or global money transfer. We have partners that enable crowd finance, P2P lending. We have our own P2P lending function but we also partner with another company. |
| | It's a 100 percent digital bank account, and most of the functionalities are processable within 60 seconds. So, within 60 seconds you do the configuration, you select the product that you want to have, and it is instantly processed in house. |
| John | It's right there. You have it? |

*(continued)*

(*Continued*)

| | |
|---|---|
| Florian | Yes, there is no paperwork and nothing to do afterward. 100 percent digital. That is what we think makes us unique because there is a lot of direct banks that have branches but still have a lot of paperwork. Usually the only paperwork that our customer sees is their credit card. |
| John | So, a couple points. Really good points. One, you mentioned before that you're the head of products and development and that you guys have this open system. So, myself as a developer, if I wanted to, I could connect to the Fidor system and not call you, you and I have never spoken before other than over the phone, and I showed up with my Echo already talking to Fidor. That is insane in America. I would usually have to call 62 people and give blood and some other things in order to get that kind of connectivity, but yet you're saying, hey, we want people to connect to us. When you do connect that becomes a product, and if I wanted to turn something like this into a product I would go through the techs group and just turn it on. It becomes sort of an app store connected to the Fidor engine. That's one of the fascinating things. |
| | The other fascinating thing to me was that you mentioned you had 300,000 community members and 110,000 bank members. Are all 110,000 also part of the community? |
| Florian | Yes. |
| John | So this is just a constant on-boarding process out of this community. |
| Florian | Definitely. Due to the fact that the community was first we definitely have more community users, but that is definitely one of our strategies to acquire customers. It is easier to acquire through the community. We have a goal to have a 100 percent digital customer journey from on boarding to how they get connected to the banks from first contact to the bank in the community, chatting with other customers, marking product suggestions, product rating. Then, if you see the value of the bank then you become bank customers. |
| John | Right. So in the community itself, is it a whole bunch of Fidor guys in there solving things, or is the community together ... |
| Florian | It is self-regulated; we call it, so definitely it's another kind of customer service. The idea is really to have P2P. Of course, |

|        |                                                                                                                                                                                                                                                                                                                      |
|--------|----------------------------------------------------------------------------------------------------------------------------------------------------------------------------------------------------------------------------------------------------------------------------------------------------------------------|
|        | there's our P2P customer service. Our P2P is very active. We have four to five moderators that are more or less . . .                                                                                                                                                                                                  |
| John   | Yeah, to make sure bad things aren't going on.                                                                                                                                                                                                                                                                        |
| Florian | But in the end, the customers really make peer-to-peer regulations. If somebody, for example, raises a question usually within five or six minutes he has the first answer. The average question gets seven answers. You can really see within the community that there is a static flow. So it's really alive. It's not a dead end. |
| John   | Yeah, I described it as Reddit plus a bank.                                                                                                                                                                                                                                                                           |
| Florian | Yeah, people are really connected with us. For example, decreased interest rates for the current account we discussed in advance with our customers. For example, our COO would go to the community or one of us in the community says, "Due to the market, we have to decrease the interest rates from 0.05 percent to 0.03 percent." Then people make suggestions and ask, is this okay? What is your expectation? |
|        | For example, at the end of last year, we were announcing a change from 0.05 percent to 0.01 percent and we really had over the year an intensive discussion with the community. In the end, we decreased it just to .025 percent.                                                                                       |
| John   | So, the community affected how you run the business.                                                                                                                                                                                                                                                                  |
| Florian | Partly, yes.                                                                                                                                                                                                                                                                                                          |
| John   | And they can speak to that. And, you know, I'm sure at this point people are figuring out why I'm here. It's a lot like credit union behavior. It feels like co-op.                                                                                                                                                     |
| Florian | Definitely, cooperation. Cooperation is the key to Fidor Bank. So, our founder is always saying you have to treat the customers like a co-manager. Not like a child and say this is how we should do it. You need to treat them on eye level. It's a very important part.                                                |
| John   | Yeah, that was just fascinating to me that you guys wanted to open up your API in that fashion. Also, that you have this community that is dedicated to financial literacy. That was another real theme that I saw as I moved through this. As a matter of fact, this was a quote from one of your folks. I'm assuming you know Stefan Weiß? |
| Florian | Our head of API?                                                                                                                                                                                                                                                                                                      |

(continued)

(*Continued*)

| | |
|---|---|
| John | Yeah, head of API at Fidor Tech, which is part of Fidor Bank here in the campus. And we're at this cool campus. There's this awesome board outside that is showing what looks to me to be all of the statistics of Fidor. |
| Florian | Our dashboard. |
| John | Just constantly, wherever you can see it. |

But, this quote from Steven is, "Another way is that we white label and license our technology that will be used by other banks to set up their own brand. This is how we will come through and rule the world someday."

So, even the idea that you guys are okay with sharing your tech outside of these four walls. I know that you have plans to move to the US and you already implemented on the UK.

| | |
|---|---|
| Florian | Yeah, in the middle of last year we launched a debit card in the UK. Customer acquisition is good. Compared to the price we invested in the UK, it is famously low compared to other banks that recently started in the UK. |
| John | I have a researcher who I asked to research Fidor, and she came back at the end of her research and told me that she joined. She bought into it immediately. So, I think the value proposition is there. |

When I look at what you're doing compared to other digital banks that have tried this, you know, I think of ING. That's the one that comes to mind. I don't feel like they connected the concept of community in their space. I don't think they knew how to engage in a digital world. So, I think maybe that's kind of the secret sauce for you guys.

| | |
|---|---|
| Florian | The one thing is that you can digitalize processes and you can leave the customer on its own. And the other thing is really to include the customer to make them a co-manager and to bring them into our processes. In product development, for example, we regularly include customers for beta tests. |
| John | Right in the community? |
| Florian | Yeah. For example, when we launch a new card product, we picked those customers from the community that were active in the card groups and have a high Karma (Fidor Community activity measure) where we see these customers are loyal, these customers know what they talk about. Together with the |

customers we found out things that even our processor didn't know.

John    Right. Because there's behaviors and things that can only be discovered en masse and just sort of crowd-funding it.

Florian    Yeah. And it's maximal effective. I don't think 150 customers sent them test cards, send them out into the world, let them test any consolation for the card. Then the feedback comes back immediately.

John    Wow! Yeah, that's just amazing to me, in the sense of when you guys are looking out there to decide on products, you have a built-in community. So many folks just put things out there blind and hope it's going to work, you know?

Florian    Yeah. It's very much a cultural issue, so one thing is to put a community in place but you really have to lift this community approach. So the community is really at the heart of any of our activities, or should be. And so anything that is not really related to the community, it doesn't make sense in the community, it needs to be crushed.

John    Well, it's a great point, because I think that if you weren't doing the community right, and I would say it's cultural but I would call it a digital culture, in the sense that they would see through that. They would know right away you're being disingenuous.

Florian    Yeah. Or if you just use the community for pushing products.

John    Yeah, if that's all it was, nobody would be interested.

Florian    No.

John    And I think the fact that you let them talk you out of your rate change, and maybe that's not a good word to use, you let them advise you on your rate change.

Florian    Yeah, we include them.

John    You included them.

Florian    And we explained to the customer why we would change the rate. We don't just change them. We explain them, okay, we have to change the interest rates because the market situation is different. On the other side, for example, we also decrease the interest rates on the overdraft so that the customers really see, okay, it's not all about maximizing revenues, but that they also get something back from this to grow.

(continued)

(*Continued*)

| John | Surely, yeah. And that might have been somebody said, "I would've been fine if you decrease the rate, but maybe if you give us a benefit here, that would be okay with us." |
|---|---|
| Florian | Yeah. And that's what feedback is, so of course people are not happy, we decrease the interest rates, but a lot of people in this community talked and said, "Okay, I'm not a Fidor customer because of the price because I'm a Fidor customer because of the full package." |
| John | The service, yeah. |
| Florian | Yeah. And that's the feedback that you never ever get from customers. No customer calls you on the hotline and says you're a good bank. But people are used to having this kind of conversation connecting bad feedback. |
| John | Online. |
| Florian | Yeah, online. |
| John | Yeah. And, you know, when I think about it, I feel like in America more and more people are moving that way because, unfortunately, in America, and I don't know about Germany, but we've not focused on financial literacy. And as a result, people are looking for help, you know. I came in here and I speak a little German, enough to read that in the center of your board there was a big circle that before you erased it said, "Gemeinsam mehr Geld," which was "Together more money." And at first I thought, was that more money for Fidor? But then I looked at the design role and it looked like the giant equation to figure out how to get more money for the member or for the consumer. |
| Florian | So this is also a good example for combining technology with cultural thing. So in the future we will more and more share the data that we collect on behalf of the customer or through the customer, share this data with the customer to give him more money at the end of month, so to make him really aware of what is happening, how other people behave, so we could use this data on our own and make analysis and enhance our product, what we do. But on the other side, we also share, for example, usually the typical customer has this and this amount of gold, for example the Fidor customer has 20 gram gold in his portfolio, how much do you have, why do people anyhow buy gold. So for example, Fidor customers get €2 bonus per month if they don't use their credit card at the ATM. So we say, okay, you get this |

|         |                                                                                                                                                                                                                                                                                                                                                                                      |
|---------|--------------------------------------------------------------------------------------------------------------------------------------------------------------------------------------------------------------------------------------------------------------------------------------------------------------------------------------------------------------------------------------|
|         | money. We don't have that much fees. On average, people go this and this, off to the ATM how much, how often do you go, so the goal is really to have more money at the end of the month.                                                                                                                                                                                             |
| John    | So it's interesting, you're using analytics to really discover who's being successful with their finances. One example would be you and I were both buying the same product from the same store but some how you were paying less for the exact same thing. What does Florian know that I don't? Oh, it turns out there's a promo code. Or there's something that you could share that across community to everybody, or if you bought it this way through this company. You know, it's that co-op mentality. |
| Florian | And that's, for example, we don't just cooperate with our customers but also wanted to enable cooperation between customers. We have about 8,000 SB customers, a small corporate. And whenever these corporates have a unique offer for other Fidor customers, we are happy to share this offer with our original customers, to have a community between retail clients and SB clients, for example. |
| John    | Yeah. You know, one of the reasons I'm here is that just so much fits in with the philosophy of BIG and what we're trying to do with our organization, some very cool stuff. And for those of you who are listening, I encourage you to Google Fidor and, you know, Florian's been very open, letting me just kind of ask a lot of questions, and one of the main questions that I know folks are going to want to know is, the US. And it is that you're looking at coming, I believe, across the ocean to visit us. And I know you can't talk about everything, but tell us what you can about ... |
| Florian | We have a partner bank in the US we are working together with, where we put our technology in place. And hopefully very soon, we can announce something either with the Fidor brand, another brand, another business model. So we will be in the US. |
| John    | Something similar to Simple? Are you aware of Simple?                                                                                                                                                                                                                                                                                                                                 |
| Florian | Yeah, maybe not the Simple way.                                                                                                                                                                                                                                                                                                                                                       |
| John    | Yeah, but something where on top of this particular partner ...                                                                                                                                                                                                                                                                                                                        |
| Florian | Yeah, but the Fidor will be more in backend for the technology part of ...                                                                                                                                                                                                                                                                                                            |
| John    | Got you. Yeah, it'll be more transparent.                                                                                                                                                                                                                                                                                                                                             |
| Florian | Yeah.                                                                                                                                                                                                                                                                                                                                                                                 |

*(continued)*

(*Continued*)

| | |
|---|---|
| John | Okay, so we'll close it with this. You've been very generous with your time, and I'm so thankful for that. What excites you? You know, I feel like this place has like been really exciting just to come and talk to people who seem to understand, you know, where everything is, fintech-wise, and can speak that language. What excites you that's out in the financial world right now? What are you guys gearing up for? What's exciting to you? |
| Florian | On the one side it's all about mobile, so I know everybody's talking mobile, but what we really want to achieve and what I'm excited also from a process side of view, to make really a full mobile bank account, not only—what is it?—channel, but mobile-only with all the stuff that comes with it and not just have a transaction list and have a credit card but everything. |
| John | Yeah, because everybody's got that. |
| Florian | Credits, insurance, all the stuff. |
| John | A bank in your pocket. |
| Florian | Bank in your pocket. On-boarding. Everything. 100 percent digital, and based on our technology, maybe with partners, and maybe it's other partners that come into play, but that's really the challenge also of our first, to make really everything 100 percent digital mobile, combined with everything that you can use with the mobile. Be it payment. Be it loyalty. Be it artificial intelligence. So we're ready to make the mobile account not only mobile but intelligent. |
| John | Document imaging. |
| Florian | Everything, yeah. |
| John | GPS. Beaconing. All the things. |
| Florian | Bringing everything together, and sooner or later also combining it with the community. |
| John | And will the community guide some of that? Will they guide what that looks like and how that product kind of comes together? |
| Florian | No. Partly yes. But on the other side, the typical user is not that much into this technology developments. |
| John | So, speaking of typical users and technology developments, one of the things I found interesting, and we'll close with this, is you're |

|          | one of the very few banks doing the blockchain and Bitcoin with your partnership with Ripple. |
|----------|---|
| Florian  | So we don't do blockchain, so we enabled our customers. |
| John     | You enabled blockchain, correct. |
| Florian  | We enabled blockchain-related clients to realize that this is more like Bitcoin.de, which is one of Europe's biggest Bitcoin P2P platforms, or Kraken, or also Ripple, which is enabled in the current account . . . We're always happy to be the banking partner. On the other side, we are always keen to make things happen. And on the other side, from a tech department, we think about and we're looking in the direction of using blockchain for a call banking system. |
| John     | And we think that faster payments in America, that's going to be probably something that we see as a matter of fact I think in the podcast that we just did. We talked a lot about that. We talked about the impact of faster payments and how the blockchain will probably be, from a distributed ledger standpoint, the de facto standard at some point, and it seems like you guys are engaging that as well. So I have a question for you. If I applied for a loan with Fidor and I stated my income as Bitcoin, would they freak out or would they just be okay? How would the underwriter react? |
| Florian  | There's no product yet, but maybe that could be part of storing with them. We are open to everything. Open up to everything. |
| John     | You're open to everything. You know, that's something we talk about a lot in America. You know, we already have people showing up and saying, I get paid in bitcoin. . . . |
| Florian  | Yeah, I have no money, but I have a lot of bitcoins. |
| John     | Well, and what's funny about that is everyone assumes if they have bitcoins, alt-coins, light coins, all of these things, then immediately they're some sort of criminal. In America anyways, that's what we think. I don't know why. I guess it's the movies, you know. But that's the sense that we get. And so the idea that, at least, if nothing else, they can be on deposit with you and have value through the Fidor interface I think is a step in the right direction. |
| Florian  | Well, you could think about a simple bank loan on Bitcoin basis. |

*(continued)*

(*Continued*)

| | |
|---|---|
| John | Well, absolutely, why not? When you say asset, I assume you mean secure line, secure loan gold. You know, that's interesting, when you said everybody has this amount of gold, you know? |
| Florian | Yeah, and people can buy gold, precious metal, and they can gold, platinum, palladium, silver in the account. |
| John | See, I'm a comic book guy, I want to buy the stuff (adamantium) that Wolverine has running through him, I don't know if that sell that here. I'll look around later. Like I said, I really thank you for your time and I'm sure hopefully we'll hear from you again in the future. |

As you can see, they are very open about their strategy to be an open API to anyone. I also found it interesting that they believe community plays an important role in the institution. These two things go hand in hand. Being open means that there will be a community, like it or not. People will coalesce around the opportunity that you are providing them and create something from nothing. We see this behavior in open source platforms where like-minded people collaborate to improve a software or service and donate their time for free.

The first step to solving this problem is to implement your own API to your bank or credit union. This should allow third parties to do everything that you do inside of your own products. Don't worry about who is going to get access to this right now; that's not as important as creating a complete interface. This interface is going to be foundation for everything you will do for the foreseeable future. Let's call this interface the FI platform. You may think that you have something like this in place already, and it is possible that you do, but before you just flip past this part, answer these questions to determine if you really have full featured and ready for prime-time industry grade API that can be used by others to create valuable services for your customer. If you are a CEO or a FI executive log into the companion website and download the following API readiness report and share it with your IT area:

- Does the API have access to all of your systems? If it is, then the API should be able to execute a command like GETALLAC-COUNTS for a single customer and data will be retrieved from each individual system such as a Mortgage servicing platform and a Credit Card platform without having to make separate calls to each of these systems.

- Is your API fully documented? Would you feel comfortable giving this document to a business partner?
- Does your API support all the features that your digital platforms currently support? Can it create a new Billpay payee or add a ACH payment? Can you reset a password with it?
- Is your API securely accessible via VPN or via the Web using state-of-the-art security such as oAuth2 or SAML?
- Does your API provide account level security that can limit access to any service?
- Is there business logic that your API should have but doesn't? A good example would be ACH processing days. If a vendor uses the API to setup a ACH payment and tries to schedule it for a fed holiday, will it go through without notifying the vendor that the payment cannot be processed on a fed holiday?
- Does your API support universal logging and reporting?

If you answered no to any of the questions above, then you have some work to do. A true API will have all of these features and more. You might be thinking that this is going to be a really long road. Don't fret: There are answers out there.

## Getting Started

### For the Technology Organization

There are software packages such as MuleSoft and Software A&G that you can purchase and create the API with your development staff. These are considered enterprise grade products and will solve most of the problems above. These products ride the line of being a pure product and being a toolkit that your IT staff can use to create the platform that you desire. You can also reach out to your industry peers to see if anyone has developed or is developing something similar for your platform. Sometimes other FIs will gladly accept the help of FI that isn't a direct competitor to share cost of creating such a platform in the form of a purchase of the application.

### For the Services Organization

There are full-featured packages that can be deployed and allow you to expose your various systems via API. Many times, these sorts of API platform packages will be provided by your core data-processing solutions providers; otherwise, there are also third-party platforms that do the same thing, such as Finnovations Concerto platform. I would suggest reaching out to your core solution provider first then if they don't have something check with your industry peers to find out if anyone is using a third-party platform that they really like and that supports your core data-processing provider.

## The Second Step

Now that the FI platform is up and running, it's time to cut off the free access that the third parties have been getting to your data on behalf of the customers. This is a relatively simple thing to do technically but far trickier in terms of marketing and customer service. For the technical side, have IT review your logs and find out the IP addresses of the systems that are scraping your data. It's usually simple to see these patterns in the logs, as these bots tend to move at a speed that no human could ever duplicate and tend to come in mass at odd times in the early morning (which is very nice of them, btw—they could run it at your peak time and add extra stress to your system). These IP addresses will also likely be associated with multiple customer accounts. Have your IT folks track down all of customers' accounts associated with these IPs as your team will need them to inform customers that the products they are using will stop working soon. You will also need to perform a WHOIS on these IPs to determine which vendors your marketing department needs to call to start the conversation of having them access your API instead of going through your home banking or mobile platform to obtain your customers' data. One of the main reasons that they should be open to having a relationship with you is that the process they are using now is very clunky and highly susceptible to failure due to its dependency on the placement of data on the screen in the home banking site (which can often be moved around by the customer, as already mentioned). This methodology will also break if it encounters a Multi Factor question or out of band password request. The customers often must regularly intervene to keep these services working properly.

## The Third Step

This is where it gets interesting. Now it's time to turn the tables on the harvesters or scrapers. Here is where you need to stand firm. Have your staff contact each of the entities that are screen scraping your customers' data and let them know that you will be blocking them from your system on this date and time in the future. However, you can also inform them that you have a new way for them to access the data and for a price of <insert amount here> per customer they can pull the data in a far more efficient and secure way. At the same time, your marketing team will need to contact every one of your customers using these services and let them know that you will be discontinuing access to your platform in their current form due to the inefficient way that these entities access the data. As an added benefit, you can let them know you have a better way for these entities to access the data, and if they truly want to continue using this service, it would be helpful for them to reach out to the entity and inform it of the new process. You can even include a nice cut-and-paste prewritten email for the customers to send to these entities in your correspondence with them.

## An Email for Customers

To whom it may concern,

I bank with <insert FI>, and the bank has informed me that the way you collect data currently is inefficient for the bank and for you, and that it would like to improve your service. I would also like for my service to be improved. I would be happy if someone from your organization would speak to someone at <Insert FI> regarding improving your service connectivity and security.

APIinfo@fi.com
Or call 18885551212 and ask for <insert Marketing name here>

I sincerely hope that your organization will work with <Insert FI here> and create a better experience for everyone involved.

Thanks for your time and consideration in these matters.

Sincerely,
Joe Customer

This may seem like a bold and kind of scary move, and I am sure that when you review the logs, depending on the size of your institution and the demographics of your customers, you will find a large number of customers that use these services. At first, these customers may be dismayed that their financial institution is forcing their provider of choice to use an API, and they may be even more dismayed to find out that you are charging this provider for the access when it has been free up until now. However, it's time to be bold and stand up for your customers and their data. Financial institutions must stop giving things away for free and plan to measure and monetize their data if they are to survive the coming digital transformation. The tragedy is that many of these customers are among your most affluent and profitable, but since they no longer visit your digital sites, choosing instead to visit the site that is harvesting their data from home banking, they also no longer see your advertisements and don't read your secure messaging, in some cases the harvesting entities will turn off alerts in favor of sending them their alerts. Moreover, each time a harvester or scraper accesses data, it cost the financial institution money by putting stress on the infrastructure and creating overhead in bandwidth and increasing storage costs by bloating the logs. In the end, all it really does is put your organization at a huge disadvantage in terms of having the opportunity to increase engagement with customers.

OK, now that you have this magical API or FI platform, it's time to leverage it even more for your customers. It's time to leverage other services and allow consumers to access your data efficiently and securely. Consider for instance the rise of Amazon's Alexa platform. Once considered a toy, it is rapidly becoming a channel of choice for many consumers to get their data, since it is far easier and more natural to interact with voice than it is to type and click on a visual interface. Once you have this FI platform to connect to, you can either find a partner to connect you to the Amazon Alexa platform or build it yourself.

---

### Chapter Review

- Implement an API at the bank or credit union. This should allow third parties to do everything that you do inside of your own products. This is the best way to provide certain services to your customers.

- Financial institutions must stop giving things away for free and plan to measure and monetize their data if they are to survive the coming digital transformation.

# CHAPTER 6

# Blockchain and Cryptocurrency

For the last two and half years, financial journalism has been dominated by the promise of the blockchain. The hype on this technology has been enormous, with predictions anywhere from facilitating world peace to curing cancer. The fact of the matter is that blockchain will not cure cancer or facilitate world peace, but it does have the propensity to be a game-changing technology for financial institutions, as evidenced by the heavy investments by large banks, insurance companies, and the medical industry. Blockchain was one of the most talked about financial topics of 2016 and continues to be a high interest concept into 2017. In order to really understand blockchain, you've got to start at the beginning, and since its beginnings are rooted in Bitcoin, I thought I would take a moment and do a brief history on the humble beginnings of Bitcoin. So let's hop in the way-back machine together and take a trip back to 2007.

## Bitcoin: A Brief History

In 2007, Satoshi Nakamoto started work on what was called the Bitcoin Plan. (By the way, this is not his real name—in fact we're not even sure this pseudonym is even just one person. There are many who believe it refers to several persons but that isn't important to the story.) Two years later, January 12, 2009, the first Bitcoin transaction happened. It happens between Satoshi and some cryptology guy named Hal. Who Hal is doesn't really matter all that much—all you really need to know is that the first transaction happened between two entities. Now here's where things get interesting. In

October 5, 2009, the exchange rate is established for Bitcoin. In 2009, one dollar would've equaled 1,309.3 BTC (bitcoin); as of this writing, the same amount of BTC would be worth around $17 million at the current exchange rate of almost $13,000 per bitcoin. The methodology they settled on was based on the amount of electricity the computers that participate in the Bitcoin network use per hour. Since Bitcoin depended on miners and these miners needed to use more and more electricity, it only made sense to use a normalized kilowatt-hour cost as a backing for the currency. So what happened? Why did it appreciate so quickly, and why is everybody always talking about cryptocurrency? What is going on?

In order to understand what all the hype is about, it's important to understand why Bitcoin was created. Bitcoin was created so that no central authority such as banks or governments could control it. It was designed to be a distributed network of computers with a transparent ledger that supported a currency that could be used safely anywhere. The transparency means that anyone can look at the ledger and validate the transactions. They went a step further and they said we're going to make it so no one could really see any of the transactions. So while you know the transaction happened, you have no idea really who it was between and what was bought or sold.

## Decentralization

Decentralization is considered one of its most innovative features. Being able to decentralize the data meant that having one big database somewhere that can be hacked is no longer needed. The distributed ledger system would keep all of the data synchronized between millions of systems. Since the data were encrypted and split up among the nodes, there was no longer one big honeypot of usernames and passwords in a central location that could all be hacked—it distributed this information all across all of these different computers in the world. Because anybody could actually download the software, the network grew very quickly. Anyone who had the desire could download the software and set themselves up as a miner. The process of mining is actually called *proof of work*. Each miner is given increasingly complex math equations to solve. If the miners solve the equation, there is a chance that there will be a bitcoin located in the complex math problem. The system was set up to continually increase the complexity of the math equations, thus making it more difficult to find new bitcoins and driving the market. At this point, there is little chance of a standard computer (even a really powerful one like I am using right now) finding a bitcoin, so miners have started pooling their processing and sharing the rewards (when they are found).

Why is Bitcoin so important? To start with, it proved this technology and started the cryptocurrency revolution that we are experiencing today. Bitcoin allowed small businesses to transact business beyond their borders. Bitcoin also proved that a cryptocurrency could exist and be backed by computing power—a fact that wasn't necessarily a foregone conclusion. Bitcoin supporters would tell you that our fiat money is based on precious metals and gold, and with this thought in mind, why couldn't we have an electronic currency that was based on a resource like electricity? Like all good revolutionary technology, it wouldn't go away easily, and the idea slowly but surely began to take hold. Now it has become so standard that you can buy goods and services from many stores online using Bitcoin. There are people all over the world who get paid in bitcoins.

Bitcoin, however, quickly earned a reputation for being the currency of the dark web. Since Bitcoin was developed from the ground up for privacy and security, it proved to be a perfect fit for criminals looking to engage in selling their digital wares. It was quickly discovered by the hacker community and used to start criminal markets. After the discovery, it became a way for criminals to do business on the web, to pay for anything anonymously and not worry about the banking system looking over your shoulder. It became a way to cover one's tracks if one was involved in a criminal transaction. Recently, and I'll cover this more on my security section, there has been a glut of what has come to be known as *ransomware*. The ransoms that the cyber criminals demanded were to be paid in bitcoins, adding yet another criminal association with the cryptocurrency.

One of the most well-known stories of criminal activity is the story of the Amazon-like site for criminal services and goods named *Silk Road* after the ancient trade routes that connected the east and the west. If you wanted to go and buy a giant file of credit card numbers, you could go to Silk Road on what we call the *dark web*. You could also hire a hitman on Silk Road. In fact, you could probably have several bid for your business. In each case, you could pay for your services using bitcoins, and as a result, bitcoins have come to be known as the currency of cybercrime.

Despite the continued criminal activity, Bitcoin is making progress as a currency. Major online retailers have started taking bitcoin. These retailers include Overstock.com, Expedia.com, Subway, Microsoft, NewEgg, and Shopify.

The advantages of a bitcoin are often pointed out by supporters and critics alike. Obviously, it's far safer. You're not carrying around money in a wallet that can be stolen. It's not traceable, so your privacy is extended. It knows no borders. I was recently in Lisbon and I saw several shops that would take bitcoins for a purchase. So it can be used around the world without having to worry about conversion rates. For many years, retailers have lamented the time it takes to settle with the large networks such as Visa and MasterCard. Bitcoin immediately settles its transactions. It is available to everyone because it is an open standard and an open-source platform. It is also a decentralized platform with no central authority and, as such, it cannot be taken away by any one country.

## Security

One thing I often hear from critics of Bitcoin is that it has had lot of security problems. While Bitcoin has never been hacked, some of the surrounding services that have sprung up to support the platform have had some high profile compromises. The most public incident happened at a company called Mt. Gox. Mt. Gox was a company that provided users of Bitcoin with a digital wallet. If you go and open up a Bitcoin wallet in the Bitcoin platform, the key to your Bitcoin wallet is this really long set numbers and letters called a *private key* that needs to be referenced each time business is transacted on the Bitcoin platform. Mt. Gox provided a service to store these wallet numbers and stored them unencrypted in a single file (wallet.dat) on a computer. Once the hackers got the private keys, they used the keys to drain the wallets of their Bitcoin.

Now where we are today is that Bitcoin is becoming a more and more valuable purchase, or a valuable system. As of November 1, 2016, the price of Bitcoin was $723.98. It has since risen to today's pricing of almost $13,000 per bitcoin. Ethereum, which is another cryptocurrency, has also risen. Ethereum was worth $19 per unit. Today, it's now worth $690.36 per unit.

So what's behind this rise? There are many schools of thought on this. One of the more popular hypothesis is that people are fearful of the economy, and investing in Bitcoin is the digital equivalent of stuffing money in a mattress. Another popular theory is that investing in Bitcoin is similar to investing in gold. What does this mean for banking and financial institutions? It means that people will be pulling their money out of the traditional savings instruments provided by mainstream financial institutions and buying Ethereum or Bitcoin to try to get a higher earning. The take away for financial institutions is that cryptocurrency has many benefits and is becoming more mainstream. Financial institutions should pay attention to this trend and continue to experiment and learn about the technology.

### Blockchain

Enough about Bitcoin and Ethereum. Let's get on to the importance of the underlying elegant technology that really turned out to be the most important part of Bitcoin for the financial institutions. The complexities involved with designing a self-governing, transparent, decentralized distributed network cannot be overstated. The basis of the Bitcoin platform is a technology called *blockchain*. The blockchain turned out to be the golden goose of the Bitcoin platform. Blockchain is a new innovative technology that will change how financial institutions transact business in the financial services system.

So here are five key points:

1. Distributed ledger technology is more than Bitcoin. So when you hear the words *blockchain* or *distributed ledger,* don't just automatically think about Bitcoin. There are a lot of other use cases for this distributed technology other than a cryptocurrency.
2. A shared distributed ledger is a linked set of duplicated transaction records. For the accountants who are reading this, it is like double ledger entries on steroids. Imagine a thousand ledger entries and a thousand notaries for each transactions.
3. All transactions on a distributed ledger are independently verified by the participants on the network and then stored on in ledger individually.

**4.** The value to financial institutions is the ability to remove the middle players by taking advantage of the decentralized nature of the platform.

**5.** Removing the middlemen will increase efficiency and security.

As if all of those qualities weren't enough, the blockchain introduced another revolutionary technology called a *smart contract.* The smart contract is the natural outcome of a decentralized network. When two entities transact business via the traditional centralized network method, the middle man takes care of contracts. Since there isn't a middleman to provide contracts to protect each side, a smart contract allows this to be done programmatically without human intervention. The smart contract has the ability to execute programs on behalf of the specific entities on the network based on contract terms. Once these nodes come together on consensus on the execution, then the results of the execution can be written to the distributed ledger and are immutable. A great example would be selling a digital asset like a book or music in a digital form. You agree to purchase a digital asset for a specific price, and the seller agrees to provide the content. In this case, to make it easier to understand, let's make it a subscription to content that is delivered monthly. In the smart contract, there is a provision that says if new digital episodes of the digital asset are not delivered by 1 p.m. on the first of every month, you get a refund. One day the subscription content is delivered at 1:01, the smart contract is triggered, and without any human intervention, your money is refunded.

So why do we care about all of this? Well, first of all, let's look at what's happening in the world. We've seen massive amounts of money poured into the blockchain/distributed ledger area in the past two years specifically by the large banks around the world. In September 2015, a group of large banks got together to try to use the blockchain concept to solve various common problems. The group formed R3 to leverage the distributed ledger and create a next generation financial services platform that would provide solutions to these common problems. The group now consists of 80 global financial institutions and through their collaborative efforts developed a financial services ledger platform called Corda. Corda was designed to allow participants to transact business with the need for a centralized switch or authority. The Corda application was also designed to allow others to build applications on top of it (called Cordapps). So if all of these large banks see this opportunity and are willing to invest large sums of money, then there must be something there, right? We agree, where there is smoke there is often fire.

Another popular distributed ledger project, built around the Linux Foundation, is the Hyperledger Project.

So with all this hype and all the things going on, what does that mean? Well, first, let's talk about the first thing. Distributed ledger is not Bitcoin. So we're not creating a new way for everybody to transfer Bitcoin back and forth between banks. As I said before, it's the elegant underlying technology that enables Bitcoin. So if Bitcoin was an application, distributed ledger would be the operating system. It's also known as shared ledger, distributed ledger, or blockchain.

So let me walk you through a theoretical transaction (see Figure 6.1). Financial Institution A wants to deliver money to Financial Institution B. Now, please understand that this is not the best use case for a distributed ledger. However, it's one that's easy for people to understand. So we'll use it as our straw man for our first experience in the distributed ledger platform.

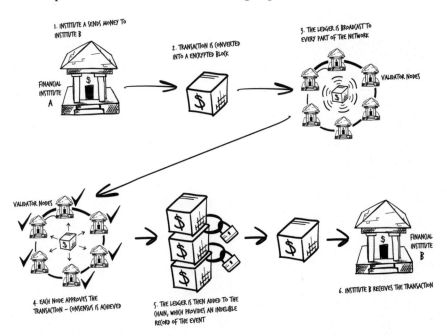

Figure 6.1   A financial transaction using blockchain

So, if Financial Institution A would like to send money to Financial Institution B and they're both connected to a theoretical distributed ledger platform, then they would reach out and put their transaction in an encrypted block. Now, this block actually would be encrypted using Financial Institution B's public key so that they're the only ones that can open it. Once encrypted, the digital box will be sent into the distributed ledger network via their node. What's interesting about the distributed ledger is that it's not like the telephone game. It's not something where you send it to one node and then that node tells another node and that node tells another node and that node tells another node. You can think of it more as like a person standing in the middle of the stadium, with everyone else dead quiet, shouting out facts and everyone hears the same fact at the same time. Once everyone hears that fact, now they can go through and validate the transaction separately. The distributed ledger creates a "single source of truth" for each transaction on the ledger that is immutable. Let's take a moment to discuss what validation and consensus look like. If you've ever been driving down a highway and you've seen a weigh station, you've seen an example of what this technology does. So when a truck pulls into a weigh station, the truck is weighed and the weight is recorded. A little bit further down the road, the truck pulls into another weigh station. If the truck weighs less, the regulating department knows something has changed. The states use this information to enforce tax and safety laws. The important aspect of this is that the people who are weighing the trucks don't need to know what's inside the truck or even who is driving the truck; they don't open up the truck and go through all the boxes. All they need to know is what it previously weighed and what it now weighs to enforce compliance. They use the weight to determine whether or not that truck is in compliance with the laws of the state. This is a similar concept with the transactions. The transactions themselves are actually hashed, and the hash is really just a digital description of the block, not the block itself. Once that digital description has been determined it is then transmitted to all of the nodes, each of the nodes run a calculation using this hash and compare it to the block to determine that the transaction has not been modified.

It's important to note that nodes don't know who the transaction parties are or anything about the transaction. This important feature of a decentralized network allows parties to conduct business without knowing anything about each other (which is why it is so popular with criminals, as mentioned before). Once everybody does the calculation and comes to consensus, then it can it be added to the ledger in the order it was received. A distributed ledger operates just like a real ledger, which means that transactions are input in the order they were executed, and if there is an error, it must be reversed out, not deleted. The ledger is considered to be an immutable source of transactions. When the transaction or block is stored, the destination financial institution will be alerted to the block, and because it was encrypted with the financial institution's public key, it can only be opened by the FI. If the block contained a transaction to pay off a mortgage for $2 million, the FI can be very sure that it is going to get that money because the distributed ledger has stored a record of the transaction that is irrefutable by the sender.

If we were to do this today via traditional means, say a wire, there will be some sort of centralized service, in this case the Fed, that would provide centralized services between the two organizations. One of the most important services that they would provide is to authenticate the remote institution. They would also indemnify the sending institution because it is taking responsibility for the authentication portion of the transaction. The most important part of any financial transaction is properly authenticating both sides of the transaction. FI A needs to know for sure that FI B is who it is sending money to. Without an authentication method, someone could impersonate the receiving FI and walk away with millions of dollars. In the decentralized network, authentication is done directly between two entities using a certificate authority. In this case, the authentication was handled with a public/private key pair. FI A was comfortable that the block could only be opened by FI B because the network authority that provided FI B's public key can be trusted. Another service a centralized network provides is normalization. In many transactions, FI A may be on a completely different kind of technology and platform than FI B. In order to transact business, the institutions must have a common language to speak between them. This service is usually facilitated by the central authority.

The third thing that a centralized service provides is funds protection through insurance. So, if for some reason FI B never got its million dollars, then the centralized provider would be responsible for recovering these funds. In a decentralized network, there is no mediator between transacting entities. The transaction is protected by the distributed network, as it can be stored on hundreds or thousands of different financial institution nodes that would provide proof of transmission for this transaction. The cooperative aspect of the technology is a game changer.

When a transaction has been sent to the ledger, each node validates the transaction and stores it in on its local ledger. Each ledger item is tied to the previous ledger item via hash. In this way, the distributed ledger acts just like a traditional ledger in that it stores the transactions in transactional order based on time and execution. Another important note is that a block is not limited to just one transaction, the block could contain a thousand different transactions or it can contain one transaction; it's whatever someone decides to put in their encrypted block and send.

Finally—and this is important—the entities that need the transaction information are identified through cryptography. And as will be discussed in Part IV, one of the people in your neighborhood that you're going to have to start looking at is a cryptologist. Cryptography is going to be the future and the distributed ledger is a very real reason that an FI might need a cryptographer in the future.

Now why is this valuable? Why does anybody care about using this distributed ledger? Well the first thing is, is that you have guaranteed availability of the stored data because if you think about, it's not just being put on one system. It's being stored on hundreds and hundreds of systems. Moreover, you can run applications (smart contracts) on all of these systems and you can be guaranteed an extremely high uptime due to the high level of redundancy on the network. You can also be guaranteed the extremely high uptime going very far into the future. The resilience of the network is directly related to the number of nodes that participate. The Achilles' heel of the platform is that if you knock out more than half the nodes, then the ledger cannot be trusted.

I know what you're thinking. You're thinking, "Hey, John, I cannot have my organization's secure and private data on some dudes laptop that is located in his basement running Bitcoin." To overcome this concern, we have to understand the difference between a permissionless open blockchain and a permissioned private blockchain. At the core, whether it is permissioned or permissionless, the blockchain will operate the same as both are just different implementations of the same distributed ledger technology. A permissioned private distributed ledger or a private blockchain is a collection of nodes where all of the participating parties are vetted and certified before being allowed to participate in the network. An ATM network is a great analogy for a permissioned network. One can't just go out and put an ATM up without getting the proper permission and licensing. This approach is similar to how a permissioned distributed ledger is governed. Like any other network, there will have to be rules just like there are rules with ATMs. These rules, however, could be enforced by smart contracts. The smart contracts could determine if proper care is being taken when handling the private keys for the nodes, much in the same way issuers and processors are audited to determine if keys for an ATM are being handled correctly.

### Permissioned Networks

Now we're going to see public permissioned networks. The first one is actually called Sovrin. It's been included in Hyperledger Project Indy, which we'll get to later. But R3, for example, is creating a private blockchain software called Corda. The credit union industry—and I'm proud to say, I was part of the genesis of this organization—has created something called CULedger, which is a private permissioned ledger that will only serve credit unions and their partners. In a private permissioned network, governance will be the most important concept, and it will be enforced by computer algorithms and real-world contracts that represent reputational risk, should they be broken.

Let's contrast the governance approach to a permissioned ledger with how rules are enforced in a permissionless network like Bitcoin or Etheruem. Why do people follow the Bitcoin and Ethereum rules? The answer is one of the many great points of a decentralized trustless network is that the network can perform self-validation by using the consensus mechanism of the millions of nodes connected to it, to validate that the software that is running on each node, and the ledger that is stored, is the correct version, and hasn't been modified in anyway. The risk is reduced because the computing power it would take to change just one node or even just one entry on a ledger doesn't exist yet. Even if one managed to magically change a transaction on a node, that person would still need to perform that same magic on more than half the networks, which is a daunting task, considering that the Bitcoin network consists of over 3.5 million nodes. Another reason that Bitcoin is resistant to hacking is because breaking it would be counterproductive to the entities that use it. In short, Bitcoin is protected because its users don't want to kill the goose that lays the golden bitcoins.

A new category of distributed ledger has emerged in the last year called a public permissioned network. In a public permissioned network there is a mixture of both algorithmic and human governance, which means contractual agreements that are also enforced by code.

Diversity is another important aspect of a distributed ledger network. A common belief is that if one were to attack the Bitcoin network and succeed at compromising a single node, they would have access to everything. But first, you have to understand how the data are actually encrypted. It's not one big encrypted block of data (see lessons learned from Mt. Gox in the previous paragraphs). It's a whole bunch of little encrypted blocks of data. Imagine that the data were on a piece of paper and you shredded it and you took each little shred and you put it in a safe, and then you took each safe and you gave them each a unique combination. For good measure, you took those safes and you distributed them to all of the nodes on the network, and then on top of that you created a bunch of empty safes, that looked exactly like the safes with the shards of information in them, also with unique combinations and distributed them among all of the nodes. This method of encrypting and storing the data makes it very difficult to find all of the data and put them back together. Breaking into a single node isn't going to take down the whole network, nor will it provide you access to all of the information on that node. A major function of the decentralized network is to track all of the elements of the data and make sure that it is distributed in a secure fashion.

A distributed network's security greatly benefits from the amount of diversity in its nodes. What I mean by that is that if every node had the same firewalls, networks, and ran on the exact same machines, the value of the targets to a hacker would go up greatly because the effort needed to get into all of the nodes, which is a necessity if you are going to infiltrate a distributed ledger, is greatly diminished by the lack of diversity. A hacker could defeat one computer operating system and use the same technique to compromise all of the other nodes and have access to everything. Because so many people are running their nodes in different environments with different firewalls, load balancers, IDS detectors, and different operating systems, it creates a diversity that helps to protect the network by making it a lower-value target due to the level of effort it would take to defeat so many different node configurations.

The data are actually encrypted using the most and current encryption standards. In this case, most of the data have been encrypted by elliptical Curve technology, which is more secure than Secure Socket Layers (the technology commonly used to secure websites) and, as I mentioned, it's broken up and spread across many nodes. The actual data are also backed up between all the different nodes and the transaction data are encrypted by the sender directly for the receiver. So you may be sitting around thinking, "Wow, this sounds like a giant database. This sounds great. I'm going to store all my data in it." But that's not exactly what it's for.

## How to Use a Distributed Ledger

One way to understand the use cases for a distributed ledger is to know what not to use it for. First, it's not a place to store all your pictures from your phone. So if you were going to store all your pictures and have it duplicated through the network, then it would quickly affect performance of the network due to the large volume of data that a high-resolution picture represents. A better real-world use would be to prove that the picture hasn't been altered. Let's say you captured a video of a crime and you wanted to give it to the authorities. If you had the software to do so, a digital description (also known as a *cryptographic hash*) of the evidence could be stored in the distributed ledger so that it could be proven in a court of law that the evidence was not altered in any way. This same technique could be very useful to prove intellectual property ownership.

Another thing I hear a lot about is, "Gee, we could use this to run our internal workflow projects like collections." This is really not something that you would use as an internal database. In fact, it is common for architects to think of the distributed ledger as a big database. However, it was not designed for this, and to try to use it this way would result in less than favorable results. A better collections use case would be validating payment information on the phone. If a call center service representative was on the phone with a customer working through a loan payment, it might make sense to store a digital description of the call (a cryptographic hash) of that approval across all of the distributed ledger nodes so that in a court of law it could be proved that this consumer agreed to actually make payment. However, you wouldn't want to store the actual transaction or the data, nor would you try to run a distributed ledger in your four walls—at least not at this point in the technology evolution.

Banks and FIs are always looking for ways to innovate in their digital channels, especially home banking. On several occasions, I have been asked about distributed ledger use cases for home banking and mobile banking, and while I can think of some home banking implications around payments, it is not a platform that is designed for home banking. It's definitely a system that could make it easier to share transactional data between digital systems but it wouldn't be a something that you would run without many other nodes involved. Cross-institutional home banking digital transactions are not going to be supported by a large distributed ledger database anytime soon due to the latency of most distributed ledger technology. It takes time for all of these systems to come to consensus, and home banking users are used to very quick speed.

What are the use cases in the financial space for a distributed ledger? The number one use case I have come across is bundling loans and other fungible assets and selling them to other institutions. The current processes to do this between financial institutions are clunky and time consuming. The distributed ledger offers the ability for two or more institutions to bid on a asset bundle, create a smart contract around the asset, and then track the ownership of the assets in the bundle down to the penny. The bidding process would be powered by the consensus function of the distributed ledger.

And then, finally, as I mentioned before, money movement. As a matter of fact, the Fed's Faster Payments Task Force in the past year has been working on different options to move money faster to catch the United States up with the rest of the free world, and many of those solutions include the distributed ledger technology as part of their core or underlying platform engines.

I would categorize this technology as evolutionary, as it will take time for financial institutions to rework their internal processes to support these distributed ledger technology. While I don't believe it will be a particularly long evolutionary path, it will certainly evolve over time. This is also a collaborative technology, and as such, it is somewhat of an anathema to the larger banks who have traditionally struggled to work together. This gives an advantage to the smaller institutions that are willing to collaborate (many because there is no other choice). The play here is to get involved in a network to see what the technology looks like. If you are a credit union, I would suggest visiting CULedger.com. If you are a community bank or some other financial institution, it may be time to start looking to your current advocacy groups to help start a network.

Now I'm going to stop here, because in the next chapter we're going to talk about identity. Identity is the strategic high ground for financial institutions across the world. If we solve the password crisis, we will have solved one of the greatest issues facing humanity. Stop laughing, I'm not trying to be funny here—okay, maybe just a little.

---

### Chapter Review

- The distributed ledger system would keep all data synchronized between millions of systems.

- Being able to decentralize data means that having one big database somewhere that can be hacked is no longer needed. Since the data would be encrypted and split up among the nodes, there would no longer be one big honeypot of usernames and passwords in a central location that could all be hacked.

- The advantages of a cryptocurrency are: It's far safer because people do not carry around money in a wallet. It's not traceable, so privacy is extended. It's accepted worldwide, reducing the need for currency exchange.

# PART

# III

## Security

# Sovereign Identity

Thete's a growing password crisis. Everyone has too many passwords, and it will get resolved somehow, someday. Consider that almost 26 percent of call center calls are from people trying to reset their passwords. For this reason alone, it would be worthwhile to get rid of passwords. I can tell you that someday we're going to look back and we're going to laugh at all of the passwords and usernames we have because we're going to have something drastically different.

Identity is a platform—it's a disruptor, and it's a hot topic for every industry. So far, all the other identity plays have failed so far. Google, Microsoft, Facebook, LinkedIn, and so many more. Banks have explored this in the past but have failed because they weren't willing to collaborate. I believe this is changing now. This opportunity is wide open. No one has solved this. So, what is *sovereign identity*? Well, let's start off with just explaining what sovereign means.

Sovereign is a rightful status; it's also known as independence. When a nation is sovereign, that means that it is independent and no one has rule over it. A sovereign identity, for individuals, gives people a digital identity that only they can control and manage. Currently, identity paradigms like social media and bank logins are actually controlled by the companies that own those websites, not by the users who rely on them. That's why people keep a long list of log-in information; one is required for every site. A sovereign identity would be controlled by only the individual it identifies. Think of it as having a *passport for the internet.* It's a single standard way to prove a person's identity without having to deal with incompatible log-in screens, username, and password challenges, multifactor with indication techniques, and all the other hassles posed when logging into secure websites and apps.

## Drummond Reed on Trust Frameworks

Before we get too far into sovereign identity, it's important to understand what a trust framework is and why it is important to this model. Fortunately, I was able to track down one of the world's foremost authorities on these sorts of models, Drummond Reed.

John     So, there's this thing called trust frameworks . . . but how do I implement them? Where do they come from? How did they start? Are they being used today?

Drummond    I'm happy to help there, John, and I'll give you a little bit of context. The idea of what we now call a trust framework was really thrust into the limelight of Internet infrastructure development shortly after the Obama administration came into power. And some of the leading lights and digital identity within the US federal government said, "Hey, you want to start using identity credentials from private providers, be it Google or PayPal or Yahoo or banks or credit unions?"

We want to be able to start using US citizens' logins to government websites without needing to register and create a new credential at every website. Lower the friction for people to start to use government websites. And to do that, they said, "We can't just accept any login from any private company or provider. We need to have a set of rules for what constitutes a sufficient security and privacy of those credentials." And so they said, "Let's create a *trust framework*, which is this combination of the legal and business rules or policies around establishing security and privacy and trust online." With the technical specifications and rules that are needed to implement those policies.

The technical tools and the legal and business rules that go with them into a single—typically—a document or a set of documents that ends up in many cases functioning then as the contract or agreement between the members of a trust community online. And that can be as small as the users of a particular company or service online, single website. But most typically, a trust framework is for a large group of websites. All the members of an industry, the citizens of an entire country and its associated government, or even global or international trust frameworks. It all depends on just the size of the network that they're applying to.

John     Well that's fascinating. So you mentioned this is like a contract. We hear a lot about smart contracts when it comes to distributive ledger. Is this part and parcel to that? Or is it something separate?

Drummond    It's adjacent to it. Smart contracts are distributive ledger technology or ways of taking contractual terms and turning them into code so that the terms and conditions of a legal contract are actually entirely adjudicated and enforced by a machine. So, a classic example of a smart contract might be that you— actually in a Ethereum you set up—and you say, "I want a smart contract that I want to sell Microsoft stock when it gets below 31," right? Normally you'd tell your broker that, and your broker would monitor it, and when it went below 31 you'd put in a sell order. And there's a human in the loop, right? Where a smart contract on a Ethereum network would continuously monitor the stock price and automatically make the sale when the the price falls below 31.

When Microsoft drops below 31, it institutes a sell order and it's all code. But it's all legally and contractually correct as long as the code's right. So then it is executed. A trust framework is legal—it is

*(continued)*

(*Continued*)

a contract. And it can be implemented as a contract between all the members of a community. Some aspects are captured in code and implemented in code. And in fact, with most trust frameworks, you want the vast majority of it to be implemented in code so the actual human element of the trust framework is as light as you can get it. That's what makes it both applicable to digital communities and scalable. But with most trust frameworks they're not completely smart contracts, they are still—they have a human element or adjudication piece to it.

Glen    Would it be fair to call a trust framework, it sounds to me like to some extent it's a membership agreement, would that be a fair way of thinking about it as well? Because if you want to play in this sandbox, you must agree with this set of rules. So you basically signed on, and if you're early enough, maybe you could help influence what those rules are actually stated as. But if the group already exists and you want to come in, you're going to sign up and say yes, I'll behave according to the standards you've put in place. Is that accurate?

Drummond    Yes, I think it would be very accurate to say that many trust frameworks would be essentially implemented and would be considered like a membership contract in a trust network online.

John    So, an example, let's say that we've been talking about sovereign identity and using that for passwordless login, but we've also—and that's kind of simple in the sense that we know they're already a member—we've validated that. But let's move into a different direction. I want to vet Drummond Reed as a member of ABC credit union. And you would like to use your sovereign identity to apply. So would it be that the credit unions would all get together and go, okay, we all agree that if a financial entity of this that you could validate this I don't know whatever regulatory piece that has validated AML, anti-money laundering, now you're a customer, in good standing? And if we can prove that, then we can accept that membership or that person in? And so we would all agree to that?

Drummond    Yes, I think that's an excellent example of if you had a trust framework that the credit union's established. Let's just call it a sovereign credit union trust framework. CU trust, okay? And part of what CU trust would say is, all right, if a member, a credit union member wants to become a member of the CU trust community, then they're going to be enrolled by one of the credit unions to do that. Then what's called a claim on sovereign is going to be issued to say this credit union member is a member of CU trust and has been enrolled by this credit union ABC.

The trust framework will say credit union ABC agrees that it's going to have performed the necessary KYC (Know Your Customer) according to, for instance, these legal regulations, AML (Anti-Money Laundering) according to these legal regulations, and the old fact check according to these legal regulations. And it's written in the trust framework so that every member, every credit union, and every individual member of that CU trust framework knows that if that claim is issued by that credit union it means those things have been done and that credit union is attesting to that.

John       Does that make them liable?

Drummond   I'm glad you brought up that question because one of the primary reasons to have trust frameworks is to actually establish the rules for legal liability among the members of that trust community. A classic example of this, John, is one of the best-known trust frameworks right now—it has actually been implemented in the UK. It was developed at the UK chapter of OIX. OIX is the Open Identity Exchange, openidentityexchange.org. And it's the international clearinghouse for trust frameworks. It's where a number of them have been developed since it was first started in 2010.

This one is developed by a public–private partnership between identity providers in the UK and the government. It's called Gov.UK Verify trust framework. I think there are seven identity providers that are certified by that trust framework today that have met the requirements that you need to issue a UK–verified credential. And if an identity provider follows the policies in that trust framework and does the vetting of the identity according to those policies, by definition they have no liability if that credential is subsequently used by that individual. If the individual falsified information or otherwise deceived the identity provider, as long as the identity provider followed the rules, the identity provider does not have any liability for the misuse of that credential. And that is established in that trust framework and then that's recognized by UK law.

## Trust Frameworks

Trust frameworks are foundations that the next level of authentication will be built on, and it's the holy grail of product positioning. There's nothing more important to users than their credentials, and for financial institutions, it's strategic high ground. Each time an organization interacts with a customer, it must authenticate the person before doing anything else. The problem is that most of us have so many passwords and so many usernames that we can't remember them all. And we've resorted to tools like 1Password or other products that will store passwords for us. This, of course, kind of defeats the purpose. If hackers get into a password-management tool, then they have access to everything.

So, what's the answer? To determine that, let's talk about the current model of identity. I want you to think of identity as your passport to get into any place. Suppose I want to use a shopping site like Amazon. I have to give my address. I have to give my name. I have to give my credit card if I would like to buy anything. And then on top of that, I will need a password and username to log into the site—and I don't want to use the same password for every site, so I might pick a unique password for the site. I can only really use the site fully after I have provided all this information. This is true for nearly every online retailer or service provider. As a result, all of us have too many usernames and passwords.

The first problem with this setup is merely an inconvenience. Imagine say you get a new credit card or move to a new address. You now have to manually update this on every single site. It's a hassle, plain and simple.

The larger problem with this deals with data security. Pieces of our identity are everywhere, all over the internet. As we've seen from breaches in the past, this creates giant enormous honeypots of data. Consider for a moment the seriousness of the Equifax breach. In one fell swoop, the sensitive data of nearly half of the adult population of the United States was stolen by hackers. Financial institutions rely on and store customers' most private and important data. When data are stored in so many different places, the risk that some of it will be stolen is incredibly high—and the effects can be dire. If someone steals personal data, they now have the ability to engage in identity fraud. On top of that, we're tracked. Our data are valuable to not only hackers. Marketers also want to know everything about us so they can sell us things. Everywhere we go, our data are harvested and sold without our consent (or, perhaps we have given our consent when we accepted the fine-print terms of use). So, if that's true, then what are our options? Why would we consider looking at this?

There's a great article about security and digital identity by Patrick Gauthier, the vice president of external payments at Amazon. He mentions that it is the time to reinvent digital identity: "For more than a decade, the financial institutions and businesses have significantly invested to protect personally identifiable information, otherwise known as PII."[1] Companies take data protection very seriously, yet an epidemic of data breaches continues to occur. Highlighting the need for a new set of strategies and tools to manage this risk. Until now, there really hasn't been a way to have a sovereign identity, an identity that exists that no one else controls.

The reason for this is because all identity plays have been built around this centralized platform. Think back to Chapter 12, which distributive ledgers and decentralized platforms. So, how can we do this? Well, let's imagine that instead of Amazon requiring your information, Amazon had a way to subscribe to you. You would be the sole owner of your personal identity. Every time your address changed or every time your card information changed, you could simply change it in one spot to be picked up by all of the organizations you grant permission to. Imagine if Apple, eBay, Facebook, Amazon, Google, your doctor's office, the government, all of these places, could talk to you to verify that the information is correct and current.

This concept was originally proposed by an identity specialist who I'm proud to say is a friend of mine, Doc Searls. Doc Searls wrote *The Intention Economy*, which I highly recommend. His idea is for individuals to become the source for proof of identity, including their correct info, their correct data, and their actual preferences. Consider that. What if your preferences followed you around everywhere you went?

## Encryption and Data Security

Imagine if you never had to touch those nasty buttons on gas pumps to select your gasoline type. The pump would know what kind of gas you wanted based on the car you were driving. Your consent, your rules. This represents an inversion of control. It's also private and super secure because it uses the encryption methodology of the distributive ledger platform and it's irrevocable due to the immutable properties of the distributive ledger. So, how would we even implement something like this, and what does it mean to a financial institution? Let's start off with the most important concept. As I mentioned before, identity is strategic high ground. Now think about this. Before we can do anything, at any bank, any transaction, the first thing we have to do is that we have to prove that you're you.

If you've been on a call with a call center recently, you know the inane things that they will ask you in order to determine your identity. My favorite one is the last two or three transactions from my account. This assumes that I'm the only one spending on my account. If they looked closely, they would see that I have a joint account with my wife, and there's a likelihood that she has spent money without me knowing. So, if I want to answer this question, I actually have to log in to home banking and look at my history. The second thing that we've seen is that when people call in to the call centers, they'll ask for some information based on personal identity information. This includes things like your Social Security number, your birthday, your last name, and so forth.

All of these critical pieces of data could be discovered on the internet. The answer is to get rid of passwords all together. What does that mean, and what does it look like? Well, first of all, it's important to understand that in a sovereign identity that is built around distributive ledger, the identity itself is actually not stored on your device. The identity is just a key in the cloud or in the distributive ledger network that's perpetuated throughout the network in perpetuity that you can access with your device. And let's think about how this might work. I call into the call center, a person picks up. Assuming I've already registered for this digital identity, the customer service rep can click a button, and my phone (or perhaps my Amazon Echo or my Google home device, or any other number of IoT gadgets in my home) might pop up and say, "The Suncoast Organization is trying to validate your identity. Would you like to continue?"

If I answer it on the Alexa, assuming that someday in the future they have voice validation software, it will know that that's me and pass that back to the organization. And, in seconds, I would be able to be authenticated and move on with my transaction. And it can work no matter where I am. Imagine that I call from my cell phone. A message pops up, and it says, "The Suncoast Organization is trying to validate your identity. Would you like to continue?" When I say yes, the call center representative knows it's me. But more importantly, I know the person on the line really is the call center representative. Not only does this guard against people pretending to be me, but it also protects me from talking to someone pretending to be a particular organization. In the world of finance and banking, this is a tremendous safeguard for institutions and their customers.

This two-way validation is at the heart of sovereign identity—and you would never need a password again. Just close your eyes for just a minute and pretend. What does it feel like to no longer have passwords? Yeah that's right, it's a big load off, isn't it? All of a sudden there's unicorns and rainbows—everything's better.

## Sovereign Identity in Practice

Let's apply this sovereign identity concept to a context that has recently come about. Not too long ago, the Consumer Financial Protection Bureau (CFPB) looked into the practices of a certain large financial institution that was setting up credit cards and other accounts without its customers' permission. The organization in question was Wells Fargo, and its sales process failed three different ways. First, it failed to get client consent. The tellers and the sales reps who were opening these fraudulent accounts had the ability to give consent on behalf of the customer. If I had to guess, I would imagine that there's some sort of software program that was intended for use in the call center that allowed somebody to walk through this process and at the end accept the terms and the agreements and the disclosures on behalf of the customer. Now, let's imagine this process in the sovereign identity trust framework, like the one I just discussed. So you're sitting at home, watching football or *The Golden Girls* or whatever it is you watch. And all of a sudden your phone buzzes or your Echo lights up or maybe even your TV displays a pop-up message that says, "Wells Fargo wants your approval to open a new line of credit. Allow or deny?" Well, you're not talking to them and neither is your spouse, so you say no and hit the deny button. The problem of fraudulent accounts—even those set up by supposedly trustworthy bank employees with access to all the necessary information and systems—disappears.

The other portion of this is that it creates an opportunity for a high level of privacy. Currently today we are tracked everywhere we go. Consider how convenient it is to log into websites using your Facebook or Google account. It cuts down on the number of passwords and user IDs you need to remember, but that convenience comes at a price. When people do this, they might not realize that Facebook or Google can now use that related data (i.e., where you have an account, what you buy there, what services and settings you have selected). They're going to sell that information without your consent. With sovereign identity, people would have to give consent before doing anything with it, so that means that no one gets any information without needing it—and without a person's explicit approval.

Now, I'm going to go out on a limb and talk about a wild idea. So here's a question, and I want you to chew on this for a minute. Does Amazon have to have your address? And before you answer, think about it. So the obvious answer to this question is that yes, of course Amazon needs my address. How else are they going to ship my magical brown boxes of awesome stuff that I get every week? But, if you really think about it, Amazon doesn't actually need your address. The only company that needs your address is the shipper. What if the shipper provides a cryptonym that you could store in your sovereign identity infrastructure? Then you could give that cryptonym to Amazon. When preparing your package, Amazon would send that cryptonym back to the shipping company, who would use it to set your real address. The result is that you no longer have your address information stored in Amazon for shipping. The same process could be used for credit card billing addresses and the credit cards themselves.

This is a whole new world to think about, and it will have a huge impact on the state of identity in financial institutions. First of all, we're going to start with home banking. Currently, a home banking credential storage is a mish-mosh of different things. I have found that in many institutions, the home banking credentials are not even under the control of the financial institution. This means that it can't be used in other applications. I call this *digital dysfunction*. Sometimes it's so bad that the mobile application doesn't use the same password as the home banking application. A good example would be Amazon Echo having to have its own authentication that is separate from a person's primary Amazon login.

The second piece is that we have something called multifactor authentication (MFA), which is mandated by the FFIEC. MFA, unfortunately, is difficult when it comes to cross-device implementation. Meaning that you can log in to home banking and if it sees a pattern or something unusual it may ask you who your favorite first-grade teacher was or what your favorite pet was or something like that. The mobile interface may not ask the questions. It may want to text you instead. The challenge with this is we're continually playing catch up with all the different channels—and they are going to continue to expand, which will create costly integration.

## Weaknesses in the Current Identity System

Our current identity platform—the user-name-and-password setup— presents a number of opportunities for illegal activity. Sovereign identity can solve quite a few of these.

### Phishing

The first one, of course, is *phishing.* Which is the act of sending someone an email and trying to trick them into typing their credentials into a fraudulent website or a façade of a website. Once bad actors get the credentials, they will go into the target home banking or mobile banking account and perpetrate ACH fraud, or bill pay fraud. Since there are no passwords in the sovereign identity model, then phishing would become a thing of the past.

### EMV

Recently, in an effort to reduce fraud from counterfeit cards, the networks mandated issuers and merchants to provide and accept EMV enabled credit cards. EMV stands for European MasterCard and Visa. This is the little gold chip that's on your card. The chip is designed so that your information is never transmitted to the POS device in the clear. The POS device transmits information to the chip which in turn returns a cryptographic payload that the merchant then ships to their payments provider. In order to duplicate a card you would have to know the cryptograms that are on the chip. It's now become much harder to duplicate a card and as result, we're seeing that the fraud is shifting to an area that does not need EMV, which are mostly online merchants such as Amazon, iTunes, and other internet retailers. A bad guy will get a credit card number and rather than try to create a physical card to use they will simply setup an account on an internet retailer and charge the card for goods and services that they can have shipped to an address to be fenced or laundered into money.

### Consumer Privacy Concerns

If you've ever started to sign up for a site, you might have the choice of creating a new user name and password or signing in with an existing account (usually a social media account). Why not use this? After all, one less password to remember is more convenient. Then again, if you're looking to be private and secure, then you might prefer to create a new log in. When you log in with one of these social media accounts, that company is likely going to share data—for a profit.

Consider the security steps any of these social media sites takes when signing up new users. When people sign up, does anyone check their photo IDs to make sure they are who they claim to be? Does anyone do a background check on them? No, of course not. In fact, you could have 10 Facebook accounts right now. As a matter of fact, with a little bit of work, I could be you on Facebook. The same thing is true for LinkedIn, Google, Reddit, and every other account. None of these systems has anything to back up their identity claims. (And let's keep that word *claims* in mind, because claims are going to be very important in the future.) But guess what? I know of some organizations that did check your license.

## An Opportunity for Financial Institutions

Who does background checks, AML checks, and KYC checks? Who is forced to verify new customers' identities? Financial institutions. This means that there's an opportunity for financial institutions to become the authenticators, and they're going to be able to create verifiable claims. Currently, if you would like to have a verifiable identity, you go down to the DMV and you get a driver's license. It's government issued and it has a picture of you on it; the license itself is actually built to be tamper proof, and it's designed to prevent counterfeiting.

So, what would a digital version of this look like? Well, to go there, we first have to understand the hierarchy of the internet. Right now on the internet there are organizations or companies that have their identity confirmed through something we call DNS. This type of website authentication relies on a security feature called an SSL certificate. How do you know you're on Amazon's site and not some hacker's imposter honey trap? Well, most of us will look up at the bar that's in our browser and see that there's a lock icon there. When we see it, we assume that Amazon's identity as a website has been verified for us. The second step of this hierarchy concerns Amazon's customers. These customers must enter all of their information into each site they set up. This is where the problem emerges. Since customers do not have a reusable verifiable identity, they are forced to either use a browser to auto fill their personal information, or type it in themselves. Each time the customers set up another identity in another site, they add one more place that must be updated if they move or if they get a new credit card. If this were a programming platform, the architects of the platform would question the design. Why? Well, the institutions or organizations are unique, but people are unique as well. Anything that is unique in a data model should only be referenced once. An efficient data model doesn't duplicate unique data; it creates pointers. On the internet, we have a way to deal with that. When you go to type in a website address into a browser like google.com or apple.com, the human readable name you typed in is transmitted to a large database that translates that request into an internet address, which is an octet of numbers, that looks something like this: 12.23.45.100. This database that translates this information from human readable to numbers is called DNS or Domain Name Server. We have a human model for this—it's our social security number. However, unlike the DNS system, it is dangerous to have a directory of people that would provide information on everyone. So how would one address this problem and more importantly, how will personal data be registered?

In the future, when I set up my Netflix account, a sovereign identity platform would verify that I am really John Best. Now, there are other people with the name John Best, but I am a unique John Best in that I have different attributes than the rest of the John Bests on the internet. My collection of attributes are what makes me identifiable to others as the specific John Best that is attempting to do transact business with them.

The first thing you have to do to understand digital identity is, you have to expand your definition of identity. I've noticed that in the financial institution space we tend to think of identity basically as a collection of attributes. Your username, your password, your real name, your social security number, your address, secondary address, your group of MFA questions, and so forth. But true identity actually has a lot more to it. For example, let's pretend that you worked for a company, I'll just name one. Let's pretend you work for the publishers of this book, Wiley. Suppose that you would like to go get a loan.

Now, today you would go to a bank or a credit union, and you would sign up for the loan and one of the things the banker would like to do is validate your employment. How do we do this today? Well, you would have to go to a website or your files and collect two of your paystubs, and you would give these paystubs to the financial institution. The FI would use the paystubs to confirm your income and employment. These are often known as stipulations. The whole procedure can take up to one or two days. There is also the danger that the FI has no way to validate the paystub without calling the employer to prove employment, since, in a world where much of our private information has been disclosed on the internet, its highly likely that a counterfeit paystub wouldn't be caught due to the fact that it may actually contain the information of an real employee.

But what if Wiley had a sovereign digital identity as a corporation and it could claim you, and prove your identity as an employee? Imagine that you go in to do a loan and you tell the banker that you have a sovereign identity. The process would look a lot like when you approve access to your local services for an application on a smartphone. Have you ever downloaded an application and been asked for your consent for the application to use the camera or microphone? In much the same way, the lending FI would solicit digital consent to your information contained in your sovereign identity using verifiable claims. The application or smart phone would inform you that the FI wants access to your address and your consent to digitally verify your employment status and the other personal information that is necessary for a loan. As part of the process, the FI's identity is also verified using a digital signature, so that you can be very sure the request is legitimate.

The safety in this model would likely incent more people to use this method than previous methods. A process like this would be far more efficient for both the customer and the FI. Suddenly, all the friction of filling out the form and typing in redundant data, as we do so frequently, is gone. Not only that, but we're certain that we have provided the most up to date and accurate information. The same process could be used to digitally sign the loan and validate the terms of the loan. The loan and its terms could then become part of your digital identity as an attribute of your finances. A smart contract could be used to enforce a direct-deposit-based rate. If the customer agreed to pay via payroll reduction or automatic payments to get a better rate and the customer then changes this by canceling the recurring payment online, the smart contract would automatically pick up this change and apply the new rate to the loan.

The backbone of this new claims process will be built around the work being done by the W3C's verifiable claims working charter group. The verifiable claims group is designing a standard that would allow organizations to transmit and validate claims. The verifiable claim is not a protocol but a syntax or standard that would allow cross-industry interoperability. What is a verifiable claim? A verifiable claim is any attestation that an entity or organization can make about you or something that they can confirm with proof. The claim is then digitally signed by the organization and digitally provided to entities that need to use the proof to conduct business with you or an entity.

In the example above, we discussed verifying employment as part of a lending process. A verifiable claim might contain an employee identifier, the amount of time the employee has been employed, and finally, a digital signature to prove that the information came from the actual employer. And they can actually submit a verifiable claim that can now be stored at the financial institution to prove that John Best is an employee of Wiley. And instead of this taking a day and a half because someone has to go get paystubs, take pictures of them with their phone, or send them in, or drop by, or fax them, or whatever they're going to do, it all happens in seconds. This is a complete paradigm shift. Imagine that you walk up to the teller line and the teller simply asks you if you're part of the sovereign. You say yes, you click a button, they know who you are. Same thing with the drive-through. Imagine no more passwords on home banking. This will solve so many problems. However, there's a lot more to it.

Today, in most financial home banking and digital platforms, there's what I call a single source of truth. And that single source of truth, or the system of record, is where all the usernames and passwords are validated. And so if you have this, you have the keys to the kingdom. And what I mean by that is, home banking could well be up. And your bill pay could be running fine and all of the other services are fine. But if your login is down, then nobody can sign in to get those services. So effectively, *you* are down. But what if instead of having just one system to validate who you are, you had tens of thousands of systems? Well, that's what this digital identity service can bring—the idea that there is more than one system to validate you.

Now let's suppose you suddenly, magically, somehow hacked into one of them, or three of them, or even five of them. And you changed information so that you could log in. It still wouldn't work because you would have to change more than half of all the systems out there in order to violate this identity. Now, people who are critics of this, they'll see a few flaws. The first flaw is that all of this cryptology resorts to a key. And key management is very important. If you lose the key, then you effectively have to start over.

What people don't realize is if we switch to an inversion of control where every time you log in to something, every time you consent to something, it checks with you first. It almost doesn't matter if your private information is out there unless someone can digitally impersonate you to say yes. However, in the world of digital identity, particularly sovereign identity, you're going to be able to put your identity back together by using your families. So, you lose your key, you may have your brother and your sister, you call them both and they can click something and restore who you are. This is a very valuable concept. Finally, why is this worth considering? Why would people move in this direction? Well first of all, normalizing authentication methods will reduce integration costs for digital platforms. This should also reduce call center calls regarding passwords. It should improve speed to market for all products. Imagine that you didn't have to worry about creating the "I forgot my password" or "I forgot my user ID" security questions.

There is so much extra overhead to get someone into a product. This would improve security drastically, simply by getting rid of passwords and checking with the person before you do anything. This would also increase interoperability between organizations due to the distributive ledger. So, if you have a sovereign identity and you would like to sign up for another institution, you could actually conceivably bring all of your bill pay payees with you.

So let's think about that for a second. Maybe you have used bill pay at a financial institution. For those of you who haven't, I'll give a quick overview of the process. You log in to the financial institutions digital services, whether it be mobile or the web, you go into the bill pay area, and you break out the envelope for the bill that you would like to pay. Let's say it's a health care bill. You type in the address of where you're supposed to remit the payment from the health care bill, from the physical piece of paper. You give it a nickname, and then you go in and you schedule a payment. And when you schedule this payment, the solution will look at the address and the name of the payee. And it will make some determinations on payment routing (or at least a good bill pay system will). So it may decide to send this payment as a check because it doesn't recognize the address or the payee information and its electronic payments registry. So its only option is to cut the check and send it. In which case, it may take a couple days to get there. It may also decide to go ahead and send this via electronic means, meaning that they have a relationship, be it Lockbox or ACH, to send money directly to this payee.

However, here's the real question I have for you: *Are those payees that you just typed into that system yours, or are they the financial institution's?* I would suggest that they are the customer's. With a sovereign identity, you could actually store all of your payee information inside your own service platform. Meaning that you could go from institution to institution and reload your payees. I can hear you now. Oh, John, we've all bought bill pay, and we were supposed to have it around because it's sticky and once people type in 10 or 12 of these payees, it's hard for them to leave, and that's part of our model. I don't disagree. As a matter of fact, I can remember in 2008, 2007, saying those very words to customers. But today is 2017, and a captured or trapped data business model isn't going to fly with consumers anymore. Why? Because fintechs will allow sovereign identity, and customers are going to go where there is utility. It's that simple.

As an industry, we either have to figure out how to start doing it or we have to figure out how to join the groups there. Because in a perfect world, you should be able to pick your payee from your preferences and then you should be able to determine how you want to pay. And one day, you might want to use the financial institution's bill pay, and that should be a button click away. But another day, you might decide to use Venmo. Or you might decide to use PayPal because you have different needs. The key is, how are we going to change the business model to support this?

So, not too long ago, I was talking to an organization that was interested in real-time balances. And one of the things that happens in a real-time balance is that when customers know what their real-time balance is, they're less likely to overdraft. Overdraft, as many of you know, means income for the financial institution. However, it's not looked upon favorably by the customers. The challenge is this, to my way of thinking: Is it right that, due to our inability to show a correct balance or data, the customers would overdraft, and we would charge them for it? Furthermore, is it right that if we were to solve this problem, we would be careful about sharing that information because we would not want to lose a revenue source? I would say, continuing to operate in this methodology is going to be a problem for all institutions.

Why not replace the overdraft fee with an artificial intelligence fee? Something that would tell people when they're getting close to these numbers and prevent it from happening. Again, this is where the distributive ledger and the identity platform can come together. So the final thought on why this is worth considering is this: If we believe that there will be a market for these claims—and by claims, I mean claims of employment, claims of identity—then the banks and financial institutions stand to benefit from this market. Because they are in the best position to identify and register the consumers.

Consider this: I once helped a friend who owned some property. And my wife and I was helping her to lease her property out. And any time someone came up to rent the duplex, half the duplex that was out there for rent, we would have to go through and do a background check on this person. That could cost anywhere from $50 to $75. The background check wasn't that useful, in the sense that we would have to go through a service and that service was related to credit reports and other things that were out there. But what if we could switch that and the person who was doing the lease could actually check with the financial institution through the magic of sovereign identity? Well, maybe I don't want to pay the $50. But I sure as heck might pay $25 or $35 for a validation that this person has an account at your institution—particularly if the customer has consented. So new revenue sources will be in play thanks to identity.

I'll close out this identity chapter by saying that the biggest impact that identity could have is in the payment space. As we mentioned before, checking with the consumer before we put the charge through is going to help reduce fraud. Imagine a purchase on the Amazon site where, before you could go through and buy something you had to validate your purchase with your sovereign identity on your phone by using your thumbprint to allow the purchase to go through. This would reduce fraud on card-not-present transactions significantly. So, if we have the opportunity to drive identity, we should take it. Identity is strategic high ground.

For more information visit sovrin.org, which is run by Sovrin, a private global foundation that is establishing a sovereign network. It is free for anyone to use. Another great resource is Doc Searls's book *The Intention Economy.*

---

**Chapter Review**

- Sovereign identity and trust frameworks can help circumvent the password crisis and mitigate hacking disasters and identity theft.

- A sovereign identity platform gives individuals a single way, which they control, to sign into all websites and apps.

- Trust frameworks rely on the same ultrasecure encryption used in the distributive ledger.

- Since financial institutions have verified, sensitive data, there is an opportunity for them to become organizations that can confirm the identity of individuals signing up new accounts in all sectors.

---

## NOTE

1. Patrick Gauthier, "It Is Time to (Re)-invent Digital Identity," Pymnts.com (September 12, 2014), http://www.pymnts.com/in-depth/2014/it-is-time-to-re-invent-digital-identity/.

# The Hacker Threat

"Hi, Bob." "Hi, Steve." "Still building the wall, I see." Bob: "Yep, still making ladders?" Steve: "Yep."

No book about digital transformation would be complete without a chapter or two or a hundred on security. As a matter of fact, the number-one issue I hear when I talk to financial institutions about digital transformation is their concern around security. I couldn't agree more that this is an important issue. As a matter of fact, I encourage most organizations that are going through digital transformation to make security their number-one priority regarding their processes. This means developing an iron-clad bulletproof security process within your organization. It should go above and beyond the regulatory standards, and it should exceed any current industry standards. For instance, if your regulatory standard is to have your digital assets penetration tested four times a year, I would consider doing it every month. If your regulatory standard is to have your organization conduct an internal penetration test once a year or twice a year, I would do it monthly or more. Simply put, you cannot spend enough on security.

Since the beginning of time, security has been a problem. I'm sure that the first caveman who found shiny rock had no idea that someone else would try to take his new treasure. The same caveman who lost his shiny rock probably found another similar one, and this time he buried it, thinking that would protect it. Sadly, the caveman didn't pay close enough attention to who was watching when he buried it, and the thief caveman dug it up and took it for himself. The same caveman found another shiny rock. This time, he hid it in a bush or behind a tree. Again, thief caveman would find it and steal it. You get the picture here; this process has been going on for millenniums. Security is a constant battle to stay ahead of the thieves. When we build a 10-foot wall to keep them out, they bring an 11-foot ladder.

The first thing to understand about digital security is that nothing is bulletproof. You must expect everything you do to be hacked. One important process around security is to conduct risk reviews or risk audits for every one of your products. The risk reviews should also include a recovery plan if the product or platform is compromised. The other important aspect of security is to have easy access to extensive documentation on all the risk controls in the organization. Understanding how a process works is very important, because with this understanding it can be audited for weak points. Without proper documentation, it can never be penetration tested fully. So, how do we go about security in the new digital world? Good news: There are some evolving opportunities in the digital space around security that can make us better. A wise man plans to be hacked, a fool hacks a plan together after they have been compromised.

A great example is a website called HackerOne. HackerOne leverages crowdsourcing by inviting their community of security experts and hackers to participate in penetration testing a product.

So, in the past when my team and I have developed software, we've hired companies to try to break into the platform or software that was developed by our teams. Usually, they will send one or two people at it and they will do their best using amazing tools to break into the platform. We will also give them account numbers and passwords so that they can log in and see what they can do inside the platform. The challenge here is that mathematically this process doesn't make sense. Why? Because we're only using two penetration testers. But in the real world you can experience hundreds if not thousands of attacks a day by different hackers. This mismatch in scale creates an advantage for the hacker community. Each of these attackers will have a different process for attacking your platform. And as a result, it would be impossible for you to come up with the number of permeations that these hackers will put against your system. HackerOne solves this issue by crowdsourcing your vulnerability testing. Rather than having one-person vulnerability testing your platform, you will have hundreds of people trying to break in. HackerOne organizes its testing into challenges with a money reward for succeeding. It's a private challenge that allows a lot of people to attempt to break into your platform. It can be run using a bounty system. For every vulnerability that's found, you would pay a bounty for it. This new approach is an important evolution in the security and risk review process that will improve any institution's security position exponentially.

## The Artificial Intelligence Threat

Soon, hackers will start leveraging artificial intelligence algorithms against financial institutions. Rather than wasting a human resource and trying to attack your website or your home banking site or mobile site, they will use artificial intelligence to try to break in. The hacker AI application will already be trained in thousands of techniques, and unlike a human, it will never give up. It will learn from every attempt and change its approach. It will be far more effective than even the world's best hacker, because it will learn from each mistake it makes.

Consider the following. Facebook recently launched a test where it was trying to teach two AI entities in the form of chatbots to negotiate with each other. To facilitate the learning process, they invented a game. The game involved trading back and forth different objects to achieve parity between the two bots. They trained both AIs by allowing them to review humans playing the same game. Facebook believes that for businesses to effectively use chatbots, they would need to be able to negotiate to be able to transact business with humans. There was cause for alarm when they discovered that the two platforms had started creating their own language to communicate with each other during the negotiation process. Neither of the platforms were trained or programmed to do this. The artificial intelligence in the system developed new approaches on its own to accomplish its given task the most efficient way. You might imagine the same technology pitted against your home banking system or your ACH processing or any other number of areas. Continually checking, checking again. Looking for vulnerabilities and learning from the traffic it sees and the errors it gets as it tries various things. It would record how long it takes for each transaction to respond and design new attacks based on its findings.

## Planning for the Worst

So how do we prepare for this eventuality? Well, the first thing that we really need to work with is understanding that security revolves around a very important process called *change control*. I did not discuss change control in the processes chapter because I believe it fits better here in the security chapter. What is change control? And how critical of a function is it? How is it related to security? Change control is the concept of recording every change in your entire system. Many times, I have been into financial institutions where there is no change control. The symptom of not having a change control process is that when something breaks, you do not know what caused the break. More importantly, if there are anomalies, they are impossible to detect without some sort of baseline. Any change to production or near production systems must be put through a process of change control.

What would this process look like in your organization? Well here is a sample model. Let's say that on a Wednesday you need to patch or upgrade your home banking servers because the vendor who provides this server, or maybe it's your own organization who has written this software, needs to do an update. Or perhaps they just want to add a new feature. So, a change control committee would allow the organization to propose this change.

Whoever's in charge of this, it would likely be someone in the digital services area. This person would put in the request to the change control committee. The committee would review the request during their normal process and work with the product owner to understand the potential impacts of the change. That means that every system that the change might touch is documented, and just as important, every person within the organization whose department this change might affect is contacted. They are all given an opportunity to give input or ask questions about the upcoming change. What this means is that all changes will be planned, tested, assessed, and reviewed before they are finally implemented. The most important part of the change control process is documenting how to undo the change. So, I will give an example.

Many years ago, when we were designing the first round of multifactor authentication for home banking at my previous company, we implemented the product and, as far as we could tell, all was well. However, over time we began to see some adverse effects. At the time, we had no idea that they were related to this change. What we saw was that the number of invalid logins or failed logins was climbing. And at some point, it was beginning to climb exponentially. In looking at this problem, we were able to check the logs and our statistics and trace it back to a start date. When we looked at the start date in the change control log, we could see that someone—or our group—had implemented a new change to the multifactor authentication that resulted in the hardest problem to track, which is an intermittent problem. By using the change control, we knew this was the problem. We rolled back what had been done. And the systems went back to normal. And at that point, we could go through and review what had happened. We then put the change back in, submitted it, fixed the problem, and moved on. If we hadn't had a record of every change that was made on that day around that time, it would've been very difficult to understand what caused the problem.

Large digital systems are notoriously complex. And they must be documented. More importantly, all changes must be documented. This also includes non-software changes. So, for example, if someone's going in and changing a configuration on, say, a communications device like a router or a firewall, this should be documented in the change control process as well. Another value of the change control process is preventing collisions. For instance, it's not a good idea to change both your home banking platform and your firewall at the same time. It's simple common sense—if something breaks during that process, you won't know which one caused the problem. So by using this change control process where change requests are documented, they're formally sent in to a committee. The committee puts it into the planning stages and reviews it. They also sign off on the testing, including signing off on your go-back plan. And then after that, it's scheduled and implemented. This is one of the most important aspects of security, because hackers thrive on organizations that do not have change control. What this means is that if there is not a process or a governance around change control, hackers find their way in by finding systems that are poorly configured. These poorly configured systems often leave holes that allow them to compromise your platform. Change control will help you with this.

So, one of the things I like to do when I talk about security is tell stories. I believe these stories are very helpful to understand some of the security processes that need to be in place. The first story I'm going to tell you happened while I was a very young engineer at a financial institution. We had installed what was likely one of the very first internet home banking platforms. And we had written this platform ourselves.

One day, I got a call from a very upset gentleman. This gentleman told me that every day he would get locked out of our home banking system. Every day, his account was not accessible because someone had repeatedly tried to use it. And when they tried to use it, they did not use a correct password. One of the security features of the system is that any account that has multiple failed login attempts will be suspended. In these days, we did not have a process such as emailing you a new password or sending code to your phone because SMS didn't even exist to unlock a password. The only way that this gentleman could get back into his account was to call our call center and unlock it. And if he happened to get locked out over a weekend or some time when our call center wasn't open, he had to wait until the next business day. Needless to say, this gentleman was very frustrated. I promised him I would look into this issue immediately, as he was implying that because of his problem he thought our systems were less than secure.

Now, the first thing I did was to retrieve the logs from where he had tried to sign in. And keep in mind, back in these days we didn't have large statistical analysis systems reviewing all the logs for login. Instead we had large text files that were loaded on our server hard drives. It was your job to be able to search through these text files to find evidence of someone's login. So, if someone had a problem, you would have to go through and figure out which one of the three or four different home banking servers that the person logged into, and then inspect those logs. Logs could likely have hundreds of thousands of entries to search through just to find the single logs for this person. And furthermore, it's not likely that each time this frustrated customer signed in, they would login to the exact same computer. So, my staff and I started working on looking through the logs to determine what happened.

The first thing we noticed was that something or someone was logging into his account frequently. As a matter of fact, our first suspicion was that it was some sort of scripted tool because the timing of the logins was very consistent. The only challenge was that whoever was trying to log in didn't know the password. The person would try three times, very quickly, and then not try anymore. Back in those days, we did not use user IDs; we used account numbers. My first suspicion was there was a member out there somewhere whose account number was close to my frustrated customer's account number. And that person was mistyping it and logging in three times wrong. However, this person would get up in the morning, try, do it at lunch, try, and do it at night like clockwork.

Also after analyzing the logs, we determined that most of the attempts were coming from the same internet protocol (IP) address. Back then, there wasn't an easy way to look up who owned an IP address on the internet. But we worked with Verizon to determine what the source of this IP address was, and we discovered it went to a business. I figured I had enough information to call this member and explain to him what happened. When I called him, I said, "Sir, I believe someone has your account number, or something close to it. And each day they try to login and they're failing." I said, "Also, coincidentally, this person either works or lives in this building." And as soon as I said the building and the employer at the building or the company at that building, the gentleman immediately went silent. I said, "Sir, are you still there?" He said, "I know what's going on." And I said, "Sir, it would be helpful if you would enlighten me in case it happens to someone else." He said, "My ex-wife works in that building." So, this was my first experience with sort of digital vandalism. His ex-wife would get up each day, go to work, have a cup of coffee, bring up our website, put his member number in, and try three times with bad passwords, because she knew this would lock him out and infuriate him. Then somewhere after that time he would call our call center, get his account unlocked. She would come back from her lunch or have lunch at her desk or, I don't know, I'm just sort of picturing her there. And she would do this again. She would log in three times, lock him out, and go on with her day. And then just before she went to bed, she would do the same thing again. And she had been repeating this process for months. So what could we do to stop this problem? Well, one thing—let me back that up.

This led to one of our first security features, which was designed to allow customers to block specific IP addresses from accessing their accounts. This turned out to be a very useful feature and came in handy later, when we started to see attacks from foreign entities. We could now block whole countries by adding their IPs to our database. For instance, if you don't live in Pakistan, then it's not likely that you will ever access your home banking from Pakistan. If you think about it, this is nothing new for the financial industry. We've been doing this for years as it relates to our credit cards. If you've never used your credit card in Pakistan, you'd better call your bank before you go there. Otherwise, your card is not going to work in Pakistan. Why not do the same thing for our digital products?

## Operation Ababil

In 2012, the financial sector experienced its first full-on attack. The official reason for this was a video on YouTube, and it depicted Mohammed the prophet. Because depicting an image of the prophet is forbidden by the Muslim faith, a group of Muslim extremists or cyberterrorists demanded that all copies of the video, called *The Innocence of Muslims,* be removed from YouTube.

Starting on September 18, 2012, they launched Operation Ababil and began attacking places like Bank of America and the New York Stock Exchange—again, in retaliation for the YouTube video. The attacks continued: September 19, they attacked Chase bank. September 21, they attacked numerous financial organizations at once. September 24, attacks against the US Department of

Agriculture. September 25, they took down Wells Fargo's website for almost a whole day.

In the midst of this string of attacks, Senator Joseph Lieberman told CSPAN in a taped interview, "I don't believe these were just hackers who were skilled enough to cause the disruption of these websites. Suspicions point toward a special unit of Iran's revolutionary guard corps called the Quds Force."

## DDoS Attacks

On October 2, analysts discovered an incredible distributed denial of service (DDoS) toolkit that was believed to be the software behind the attacks on Bank of America, Chase bank, Wells Fargo, and PNC. The toolkit was capable of simultaneously attacking components of a website's infrastructure, flooding the targets with millions of packets to overwhelm their ability to serve their customers. These attacks continued throughout 2012 all the way into 2013. These were distributive denial as service attacks or, as I said, simply just shutting down the website's ability to service their customers. However, it was determined that many of these cyberattacks were distractions. They were created to distract the security team at the financial institution from their real purpose. Their real purpose was to steal money from the bank. So, while the entire staff from the organization is trying to deal with the website being down and the thousands of calls coming in about the digital services being down, the cybercriminals were stealing money from accounts. They knew that no one would have a chance to look at the actual files for transfers in detail.

On October 15, 2012, Bank of America, Chase, and Citibank were notified that they were the targets of a planned cyberattack. A total of 26 banks and credit unions were identified initially, and more than 100 criminals were believed to be part of the cybercrime ring. By March 2013, the financial sector replaced the government as the top target of cybercriminals. Several of these DDoS attacks were also accompanied by crippling viruses. Here's one story from a company called Aramco:

> More than 30,000 computers infected at the Saudi oil company Aramco were rendered useless and had to be replaced. Imagine what would happen if your organization was hit by a virus such as this. The virus called Shamoon was a dormant virus that got onto

every single computer at Aramco and was discovered by one of the security specialists. While the security specialist was researching the virus he accidently tipped off the cyber criminals that he was aware of them and the cyber criminals initiated a process called Wiper, which destroyed all the data on all 30,000 computers at once. I cannot overstate this, 30,000 computers instantly deleted all at once. Imagine if this happened at your financial institution.[1]

A Christmas Eve cyberattack in 2013 against a website of a regional California financial institution helped to distract bank officials from an online account takeover against one of its clients, netting the cyberthieves more than $900,000.

As a matter of fact, what we are seeing now is different organizations partnering together to accomplish these sorts of attacks. So, here's some things that we can do to mitigate risk. One, were going to have to think outside the box in terms of security response teams. My suggestion is that each organization needs two separate incident response teams. Incident response team one is assigned to deal with whatever threat problem or disruption has arisen. In the case of a DDoS attack, incident response team one would work with the security vendors and other consultants to stop the attack. Meanwhile, incident response team two would be instructed not to participate at all in the current attack scenario and instead to focus on current operations of the organization, looking for anomalies in their security files, their transmission files. They would be specifically looking through money transfers to make sure that the attack was not a distraction to accomplish some other sort of loss.

## Be Afraid When Things Are Down. Be *Very* Afraid When Things Are Going Well

In 2007, major retailer TJ Maxx disclosed that hackers had infiltrated its system and stolen credit card data that exposed over a 100 million credit cards to fraud. At the same time, TJ Maxx disclosed that the hackers had had access to the network for almost two years. The main hacker, Albert, who at the time was working as an undercover informant for the Secret Service under the moniker "Soupnazi," was able to gain access to the TJ Maxx corporate network by using a practice known as *wardriving*. Wardriving involves driving around with a laptop and looking for Wi-Fi networks that can be hacked. TJ Maxx at the time was using the WEP (Wireless Equivalent Privacy) protocol to secure its wireless network. WEP had been cracked in 2001, and yet TJ Maxx was still using the protocol to protect its Wi-Fi network in 2005. Gonzalez and his group were able to easily infiltrate the network via the Wi-Fi and then escalate their privileges within the network by stealing TJ Maxx users' credentials. Once they had enough access, they set up accounts on the retailer's mainframes and started collecting credit card data by reviewing files that were unencrypted and being sent to banks. Gonzalez and his group of hackers would take turns managing the account.

This is where it gets interesting. In order to send the stolen credit card information to their servers, they had to transmit over 80 GB of information. Since the TJ Maxx firewalls were poorly configured, they had to fix problems on the network so that they could transmit such a large amount of information. They also had to close some of the backdoors they had discovered so that other hackers wouldn't get in and take the data they had collected. The hackers had access to the TJ Maxx network for over 18 months and during this time they would have to fix things to keep unwanted IT people from looking for problems and inadvertently discovering their access or shutting off access to the areas they needed to complete their criminal activities. They developed a communication system by leaving encrypted messages for each other on the systems they were accessing to make sure that everyone knew what the last person had done.

I know many CTOs that start to freak out when seemingly random events happen in their systems. They often immediately jump to the conclusion that someone is trying to hack their system. This may very well be true, but I would also be concerned, based on the TJ Maxx incident, when things are working too well. This is because the last thing a good hacker wants to do is draw attention to his or herself by setting off alarm bells in your system. Sure, destructive hackers that want to perform distributed denial of service attacks or deface a website will leave their mark, but these are just vandals. The real cyberthieves, criminals who actually want to steal money or other valuable information, will do all they can not to leave any tracks or set off any alarms. So instead of freaking out when something happens, you might want to be more concerned when things magically fix themselves. If your users can suddenly access a website that they couldn't access before, or if a firewall problem that prevented you from transmitting large files suddenly fixes itself, and you cannot find anyone who knows why it suddenly started working, then I would be much more suspicious.

## Security as a Process of Innovation

Some of the most valuable innovations can and should be security related. For instance, the story of the angry ex-wife that I mentioned earlier resulted in a feature that allowed financial institution customers to block out access from certain IP addresses. This turned out to be a very valuable feature for the customers, because as time went on, account takeovers became more and more common, and while eventually hackers started spoofing addresses, this measure on our part caused them to move along to greener pastures. Security innovations will continue to go forward.

Some of the most difficult processes to digitize are security related, such as the FFIEC mandate that specifies that you must have multifactor authentication login. When digitized, this process is inconvenient for customers and ineffective against today's hacking techniques. Having to answer questions like "Who is your first school teacher?" and "What's your favorite pet?" are often inconvenient when you're trying to do something quickly. Especially if you did not set up these questions to begin with. I don't know about you, but I don't know the last name of my wife's favorite schoolteacher. So how will we look at security as innovation in the future? I believe that the evolution of security is going to be built around artificial intelligence and cryptography.

As a matter of fact, the same artificial intelligence that the hackers will be employing will be employed by financial institutions to defend against these new attacks. For example, consider the Facebook chatbot experiment I mentioned earlier. One chatbot was pitted against another chatbot in a negotiation game to determine if two chatbots or AI mechanisms could negotiate with each other. Much in the same way these two systems interacted, I believe that defense artificial intelligence bots will, in the future, protect our digital systems. These artificial intelligence bots will learn from the attacks that are levied against them, and they will create their own countermeasures. As they begin to create their own custom countermeasures, they will also work together with other financial institutions defense bots to collectively learn from the attacks happening at other institutions. Through cooperation and aggregation, we will create a much stronger defense against cyberterrorism and cybercriminals.

We will need to reexamine the security paradigms and conventional security wisdom if we are to succeed in a more dangerous digital environment. For a long time, digital security has been designed around a castle methodology. The castle protects the crown jewels and is fortified with tall walls, moats, alligators, soldiers, hot oil, and dragons. Each fortification is designed to be a defense against failure of the previous defense. The flaw in this design is that it is assumed that no one will ever breach the castle because the likelihood of all the defenses failing at once is low. But unbeknownst to the head of castle security, the king of the castle likes to throw parties, and during the parties he will let almost anyone in the castle. Sometimes during these parties, he orders the guards to raise the drawbridge and turn off the alarms so his friends aren't inconvenienced by the excessive security. The king's enemies closely monitored the habits of the king and the guards and eventually took advantage of the human error to gain access to the castle and steal the jewels.

The castle approach is highly susceptible to human error. All it takes is one unpatched system and the hackers are in. How can we think differently here? We must assume that the castle *will* be breached, and as a result, the assets must be protected even if they are in the hands of criminals. This is where cryptography comes into play. If all assets were protected with high-level cryptography, it wouldn't matter if the criminals were able to get their hands on it, because they wouldn't be able to access the data. This means we don't need alligators, moats, drawbridges, or dragons to protect our data. I can hear your argument: What if someone gets the keys to decrypt everything? Again, we need to change our thinking. There shouldn't be one encryption key to decrypt all the data. Instead, we allow the members to encrypt their own data, and through the magic of distributed ledger we can leverage a key management system that allows us to disburse the keys among all the customers. With this in place, a hacker would have to compromise every customer of the bank to make the data useful. I call this approach "hiding in plain sight."

## The Equifax Breach

Consider the Equifax breach that was reported in September 2017. Equifax is a credit agency that collects information from banks and other credit sources and, as a result, has a huge amount of data on millions of people. The announcement included the fact that more than 143 million people in the United States may have had their names, social security numbers, birthdays, addresses, and even photo-based identification like passports or licenses accessed.

At this writing, the nature of the attack is not known; however, I would bet that Equifax wasn't completely at fault here. Many believe when these breaches happen, it is due to carelessness or lack of security. However, I have worked with many of these organizations, and they work very hard on security. The simple fact is that the castle approach is destined to fail due to the modern tools that are available. If, however, Equifax had employed a cryptology approach and encrypted the data individually, then hackers wouldn't have been able to use the data even though they had gained access to it.

Furthermore, the castle approach also results in the biggest castles being targeted, in this case the hackers probably spent more time on gaining access to Equifax than other organizations because they clearly understood that hacking this platform would bring more gains than any other organization. Equifax is delivered data from over 91 million businesses worldwide. So rather than attack 91 million businesses why not just attack a place where data are centralized? Identity expert Phil Windley, the chair of the Sovrin foundation and an enterprise architect at Brigham Young University, explains it like this:

> So long as we insist on creating huge honeypots of valuable data, hackers will continue to target them. And since no security is perfect, they will eventually succeed. Computer security is difficult because computer systems are nonlinear—small errors can result in huge losses. This makes failure points difficult to detect. These failure points are not usually obvious. But hackers have a lot of motivation to find them when the prize is so large.[2]

So what is the answer, other than cryptography? Well, if a centralized database draws hackers, then it stands to reason that a decentralized database would be a better approach. The challenge up until now has been that good technology for a decentralized database wasn't available. However, in the era of cryptocurrency, it turns out that a decentralized database technology has actually been around for the last nine years in the form of Bitcoin. Equally important is removing correlatable identifiers such as login names, CC numbers, and so on. These identifiers allow others to correlate who you are. For instance, if your login is always "CryptoGuy2477," then Google and other sites will be able to correlate this knowledge with your search history and determine who you are. Again, the underlying technology of the Bitcoin platform comes to the rescue; along with the decentralized network, decentralized identifiers are also available.

Speaking of cyberterrorism, I would be remiss if I did not mention that all financial institutions are covered under the National Infrastructure Protection Plan devised by Homeland Security. As a matter of fact, financial institutions belong to one of the 16 critical infrastructure sectors identified by the government that need to be protected; in this case, the financial services sector. The department of the treasury is designated as a sector-specific agency for the financial services infrastructure. Consider what would happen if cybercriminals were able to destroy the trust between the population and our financial institutions. What if you didn't trust what your balance was? One popular notion of an attack is the idea of going in and altering ledgers but not in a way that everyone would notice. The idea is that most financial institutions have moved to a point of replicating their ledgers between active infrastructures to gain high availability.

What this means is that if you were to go in and attack a system and make some subtle changes to, say, a couple hundred thousand accounts, no one would notice. Over time, these errors and changes would be replicated to other systems. Eventually, it would be nearly impossible for the financial institution to restore from backups to erase the changes made by the criminals. In this way, it would reduce the trust that customers have in the financial system, and this could be catastrophic to our economy.

So what does this mean for you? It means that you're under heavy regulatory scrutiny with regards to security as a financial institution. Because of this, it would be very easy to throw in the towel and give in to the forces within your organization, particularly internal security forces that typically will fight against new innovations out of concern for security. However, while this may seem like a safe move, you can also secure yourself right out of business. The challenge with the security is not to say no to everything; the challenge is to create an environment where the security group is involved in all new features and innovations and to create a culture that encourages them to find solutions and reduce risk, as opposed to being an obstructionist in projects.

Security is a critical function that must have a seat at the table for all projects. That said, security should also have checks and balances to make sure that it is not slowing down projects. I knew a security officer who was super innovative, and instead of stopping ideas because of security concerns, she would work with the team to come up with solutions to security problems. I believe it would be useful to manage security personnel based on the ideas that they help get out the door. Executive leadership should measure security based on consistent process and being innovative. Creative thinking is going to be a highly sought-after trait in future security professionals.

When developing your own platforms, security takes on a whole new meaning. When an institution builds a product internally, it usually undergoes a lot of scrutiny by the staff, but there are steps that would be done in a professional fintech development shop that are often overlooked in an in-house development project. Three important security considerations should be noted as FIs continue to round out their development capability:

1. Since there is code being created in house that will be exposed to the general internet it is critical that a code review be performed.
2. Web application and network penetration testing should also be complete and all issues remediated before any production rollout.
3. Stress testing should be performed before any product or project is deemed production ready. This is particularly important when there is a latency problem in a project.

Many credit union CEOs and CIOs that I have talked to about in-house development have cited security as their number one reason for not allowing their staff to develop customer-facing products in house. They fear that if a vulnerability was found in the software, they wouldn't have anyone to fault but themselves. These CUs would rather get software from a vendor that they trust. However, even when getting software from a vendor you cannot be sure there aren't vulnerabilities.

It is important to have a process to review the security procedures for software platforms that you depend on, whether you build it yourself or buy it from a vendor. It is also important to have a risk review for all platforms to understand what the damage would be in the case of a breach.

## Scenario Planning

One great way to think and learn about digital security concepts is to do some scenario planning. What follows are some interesting and in some cases outlandish scenarios to think about. (See this book's companion website for scenario worksheets.)

### Scenario 1: NSA Backdoor

What if you woke up one morning to discover your FI on a WikiLeaks list of institutions to which the NSA had gained backdoor access?

Recently, I was fortunate enough to attend the Temenos Community Forum in Lisbon, Portugal. This was a big conference focused on "real-world fintech," tailored for an international audience. After filling my buffet plate and searching for a lunch seat one afternoon, I joined a gentleman sitting alone at a round table. We engaged in conversation and I learned he was from a bank in Dubai.

Immediately, I felt a bit awkward—not because of anything he said but because WikiLeaks had just revealed that the NSA, the US government's information spying platform, had hacked a group in Dubai that provides SWIFT payment services to banks in the region. I wondered what he thought about this, and how I would feel if the situations were reversed. Intellectually, I understood that neither of us was involved in the hacking, but when abroad we all become the embodiment of our country's actions to the people we encounter. The topic never came up, and we had a delightful conversation. The thought stuck with me, however.

Let's take a trip into a hypothetical bad day at your FI.

What if one morning you woke up to find your own institution's name in the news? Here's how it might play out for a CEO or CTO of the organization. Imagine driving into work as usual on a bright and sunny morning, thinking about the day's work ahead. Your phone begins buzzing and binging frantically. You are curious, but of course, safety comes first, so you pull over before checking your messages. Your marketing team would likely be first to know, because they have a Google alert set up to track the institution's name. They've already left you voicemails and forwarded links. After reading an article or two, you learn your system has a "backdoor" that the NSA has been using to monitor some of your customers' data. This backdoor is referred to as a *zero day*, a software hack that is coveted by hackers and organizations like the NSA because they are unknown to software providers like Microsoft and therefore never get fixed. Microsoft depends on the *white-hat* hacking community to report these issues so they can be resolved. When a nefarious individual or a state actor finds one and doesn't report it or share it with anyone else, it's a zero day until discovered by either the software company or the white hats.

You now know you have a backdoor in your system and, more importantly, the world knows. The logical first step is to plug the hole the NSA was using to get in. On the surface, this seems straightforward, since the issue is documented on the WikiLeaks site. However, if you have ever reviewed WikiLeaks' data dumps (and I have), you know that finding the necessary information isn't that easy. You will likely need to use a Torrent product to download the detail you need to close the hole. Meanwhile, your call center is besieged by customers wanting to know if their account was compromised. Do you console your customers by reasoning, "Relax, it's the NSA, they are working to keep us safe"? This approach may play better with certain fields of customers than others—and will almost certainly not be unanimous.

From here, the plot thickens. You confirm that the NSA has been regularly monitoring the accounts and purchases of certain customers. Do you tell the customers? Was the NSA watching them for a sound reason? Do you need to research the customer to ensure you performed proper vetting (OFAC, etc.)? Does the NSA call you? What if you get a letter from the State Department instructing you not to inform your customers? If you follow its direction, your entire customer base might conclude that their accounts have been compromised and lose trust in the institution.

While your team is sorting through the details to determine root cause and full impact, curiosity builds over who was hacked and how. News organizations are calling everyone related to your FI in the LinkedIn directory, trying to find somebody willing to dish.

Meanwhile there's mundane everyday banking business to perform. Good news: Someone on your IT team figured out the puzzle. Bad news: The hack involves a critical piece of software that can't be fixed without Microsoft's help. While IT is on the phone with Microsoft, others move onto the important business of determining what has happened to whom.

More good news/bad news: Microsoft has designed a work-around, but it will take four days to code and implement. You are now faced with the unappealing options of leaving your online banking running with the now well-documented hole (within the hacker community) that let the NSA in, or depriving your customers of online access for an extended period. By the way, your security team has detected high levels of suspicious traffic on your websites and mobile sites. You discover hackers are trying to use the same backdoor the NSA reported to compromise your site.... Decision made.

You choose to take your site down. The call center is melting down, the camera crews are in the parking lot, and you are reduced to the fetal position in the breakroom.

How do you respond to this? Download the scenario response form from the companion website.

### Scenario 2: Ransomware

On May 12, 2017, users from all around the world woke up to find a message on their computer screens (Figure 8.1).

Hospitals, banks, and other large organizations around the world reported their computers were affected by this virus. In a bizarre twist of events, a security researcher named Marcus Hutchins, also known online as MalwareTech, was reviewing the code of the malware and accidentally discovered the kill switch and stopped the attack. According to Hutchins, during his review of the code, he discovered a list of URLs (domain names), and when he researched them, he noticed one of them wasn't registered. After he registered this URL, the malware stopped working, which is incredibly fortunate because the ransomware (aptly named WannaCry) had infected over 400,000 machines—98 percent of them were running Windows 7. The hackers were demanding $300 or 0.1 BTC (bitcoin) to unlock the machine. Further analysis of the virus by security experts exposed the fact that the hackers weren't prepared to get all of the bitcoin

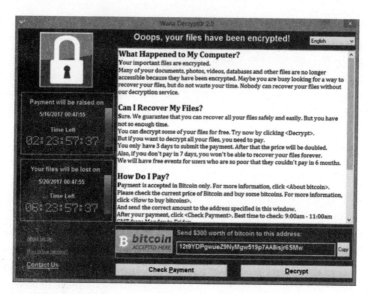

Figure 8.1    Encryption ransomware message

that the system had created (in fact, according to most experts, only 300 or so people paid the ransom).[3]

So, what if you woke up tomorrow and got that call from your security team that 70 percent of your systems were locked up with ransomware and even with restoring backups it was going to take a least a day to get back to being operational? How would you handle such an event? Do you pay? Do you admit to the public that your systems are vulnerable? What if your ATMs are among the infected systems and now are vulnerable as well?

### Scenario 3: Cyber Infrastructure Attack

On December 23, 2015, hackers were able to gain access to three of the energy distribution companies in the Ukraine and temporarily disrupt their services. More than 230,000 people were left without power on one of the coldest nights of the year. It took 6 hours for some customers to regain power. The attacks were traced to IP addresses owned by the Russian Federation. Like something out of a movie, operators at the power companies reported their mouse pointers moving on their own and being powerless as they watched whoever was controlling the mice turn off the power to hundreds of thousands of people.

It is widely believed that this is just the beginning of these kinds of attacks. While it is interesting that they cut off power, most of the major financial institutions have backup power, however what if they specifically targeted the financial sector, what would it look like if hackers disrupted the payments system on Black Friday? What would happen if VISA/MC/Discover suddenly stopped working on December 23?

### Scenario 4: Internet of Things Breach

The rise of IoT (Internet of Things) devices has created a new security threat. Case in point, on October 21, 2016, the internet experienced the strongest bandwidth attack ever recorded in its history. A company that maintains the domain name system for much of the internet's most popular sites was attacked with a distributed denial of service (DDoS) weapon that generated and hurled over 1.2 terabytes of data at their infrastructure. This DDoS attack was twice as strong as any attack ever recorded in the history of the internet.[4] In addition to being the strongest, it also was a sustained attack that took down sites like Twitter, Netflix, Reddit, CNN, and other large sites for many hours. I was online this day, and I must say, it was unnerving to see that a site like Twitter wiped off the internet. If you typed in its domain name, it looked like a site that wasn't configured—not even an error page came up. The combination of bandwidth and sustainability proved to be more than any defense that was available at the time could handle.

What made it more interesting was that the method of attack used consisted of hundreds of thousands of IoT devices such as webcams, thermostats, DVR players, and other internet-enabled products. The IoT explosion has been well documented in technology circles—everything from refrigerators to bird feeders has been internet-enabled in the name of innovation. Sadly, in the rush to corner the market, it appears that security wasn't a high priority for many of the creators of these products, and as a result, hackers were able to conscript hundreds of thousands of devices and turn them loose on a critical piece of infrastructure that crippled many major sites. When devices are taken over and used for nefarious purposes without the consent of their owners, the device is called a *bot;* when you have multitudes of these devices that can be controlled from a single source, it is referred to as a *botnet.* A botnet is a command-and-control platform that allows a single bad actor to control hundreds of thousands of PCs from a single console. Botnets are considered highly valuable in the cybercrime world and can be bought or rented to perform various actions, such as delivering spam, spreading ransomware, or attacking DDoS.

Up until this point, no one had seen a botnet that was exclusively made up of IoT devices. An analysis of the attack revealed a new botnet console specifically made to control IoT devices, called mirai (Japanese for "future"). In retrospect, it should've been pretty obvious that these smaller devices capable of high bandwidth would be high-value targets for hackers. Most experts believe that this is not the last we will see of these sorts of attacks.

So here is your scenario. I have already noticed financial institutions putting these devices in their branches and headquarters. So assume that another attack happens, and you discover that some of the devices that were involved in the attack were inside your firewall. Once you discover these devices are part of the attack, what are your next actions?

### Chapter Review

- There is no such thing as bulletproof digital security. You must expect everything you do to be hacked.

- Conduct risk reviews or risk audits for every product. The risk reviews should also include a recovery plan if the product or platform is compromised.

- Have easy access to extensive documentation on all the risk controls in the organization. Understanding how a process works is very important, because with this understanding, it can be audited for weak points. Without proper documentation, it can never be penetration tested fully.

- Common security risks come from four sources: government surveillance, ransomware, cyber infrastructure weaknesses, and IoT.

## NOTES

1. Tim Wilson, darkreading.com.
2. Phil Windley, www.windley.com.
3. Jonathan Crowe, "WannaCry Ransomware Statistics: The Numbers behind the Outbreak," *Barkly* (May 2017), https://blog.barkly.com/wannacry-ransomware-statistics-2017.
4. Nicky Wolf, "DDoS Attack that Disrupted Internet Was First of Its Kind in History, Experts Say," *The Guardian* (October 26, 2016), https://www.theguardian.com/technology/2016/oct/26/ddos-attack-dyn-mirai-botnet.

# PART

# IV

## People

CHAPTER

9

# The Digital Change Is for Everyone

One critical piece to digital is getting the entire organization to invest in it. Some departments in the average bank or credit union are often overlooked when it comes to digital transformation, yet they are critically important to the transformation. Each department has a part to play, no matter how removed they may think they are from the basic business of the organization. What follows are some of the things that must be considered in these important departments.

## Human Resources

### *Remote Employees*

The talent we need will often not be in our backyard. I find that in smaller institutions, there is resistance to hiring remote employees. Unfortunately, this often results in organizations in more rural areas not being able to attract the talent that they need. Organizations that are going to survive the transition to digital will need to think about how to deal with employees who may only set foot in the office once a month, or even once a year. Here are some of the challenges that must be overcome.

### "A remote employee cannot be effectively managed."

I discussed this in a previous chapter from a manager's point of view. However, it is just as important to discuss it from the HR perspective. So when a manager identifies a resource that could be very valuable and allows the employee to work remotely, it will be up to HR to provide the tools to manage this person remotely. In this case, it is recommended that HR consider finding remote management software that allows managers to view screenshots during the work day and track the time of remote employees.

### "The benefits we offer are only available in our state."

This is another common issue that managers face when trying to hire remote employees. Even if HR and the manager agree, the next challenge is extending benefits to an employee in another state. To prepare for this, HR should work with their benefit providers to implement flexible health care options that are available in any state.

### "The remote employee doesn't feel like part of the team."

Another issue is that remote employees are often left out of cultural events, benefits, or even simple things like remembering their birthdays. Email, video, and other technologies should be used to include remote employees as much as possible in events. For instance, if there is an all-staff meeting and it is feasible, fly the employee in. If it doesn't make monetary sense, use a video-conferencing product to include the remote employees. The best approach is a mixture of both—flying them in for some events and always providing a video service.

### "Employees are in a different time zone and are not available when we need them."

Depending on the job, this could be true. There is a need for the remote employee to be available when needed. There are several approaches to this problem. The first and most obvious one is to ask employees to adjust their hours to be available to the company. Since they are working from home, they have much more flexibility. I would also consider the concept of having an employee during off hours to be valuable in some situations. For instance, a West Coast company might find having an East Coast group valuable to do after-hours work. Since the East Coast is three hours ahead of the West, much can be done before things start happening on the West Coast. In a similar fashion, if you need to cover later hours, an East Coast company might find a West Coast group valuable. Larger financial institutions have already conquered this problem, as they often have offices in different time zones, but I find that medium-size organizations struggle with this concept. Also, for goodness' sake, think of the time zones before you schedule meetings. Remote employees struggle when they are asked to attend a meeting at 4:30 West Coast time and it's 7:30 East Coast; this a training issue. I suggest a time zone sensitivity class for all employees.

### Evaluations

Evaluations in the digital age will be different than the traditional evaluations that are delivered today. As mentioned in the culture section, it is important that your evaluations are aligned with your organizational culture. If you are trying to foster collaboration, then individual goals on evaluations will be counterproductive. The evaluations should reflect the employees' work environment. Organizations that are pursuing organization agility will want to reward collaboration, inclusion, and participation.

### Career Paths

Career paths are among the biggest issues I see in financial institutions that are attempting a digital transformation. Often, a department such as analytics evolves as opposed to being planned out. The evolution usually involves hiring a person for a position that is new in the organization and placing that person somewhere that is the closest fit. Eventually, as the position and the value it brings evolves, the organization will decide to formalize the area into a department. In this model, the evolution hurts the employee and sometimes the organization. New positions can often become a place where good employees go to wither away. While most of the mature parts of the organization have well-defined career paths, this new area doesn't, and as a result, the employee doesn't have clear goals or expectations.

It is important for human resources to do research and map out a career path for every department long before the department positions are filled. Technical employees want to know what their options are to move up in the company. If the department has a well-defined career path and that is communicated to the employees clearly, it will help with motivation and teamwork. To accomplish this, I would highly recommend that human resources visit other tech-heavy industries and review their organizational structures—if possible, visiting a larger bank with a programming department or technical department would be a valuable experience for the HR team.

### Incentives and Compensation

In the technical area, incentives are a valuable resource. I once put a $1,500 challenge out to my staff to build a financial application for the Xbox, Apple TV, or any TV streaming device that supports applications. In less than a week, an employee delivered a financial application that showed balances, pulled history, and displayed check images on a ROKU (this is a common TV streaming device). You haven't lived until you have seen a check image on 55-inch 4K television. The challenge I had was getting the person paid, because HR didn't have anything set up to do this. I knew that we had a budget for this sort of thing, as I had set aside money for these sorts of challenges. What I hadn't considered was that HR didn't have a way for me to deliver the incentive without doing a 1099 for the employee. I wound up having to give the employee $1,500 in Visa gift cards. HR should encourage innovation and work with department heads to have an incentive program that allows departments to motivate, provide rewards, and foster innovation.

Compensation for technical employees changes very rapidly in the finance space. I have seen many financial organizations lose great technical talent to other industries because HR didn't keep up with the market. For an organization that desires to be a technology company, it is very important to monitor the market as it relates to your technical positions and stay competitive. Financial organizations often struggle with this because the rest of the organizational chart is very static in comparison to the technology area. Many companies provide these services, so I would suggest that at least once a year, technology area compensation be reviewed.

### Recruiting

Recruiting top technical talent is the place where I see the biggest need for improvement. In almost every financial institution I have worked with, technical talent is recruited by managers from within the technical areas of the organization. While this is certainly not the worst situation in the world, it does take away from the daily duties of these managers. Human resources should consider partnering with universities, technical schools, maker spaces, and other areas where technical talent can be cultivated. A pure technical recruiter position should also be considered for organizations that wish to operate as a technology company. This recruiter would understand the markets for the skillsets they are seeking and talented enough to do first-level interviewing.

### Training

Bank Security Act or BSA training has never been more important in a financial organization. In the current world environment where cybercriminals are targeting financial institutions' employees more than ever before, it is important for employees to understand the techniques that will be used against them in their everyday job. For instance, in the past, my security people have dropped random USB sticks in the employee parking lot to see who would pick them up and put them in their work PCs, sent fake emails from the CEO with an attachment that emulated a virus, and tested social engineering by pretending to be a system administrator and calling employees and asking for their passwords. The point I am making here is that BSA isn't enough. Like all security-related regulations, I believe a financial institution should exceed the requirements as much as possible. One thing I have seen recently are increased attempts by cybercriminals to gain access to specific employees systems by targeting them with emails containing viruses that would allow the hacker to take control of their system remotely. Many times I have been asked, how do they know whom to target? A simple LinkedIn search for ACH and the bank or credit union being targeted will give you numerous targets. Even if their email isn't listed on LinkedIn, it is not hard to learn the patterns of email at an organization. For instance, if the CEO's email is Jsmith@bigbank.com and your targets name is Jane Doe, it's likely that Jdoe@bigbank.com will be the email address. I would encourage financial institutions to ask employees with significant access to moving funds to keep their names and information out of social media. It is likely that these threats will continue to escalate in the coming years and the quality of the training programs instituted by the HR department will play a key role in how well employees respond to these attacks.

Training takes on another dimension completely when it comes to developing technical employees. While roles like accounting and risk evolve each year, they don't evolve at the pace that technology is currently evolving right now. Technical employees will continue to need to be trained in new platforms, new paradigms, and new services on a regular basis. Unfortunately, this training isn't cheap, and as a result, I find that most employees' technical areas wind up either self-learning or paying for courses and training themselves. In both cases, once the employee acquires the new skill, they will often leave the organization. This is usually because their effort isn't rewarded by the organization, and since the organization didn't provide training with career development opportunities, there is no incentive to stay. Millennials highly value developmental training and will seek out organizations that provide career development resources.

The good news is that there are lots of ways to do this now without breaking the bank (no pun intended). At my company, we have corporate access to video training sites that we encourage our employees to use. Sites like Lynda.com or udemy.com are excellent resources to learn new concepts, explore new platforms or just sharpen their skills on the current platforms that your organization already has in place. The key to getting your employees to use it is to provide easy access to the resource, provide them with the time, and measure their progress. I also believe that all employees should be able to order technical books without having to ask management. There are many sites that allow access to as many technical books as you can download. Providing your employees with a cost-effective e-reader like a KOBO would pay off very quickly in employee advancement by allowing them to download a multitude of technical books and have them at their fingertips at all times. A final way to encourage employee training is to give employees time off to attend local meetings of groups that focus on their specific skills. For instance, if your organization has chosen to move resources to a cloud provider like Azure or AWS, there are likely groups that meet to discuss these platforms, and your organization could benefit from the relationships formed at these meetings. In fact, it can also be used as a recruitment opportunity. It's a simple recipe: If you want to find mobile developers, go to where the mobile developers hang out—or better yet, create a place for mobile developers to hang out and have them come to you (more on that in the next section).

### Dress Code

One challenge the financial community will face as it courts the upcoming millennial generation is their dress code. The next generation of programmers and technical experts doesn't understand how a tie will make them a better employee. As a matter of fact, they have been repeatedly taught not to judge books by the cover, and moreover, they are a generation that is used to personalizing everything, from their phones to their cars. However, it is difficult for the average financial institution CIO to get past full-length arm tattoos and large gauges in someone's ears (these are the big circles you see in people's ears—which, by the way, look far worse if you make them take it out). The challenge is that banking has always been a suit-and-tie industry. Fintechs, however (which is our greatest competition for top technical financial talent), don't care if you come to work in board shorts and a tank top. In fact, they pride themselves on their laidback environment, and it's a selling point to their employees.

There are several options for solutions here. One is to house your development and programming team elsewhere. When you read the "Facilities" section, next, you will find that the workspaces needed to support technical talent and development are different enough that it might be worth your while to find a space that can be retrofitted into a technical lab. After all, you only must get one or two of them to dress up now and then if they only come to a meeting or two at the main office, or bring them to your senior staff meeting. The other option is to contract these workers. I have been in many cities where in the same building park as the financial institution there is a technical company just waiting to be bought. There is value to buying an established culture and integrating it into your organization rather than trying to create it from scratch. A final option is to allow some of the staff to work at home a few days a week. I find that most technical workers can work at home and they relish the opportunity to have a day where they won't be bothered by other employees. When they are home they are welcome to wear whatever they want.

## Facilities

It may seem kind of trivial, but your workspace says a lot about your organization. For instance, a room filled with high walls and closed-off cubicles doesn't scream collaboration. We live in a world of standing desks, high-end headphones, multiple screen, and open spaces. It is important to understand that how you design your facilities will become a key driver of your culture.

### Workspaces

The thinking behind technical workspaces has evolved in the past 10 years, from high-walled cubicles to open wooden desks (like you might find at a Apple store) that can be moved around to accommodate new projects. Open meeting areas, with ceiling-to-floor whiteboards and private sitting areas with furniture that has built in charging mechanisms, are the new norm in tech companies. If financial organizations want to compete, they will need to design their facilities to be more tech friendly. The challenge is that this approach doesn't work well in other departments. For instance, accounting will not want a large wooden desk where the accountants sit buffet style and work side by side. They are more partial to the high-walled cubicles and filing cabinets. The challenge is how to mix these things together.

The new facility is important in an agile environment. In new tech companies, the development areas are flexible and can be reorganized if necessary, so if your next project requires two developers, a UX professional, a project manager, scrum master, and QA person, this group may reorganize the space so that they all sit together for the duration of the project. The QA person will be present and can give instant feedback on the developers' efforts, the developers will be next to the UX professional who can answer questions about how things are supposed to work as they come, and the project manager and scrum master can track the project continuously. This shortens development time frames, increases productivity, and fosters a team mindset for projects. Open areas that can be used for impromptu meetings will be necessary in this environment because the flexible spaces don't lend themselves to private meetings. If the UX professional and scrum master need to meet together and work out an epic, a small conference room with glass walls (this is important, by the way) and a floor-to-ceiling whiteboard is a perfect working space for them. The glass walls allow your team to know where someone is; closed conference rooms send a message to technical employees that meetings are private and don't foster collaboration. It's important to have an open environment.

## Wi-Fi

Dear financial institutions, for goodness' sake, figure out your Wi-Fi. I have been to organization after organization where Wi-Fi is a mess. Among the technical employees, Wi-Fi is considered a joke. It's too slow, too burdensome to use, or so locked down that it is useless to the average technical employee. I realize that Wi-Fi has been a security concern; however, this is 2018, and we have conquered these problems. If you are going to have a flexible workspace, then a good Wi-Fi system is absolutely necessary.

Again, I am not saying that you need to put in a Wi-Fi system that is less than secure. I am saying that you need to spend the money so that there are no dead spots, and there is a good security apparatus in place that allows productivity while protecting the organization that doesn't need an act of God to change. Nothing is more frustrating to a highly technical individual than not being able to get to the resources they need to do their job. It sends a message to them that the organization doesn't understand what they do; otherwise, they would have these resources available to them. This, in turn, creates a perception that the organization doesn't want technical people. Wi-Fi is also important if you are going to outsource. I have seen situations where contractors are sitting around being paid for days and weeks while they wait for security to grant permission for them to get to the resources they need to do the job they were hired for. This results in cost overruns, shifting deadlines, and excessive errors due to playing catch-up on the project. Having a bad Wi-Fi system will cost you money and employees.

## Equipment

I have watched programmers press build on their laptop or PC and walk away for 30 minutes while they wait for the build to complete. When I asked them why this was happening, they would inform me that their machine has an i5 processor or it has very little RAM. This is always baffling to me—why would anyone hire top technical talent and then give them subpar tools to work with? Again, this sends a message to the programmer that the organization doesn't understand what they do or how they do it. It's a little like hiring a carpenter but not buying a table saw, nail gun, or any of the other tools that he or she needs to work. As new platforms evolve like blockchain, artificial intelligence, and machine learning, the average IT professional's processing power needs are going to double. I prefer to buy laptops for all technical staff so that they can roam with their devices and work off-site. One good strategy is to continuously cycle the technical staff's devices down to other departments every year so that IT is continually upgraded. Another way to handle this is to move your entire development environment to the cloud (see the cloud computing section for more on this) where the development platforms can be housed in the cloud and processing power can be used in a more efficient manner. When more processing power is needed for a particular developer or technical expert on a project, the system administrator can allocate more power to the system without a costly upgrade, or design a build system that can be used by the entire staff. The point here is to not underpower your technical team—don't underestimate the frustration of technical experts trying to do their job with a underpowered system; they will eventually leave.

### Meet-ups

When my kids were young, my wife and I encouraged their friends to play at our house as much as they wanted. We figured if they were at our house, we knew where they were and they were safe. I think this same approach can be true for attracting top talent at your organization. If you have built a nice workspace for technology, why not allow it to be used (with appropriate security of course) by technical groups that have synergy with your organization. In the cloud example I mentioned above, your organization could host a meeting once a month and as a result technology professionals would get to experience your culture and facilities. Again, this could be a great recruiting tool. It can also be a great way to get customers.

## Accounting: Software Depreciating

There are several techniques that accounting experts in the software and infrastructure industries have adopted to capitalize technology and development projects that would benefit financial institutions. The first has to do with how to capitalize software development. I will preface this section by stating *I AM NOT A CPA OR ACCOUNTANT,* so I would advise you to get expert advice on these concepts. I will share with you the way the accountants I have worked with in the past have capitalized software development and other technical assets.

The approaches break down into three distinct categories: software that is developed in house to be sold to other organizations; software that is developed in house to be used solely by the organization with no intention to sell it or commercialize it; and website development. The first step for each of these approaches is to make sure the software is versioned. The version will establish the cut-off points and signify when significant changes have been made to the software. For example, if you build a teller platform called TellerMagic, the first version of that software that will be capitalized is version 1.0.0. Where 1 is the major release, the second position is considered a minor update and the third position is considered a patch. The important understanding here for all three of the categories is that you can only start depreciating on major releases. So if you release TellerMagic 1.0.0, and then TellerMagic 1.1.0, the capitalization period doesn't start over. However, if you release a significant upgrade and call it 2.0.0, then you can capitalize this as a new product or process.

The word *significant* is important here, as you cannot release major versions just to recapitalize your software. A significant release should include new technology, and a significant amount of code should have changed because of the release. Once the product is in production, then you cannot capitalize the effort it takes to create minor updates and push patches. I have had many accountants tell me that this is a conservative position, and in point of fact, it's the only approach I have ever seen used. I am sure there are more aggressive approaches, but from what I have seen, this approach raises the fewest red flags with auditors.

If your organization is considering creating software and reselling it to other organizations, then there are specific account rules that apply that will allow your organization to capitalize the expense of the development. The key to this approach is that the software is well defined, it has been reviewed for risk and feasibility, and the organization was reviewed to make sure that it had the resources to create it. The cost to market the software, the cost to maintain the software, and cost to test the software should all be capitalized. The organization will need to provide detailed documentation for any development that includes specific times and efforts of the resources involved to back the capitalization process. Also, there is usually a productivity percentage that can be applied to these sorts of programming efforts, meaning that it is not likely that a programmer was programming all 8 hours of his day, so many organizations will reduce the programmer's hours by 25 percent to make up for bathroom trips, meetings, and other nonprogramming activities. Again, this is something that would be favorable to auditors.

If your organization is creating software that will only be used inside your four walls and will not be sold, then you can only capitalize the development effort. The project development, design, and care and feeding in the production model are all expenses and cannot be capitalized. If there is a data conversion (like a Billpay platform is changed out), the conversion cost cannot be capitalized, but if you purchased a tool to help you with the conversion, then the tool can be capitalized. In this model, the only thing that can be capitalized is the actual programming that is done to create the software. Once the software is in production, then everything else will need to be capitalized.

Web development is the final category, and the capitalization process is very similar to the in-house software process. The difference in this model is that the graphic development and creation process can be capitalized, as it is considered similar to programming. The programming that takes place to build the website can also be capitalized, along with the server or hosting platform, as well as the domain name registration.

Documentation is very important in each of these approaches. Leadership will need to be able to provide solid documentation of programming practices, project management, risk reviews, and the processes that support it to back up the practice. So the first thing to do is to make sure that your technology area is operating in a manner such that it could provide this sort of documentation. A financial institution that is shifting to becoming a technology company or even a quasi-technology company should start considering these accounting practices to determine what benefits can be gained by capitalizing its development projects.

## Chapter Review

- People across departments are needed to break digital gridlock.
- Gridlock commonly emerges in human resources, facilities, and accounting.

CHAPTER

# 10

# Who Can Break Gridlock?

The most important aspect of any organization is its people and its culture. Your people are the key to breaking the gridlock. Sadly, they are most likely to be causing the stoppage somewhere up ahead. It could be for many reasons—they could be afraid of risk, or perhaps they are not in an empowered position, or worse yet, in over their head. In the evolving digital world, people need to be organized in the right way to have a fighting chance.

The first step to breaking the gridlock at your organization is to assess your organizational chart as it relates to digital. The goal of this assessment is to identify the people who are currently driving your online offerings. For many years, any technology or online products have been pushed into departments that aren't necessarily the right place but the closest fit at the time. ATMs pushed into payments, home banking is often found in IT, even sometimes marketing, and now analytics seems to be getting forced into the accounting division.

It's OK to temporarily house a new, emerging, or evolving channel or service in the closest fitting area, but it must be reviewed to make sure it doesn't deserve an area of its own. This challenge often leads to difficulties for the program owners to get the resources they need and to be understood by their leadership. Here is a great example: If every time your analytics people need a new tool (this is an evolving arena, and as such, new tools come out every day), they have to explain how the tool works and what they are going to use it for to three or four different people, they are going to eventually leave your organization, and if they don't, they are either really nice people (rare) or subpar analytics experts who cannot find another job. A true expert doesn't like to have to repeatedly explain the need for tools to people who don't understand what they are trying to explain. They expect the leadership to understand their needs and work with them. They are usually passionate about what they do and feel demoralized when they feel as though they are being prevented from doing their job. I want to be clear: I am not saying that an analytics expert should have carte blanche for all of the things they want without oversight, just that they should have leadership that understands what they are saying and knows how to access the request.

Accessing your organizational chart to determine who is handling your digital offerings is the first step to breaking gridlock. Figure 10.1 is a common top-level org chart I see at many banks and credit unions.

There are many missing roles, among the most notable a chief digital officer (CDO) and a chief analytics officer (CAO). Usually, when I am called in to review an organization such as this, I quickly discover that these roles are not missing, they are just buried in the various departments. For instance, the chief digital officer might

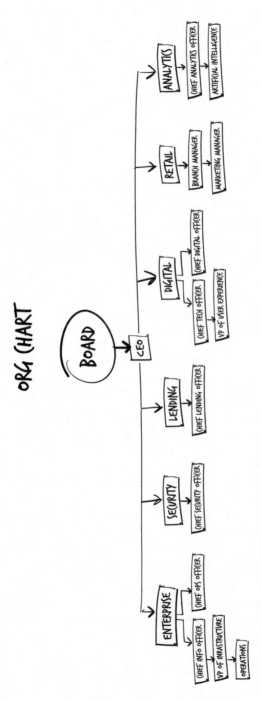

**Figure 10.1   Sample executive organizational chart**

be buried in the chief technology officer's organization, or a chief analytics officer is buried in the chief financial officer's organization, or even in marketing. Once we track down the individuals responsible for these roles, we usually find that they are woefully understaffed and usually not empowered. A twenty-first-century organizational chart must have a role for digital services and analytics that reports directly to the CEO.

## Common Symptoms of People Problems

### Lack of Consistency

If you can pay your mortgage online but not through your mobile application, it is usually as a direct result of not having someone overseeing the digital platform and planning for channel integration as the financial institutions systems evolve. A chief digital officer should roam between all areas of the financial institution helping to make sure that systems that are purchased or implemented in all departments can support digital transactions. When this doesn't occur, it leads to a form of gridlock called *feature paralysis* that many people experience regularly in their organization. Feature paralysis gridlock is when you are waiting on one company to make something for another company to facilitate what seems like a simple transaction, such as a credit card or mortgage payment. More importantly, your customers don't understand why this is happening, and at some point will opt to leave the institution for an institution whose services are digitally synched up.

### Cost and Time Overruns

Projects run long and staff augmentation costs drive up project costs and create variances when we try to get them back on track.

Digital products, by nature, tend to cross organizational boundaries on a regular basis. Take, for instance, a project to create a digital credit card balance transfer process. This project would likely include lending, technology, operations, risk, and audit. In this situation, which department is in charge? Who makes the key decisions for the project? In theory, it should be lending, since the process is a lending function, but since they are not well versed in digital processes, they tend to defer. In my experience, since lending will defer, it's usually a fight between risk and technology. Risk is doing its job and trying to add protections into the process; technology is advocating for cool innovative tech that excites its group. Sometimes risk wins by pointing out regulatory issues; sometimes technology wins by innovating around the regulatory issues. In the end, no one really wins because the endless back and forth creates scope creep and unnecessarily bloats the timeline, which increases expense and reduces time to market on critical services and features for the organization.

## Human Solutions

To solve these problems, you need to address your people. They are at the center of your solution.

### Chief Digital Officer (CDO)

When it comes to both lack of consistency and cost or time overruns, a CDO can help. The role of the CDO is to convert analog processes into digital processes. The CDO is more than just a technologist. He or she is also seasoned in understanding the digital user experience and has a background in all areas of banking. The CDO is responsible for the digital transformation of all aspects of the organization. In banking, I see the CDO as having the following primary responsibilities:

1. Design, implement, and oversee an organization-wide digital strategy.
2. Chair a digital governance committee that is made up of all areas of the organization—all purchases, new products, new delivery channels, and new processes.
3. Oversee all digital projects, both internal and external.
4. Advocate on the behalf of the customer in terms of digital processes.
5. Balance features and functionality with time to market.

In 2012, Gartner predicted that 25 percent of organizations would have a CDO. Well, it's 2017 now, and I think that 100 percent of the financial institutions that want to survive should have this position filled. Many times, the role is filled by a talented IT professional such as a CTO or CIO, which I believe is just fine, so long as you backfill his or her position and give that person a seat at the table. The challenge with having someone both running IT and trying to balance digital initiatives is twofold. The first is that the work of a IT department includes updating systems and dealing with operational issues, and these can sometimes be counter to the goals of a CDO who is trying to deal with introducing new technology or processes, and seeking to align departments around digital goals. The second is that the CDO needs to have a seat at the table in the sense of creating business strategy. This person should be involved at the highest levels of the organization, helping to educate the executive suite as well as the board by laying out a digital strategy that is aligned with the strategy of the organization. Finally, this person will have to battle the internal forces that naturally seek to slow down or block digital processes by quoting regulations or other means.

### Chief Analytic Officer (CAO)

The other missing role is the chief analytic officer (CAO). This person is responsible for turning data into information. Initially, you may think that this role is another role that you can push into information technology, or maybe even under your chief financial officer's part of the organization. While this might seem like a good move, it would be underestimating the role that analytics will provide in the survival of your organization while becoming a digital organization.

Digital, by its very nature, creates a massive amount of valuable data that needs to be collected and curated. Every time a customer visits your website, important and valuable data are available to your organization. You can collect information about where they came from, how they got there, what kind of browser they used, and even instantly figure out how long it has been since their last visit. Imagine if you tried to do this in a physical branch—you would have to have someone sitting by the door with a clipboard or (if you are high-tech, an iPad) surveying the customers as they come in. "Excuse me, ma'am, what make is your car? Also, where were you before you came here? Do you remember the last time you visited us?" The same is true of a loan application or your home banking site. The mobile application produces an amazing amount of data that can be used by your financial institution to its advantage. The challenge is doing "something" with the data. This is the CAO's purpose, to collect, categorize, and analyze all of your data and turn the data into insights that your organization can use to improve its customer service, make more loans, or find new customers. I often find that when I explain this to executives they are surprised. In their minds, they had equated the role of an analytics person as a new name for a report writer. Nothing could be further from the truth. Reports are historic, and therefore, report writers are like historians. A good analytics officer will be more like a psychic, using data to make astonishing predictions that will help you shape your organization's future. In banking, I see the CDO as having the following primary responsibilities:

1. Chair the data governance group.
2. Find actionable insights within your data.
3. Be responsible for ROI on projects.
4. Review all new projects to determine data needs and opportunities.

So why does this person need his or her own department? Great question. The first reason is because the data that the group (notice I said group—this is not just one person) must deal with exists everywhere in the organization. It can be in lending, the call center, collections, the branches, and even on your employees' cell phones, and for this reason, they must be able to cross all organizational lines in pursuit of acquiring data.

## Data Is Money

Data is money. It is a simple truth. If you put this book down right now and don't read any further and all you walk away with is this statement, you will be better off.

When you think of it in these terms, you will think twice when your staff comes to you about budgeting for higher storage costs to preserve data. When data is purged, it's like burning money. The second reason you need a CAO is because this person is going to be part of your business strategy and will work very closely with your CDO. This can be the difference between succeeding or failing on digital initiatives.

One way to think of it is like this. If banking were a fishing boat, opening branches would be like throwing a huge net out to catch fish. It's effective and you do catch a lot of fish, but you also catch a lot of boots, old tires, and other things. Also, you can't be sure of the type of fish that you catch and the quality. Digital is like spearfishing, dropping down into the ocean looking for a special fish that is worth more to your organization. You can catch 10 of these fish and it would be worth 30 days of fishing with a net and be less work for your boat workers to clean. (FYI, I am not a fisherman by any means.) Your CAO will help identify which of the fish in the sea you want, where to fish, and what kind of bait you need, and your CDO will go out and catch them.

OK, so you have bought in and you believe me, and you just did a Google search or asked your HR person, and you discovered that each of these positions are expensive and difficult to fill, and as a result you fainted and had to be revived by your staff. Once you woke up, you also realized that neither of these are one-man departments, which has made the expense that much higher in your mind. Never fear: That is what this book is for.

If the CDO or CAO position is too expensive for you, there are evolving services and consultants who will come in and help you with digital strategy. They can place boots on the ground at your organization and play this role. I would argue that it won't be as effective as having someone on staff full time, but it is better than not doing anything. This can be much more cost-effective because you are sharing this individual with other organizations, and as a result the person is usually a very high level and qualified professional. Second, these companies often have the necessary resources to support the positions they are filling within your organization. This approach can be very valuable because it allows your organization to learn how these positions will work within the organization without hiring a FTE right off the bat. You can learn from how these groups operate, what works and what doesn't work in your culture, as well as what level of expertise is needed to fill these roles. You can also find your shortcomings. For instance, the acting CAO consultant may come to your executive group and report that your data aren't in a usable format, and that before anything can be done, the data must be scrubbed and cleaned (just like the fish analogy) and yes, these are actual words they will use. The CDO may come to your executive team and announce that many of your systems aren't prepared for digital in that they aren't accessible via a normal digital means and that these systems must either be replaced or retrofitted to fit into a digital ecosystem. Finding this out ahead of hiring someone (ostensibly forever) is a good thing. These problems will be dealt with by your IT department or the departments who are responsible for these systems. If you were building a house, you wouldn't want to bring in the painters until the walls were finished; otherwise, they will stand around and charge you for doing nothing.

The second approach, if you cannot afford to hire consultants, is to grow your own. Your current CTO may be a perfect fit to become a CDO and may even long to do this job. However, you must be careful not to expect this person to be a CIO and CDO at the same time. If you are going to grow a CDO internally, I would suggest that the first thing you do is to tell this person to replace themselves. In Chapter 1, I mentioned my mentor Tom Bennett at Suncoast, and that he often gave me life advice. Another great piece of advice he gave me was this: "If you want to advance, the first thing you have to do is replace yourself." This ran counter to what I was thinking at the time. I was all wrapped up in learning new systems and making myself indispensable because no one else could do what I could do. After Tom gave me this advice, I realized he was right. I started the very next day by holding an impromptu class for anyone who wanted to learn how to set up new users on our newly installed network. I found this to be invigorating, I enjoyed teaching, and the others were happy to learn. After that, I moved up quickly. It was easy because there was always someone who was excited to do my old job. I would encourage this line of thinking within any banking organization, and especially if you are looking to grow your own executives. This approach has the added value of creating cohesion between the outgoing CIO and the new CIO (likely trained by the outgoing person) and thus fostering better teamwork between them. The second thing to do is give them free reign to buy books, take classes online, and go to conferences to learn to become a CDO. When I give this advice, I often hear people say, yes, but what if they leave us? My answer is always the same—but what if we never train them and they stay? If you are concerned about this, there are things you can do to protect your organization from investing in individuals only to have them leave, such as offering a bonus for completing the course, or having them sign something stating that they will stay for a certain amount of time.

Finally, and this is the most important thing to do, I have found that in the banking industry, everyone knows everyone, and that usually CEOs and other executives have friends at other banks. So send this person to one of these other organizations where you know there is good digital leadership and have them spend time learning what the CDO does at that organization. It doesn't even have to be a banking organization. As a matter of fact, if you have access to someone in a different industry, say health care or investments, all the better. Have them provide a report of their findings and ask them to write down what can be applied at your organization, and when they come back, review it with the entire executive team.

Once you have grown this individual, you can start him or her out as one-man departments by allowing them to outsource their needs. This can be very cost-effective, and again has the added advantage of allowing for learning on the job. A CAO, for instance, will likely need to have a data scientist available. If you thought the CDO and CAO were expensive, Google what a data scientist makes. OK, I apologize for making you faint again (I should've warned you), but I wanted to see the look in your eyes just before you passed out. Yes, these resources are expensive, but ask yourself why. I would reason that it is because they are effective and as such, in high demand. So this is another opportunity for outsourcing; the key is having someone who understands the area running the rodeo. A CAO will know what questions and what key things to put a data scientist consultant to work on. An experienced CDO can work wonders by outsourcing digital initiatives to experienced firms while working hand in hand with your organization to integrate the results.

So to recap, I can't stress enough the importance of these positions in terms of digital transformation. You can think of both these positions as the guardians of your digital future.

---

### Chapter Review

- The first step to breaking the gridlock at your organization is to assess your organizational chart as it relates to digital. The goal of this assessment is to identify the people who are currently driving your online offerings.
- People gridlock often begins in the executive offices. The chief data officer and chief analytics officer can do quite a bit to get things moving again.

# PART

# V

## Culture

# 11

# Culture and Innovation

I never said I was going to fire anyone that didn't work this weekend, I said I was going to **HIRE** someone to work the weekend!

**M**ost technology books wouldn't dedicate a part to culture, and I think that mindset is a tremendous failure in other digital transformation approaches. Accessing and adjusting your culture is the most important step in your digital transformation process. The culture of your organization will dictate a great many things, such as your organization's willingness to accept innovation, your organization's ability to adapt to change, and the organization's ability to resolve internal conflicts. Culture will also dictate habits; your organization's muscle memory is dictated by your culture. Muscle memory is the default reaction for how an employee responds to a situation. For instance, I once worked with an organization that had a problem with reversing fees. Customers would call in to the organization and ask to have fees reversed, the call center representatives (CSR) would look to see if it qualified to be reversed based on rules set forth by the organization, and often the CSR would deny the reversal, only to have the customer ask to speak to the manager and the manager would override them and reverse it. After a while, the CSRs realized that the manager was going to override them every time and started reversing fees by default, which led to a loss of income for the organization. Reversing fees became muscle memory for the organization because the culture of the organization was to always give the customer what they wanted.

## Where Does Culture Start?

I find that culture at a financial institution is established at the top of the organization and dwindles down to the various departments, sometimes getting changed, usually for the worse along the way, much like the old telephone game that we used to play where one person would whisper a story in the ear to the person next to them. This process would be continued person by person until the final person was reached. When that happened, the last person would repeat what he or she had been told and it would be compared to the original story, and of course the two stories would be drastically different. Here is an example of this happening at a typical financial institution.

CEO → Senior VPs at executive meeting: It is important to get this project done on time and within the budget.

Senior VP → VP: It's critical that we get this project done early under budget.

VP → Managers: Either we get this project done two weeks early and under budget and or we are going to need to look at budget cuts.

Managers → Employees: The CEO wants us all to work this weekend until we get this done.

Ok maybe it isn't quite this extreme, but it is a fact that communication changes as it filters through the organization. How people respond to these changes is dictated by their muscle memory from previous experiences. If the employees' experience has been that "every project" in the portfolio is considered critical, must be done early, and must be completed under budget, they will eventually just ignore the urgency. This creates the "organization that cries wolf all the time" culture. If the employees' experience is that when urgent communication is handed down, it should be taken seriously and they have seen people lose jobs, then they could either buckle down get the work done, or they could look for a new job. As you can see, there is an incredible need to cut out the middleman when communicating throughout the organization. In one place that I worked, the CEO installed a full video system and had everyone in the company come in early once a month to watch a well-produced show that included messages about the objectives and goals of the organization and upcoming events, and finally, it always ended with a direct message from the CEO. During the downturn of 2008, this communication channel became critical, as he used the medium to hold the organization together and guide us through very turbulent times. In the end, his direct communication became part of the culture, and as a result, the employees found him to be very approachable and they were willing to share their ideas and concerns directly with him.

An often overlooked tool to promote culture is storytelling. Story is an incredibly powerful tool to help employees understand how the organization should work, and what the value proposition of the organization really is. For instance, at Microsoft, there are many stories that are often told and retold about Bill Gates. Steve Jobs had almost a mythical status at Apple and Pixar. These stories or parables were often used as motivators in down times, or as a guide in a difficult situation. A story is a far better tool than any procedure manual or electronic process. I have been blessed to be around some amazing people in the credit union world who shared many stories about things that happened and how they handled them. Stories about customers that they helped, situations that they found themselves in, and problems they solved. As I mentioned in the previous paragraph, your employees need a measuring stick for the decisions that they have to make every day, the stories help the staff make these decisions. In my case, these stories stuck with me all throughout my career and often served as guidance in my own decision making in similar circumstances.

Culture starts from the first day the FI opens its doors. For example, during the genesis of an organization, culture is often created around the founder's values and morals. Much like a real birth, genesis can be a very turbulent time in the life of an organization, and in the case of most financial institutions, many of its current employees weren't present for the genesis process. During the genesis of the organization, many decisions are made that will forever become part of the organization's cultural DNA. For instance, in a financial institution model the decision as to whether to support commercial accounts can change the way the institution evolves culturally. A company that supports charitable events from the day it is established is more likely to have a charitable culture. These values are passed down from the top. The behavior modeled by senior leadership will serve as the guide for the rest of the organization. Like it or not, if you are in a leadership role, your behavior, decisions, and communication techniques serve as a guide for the rest of the organization. Culture always starts at the top.

## Culture Breakdowns

Culture can evolve as the organization matures. During times of crisis, the culture is often either validated or in some cases it is forced to change. I witnessed an incredible example of culture in crisis during the 2008 recession. A large organization I worked with was experiencing the results of the recession and was faced with several options, one of which was reducing the number of staff that worked for the organization by closing branches. I spoke regularly with the CEO during this time and witnessed his profound concern at how letting go of people would affect the culture of the organization going forward. He was concerned that the move would run counter to the family culture that was core to the values and the mission of the organization—after all, you wouldn't stop taking care of your family in a crisis. In the end, the organization found a way to survive the downturn without closing a single branch or losing a single job. This move spoke volumes about the culture of the organization and more importantly sent a message to every employee about how important their contribution to the organization was.

Another culture trap that I often see financial institutions fall into is the sales-versus-service culture conundrum. The sales culture is defined as an organization that is always looking to sell the next product, and usually is equated with profits. A service culture is defined as an organization whose primary goal is to solve problems for their customers. The organization believes that providing good service will result in the customers' choosing to do more business with them. Each of these approaches has their strengths and weaknesses. An improperly managed sales culture can lead to situations like the most recent Wells Fargo incident, where employees felt compelled to open false accounts for customers because their quotas were unachievable. An improperly managed service culture can result in the situations where the financial institution's staff is giving away too much and directly impacting profitability because of the perceived service culture values that are expected of them.

I think that both approaches are a myth in the new world. A good organization will turn sales into service, and vice versa. The key to this kind of culture is ensuring that the moral compass of the organization is pointed to true north. If the employees have a measuring stick that they can use to gauge their behaviors as it relates to customers, and that measuring stick is rooted in finding a win for both the customer and the FI, then there is little chance that the organization will need to build a service or sales culture. This by no means exonerates an institution from having the ability to measure their success or failures, it also doesn't mean not setting goals. Simply put, it is aligning the organization's goals with the organization's stated values.

## Culture and Talent

Why is culture important to digital transformation? The main reason is that your culture will dictate the type of talent that you attract. People tend to seek out organizations to work where they feel they would belong. A highly technical person might look at an organization's culture and see that they don't feel like there is a fit for an engineer or a fit for someone who thinks in the ways they do. They may also decide that the organization doesn't value technical contributions. Conversely, a highly skilled sales consultant doesn't want to work at a place where a high value isn't put on delivering sales (for instance, a service culture) and would not consider applying at an institution where there isn't a sales incentive program.

Young millennials seek out cultures where they believe they will be heard and their ideas will be embraced. Millennials possess a unique talent to sniff out hypocrisy in an organization. If your organization doesn't have consistent rules across the all departments, millennials will see this as hypocrisy and immediately dismiss the organization's values altogether.

An innovative culture will attract the future leaders of your organization. These innovators will have a growth mindset; a less than innovative culture will attract those with a fixed mindset. Fixed-mindset people like a consistent environment and look for structure supported by rigor and consistency. They are also highly resistant to change because they don't believe they can learn new skills—their belief is that they are either good at something or they are not. A growth mindset person believes that he or she is in constant evolution and enjoys the challenge of mastering something new. In the current evolving banking environment, there isn't much room for fixed mindset people, as all processes are subject to change based on the digital transformation that the industry is currently undergoing. So ask yourself this question: Would your 19- or 20-year-old kid want to work at your financial institution? It's a good way to understand how your culture is viewed from the outside. Your outward branding, technology, and services will all tell a story about your culture. If you still have pens chained to the desk at the teller line, this is a message to the average professional that your organization has not culturally evolved.

Evolution is inevitable. I have spoken with many leaders in the banking industry who have lamented over losing a talented employee to a "work at home" position. In many cases, these employees will take less compensation in order to work at home. When I questioned why they couldn't let the employee work at home as well and keep them, they either stated it was their belief that work-at-home employees were not as productive as those that came in to the office to work or that there was a barrier in human resources or some other department that prevented them from offering the option to work at home. In today's world, you can have a video conference with five people at once, share screens, collaborate all at once on a document, and do it all securely through VPNs or cloud-based systems. Sadly, many financial institutions have not embraced that fact that many of the organization's digital positions could be filled with top talent who want to stay home and work. For those who are concerned with the productivity of a work-at-home programmer or project manager, there are tools that will monitor the productivity of a remote worker by taking screen shots at various intervals and uploading them to that employee's "work diary" so that management can review their work at any time. Working 40 hours in 8-hour intervals from 9 to 5, five days a week, is fast becoming a thing of the past. It is more likely that a knowledge or digital worker will work 60 hours, spread out through various times of the week and do it all from the comfort of their home office, on the road, or at a sporting event. Organizations that cannot evolve to provide workers with these options will be viewed as less than desirable workplaces by highly technical and sought-after talent.

If having an innovation culture is important to attract the next generation leadership, how do you go about creating an innovative culture when one doesn't exist currently? The first and most important step to evolving an innovative culture is to remove the stigma of failure in your organization. A culture that doesn't tolerate failure is not innovative. Failure is a symptom of trying new things. To be clear, I am not talking about tolerating incompetence, I am talking about not punishing people for trying something new and failing.

**Here are some examples of tolerable failure:**

- Implementing a marketing campaign on Reddit and not meeting the expected goals.
- Changing a process after researching with the staff with an expectation that it would save time, only to find that it added time and the process had to be reverted.
- Implementing a new voice technology and not getting the adoption that was expected.

**Examples of failures that should result in administrative action:**

- Updating technology without testing and finding out that the new technology isn't compatible with the FI's current software and is causing a major service interruption.
- Implementing a new process without conferring with the stakeholders—expecting it to save time only to find out that it added time and had to be reverted back.

Recently, there has been a trend in technology circles of celebrating failures. Take, for instance, a recently formed group called f--- up nights (you can fill in the blanks here, this is a family book);

this group meets regularly to share failures, and by sharing these failures they help others avoid the pitfalls that cratered their project as well as get ideas from others on how to pivot from a failure. Here would be a good place to calculate your *failure tolerability index (FTI)*. (I just made this up but I am going to trademark it, so don't think about stealing it.)

---

### Failure Tolerability Index (FTI)

To determine your FTI, answer the following questions. The first question is multiple choice; the others require a simple yes or no response.

1. When was the last time you tried something that failed?
   a. Today
   b. In the last month
   c. This year
   d. More than a year go
2. Would you be comfortable going to your boss and admitting a failure?
3. Would your employees or coworkers be comfortable discussing a failure with you?
4. Does your organization have a formal process to review failures?
5. Does your organization have a place for staff to submit innovations or ideas?

Scoring

For Question 1, use the following point assignments:

   a = 2 points
   b = 1.5 points
   c = 1 point
   d = 0 points

For the other questions, use the following point values:

   Yes = 2 points
   No = 0 points
   Kind of, sort of = 1.5 points

Add all points up to calculate your failure tolerability index.

A perfect 10 represents an organization that is extremely failure tolerant and, as a result, is likely very innovative. A score of 5 or less represents an organization that is intolerant of failure and is not likely to embrace innovations.

A *Harvard Business Review* article titled "The Failure-Tolerant Leader" describes how to determine if failure was a result of mismanagement or just a simple failure by asking questions such as the ones below:[1]

- Was the project designed conscientiously and vetted by the proper departments?
- Could additional research or preemptive feedback prevent the failure?
- Was the project developed collaboratively, or was important feedback rejected?
- Did others in the organization conspire to kill the project?
- Was the project propelled by its agreed-upon goals or was it taken over by special interests and individuals?
- Has anyone else anywhere else succeeded with a similar project?
- If so, what were the differences between the project at your FI and the project at the other organization?
- Were the mistakes repeated during the process?

Your FTI, combined with the attitude toward failure in your organization, will be the yardstick that innovation professionals use to measure your organization. An innovative person by nature will want to push the limits of the culture, and if he or she sees that is not possible that person will find another place to work.

## Steps to an Innovative Culture

Now that we have covered failure, what else does it take to create an innovative culture? The next step is to make sure that it's okay to admit mistakes as long as you have a plan for fixing them. It's also okay to ask someone to help you. Employees or staff members should be the same heroes in the organization whether they solved a difficult challenge themselves or they reached out for help via Google, consultants, or other means to solve a problem. It's important to identify problems quickly and have a plan for resolution. Keep in mind that I didn't say resolve the problem quickly, just to have a plan.

An organization with an innovative culture will want to build a relationship with its consumers that is built on trust. A consumer that deals with an organization that is innovative will expect failures from time to time, and when the organization quickly acknowledges these failures and has a plan to make it right, then consumers can be very tolerant. This is because most people don't expect a quick fix to everything in life, but they do expect to be told the truth. If a problem arises and the organization says it will be fixed by a certain date, the consumer will expect this fix, and unless they hear otherwise, they will expect that it will work on the day that you promised.

An innovative culture teaches people not to dwell too long on a problem before they reach out for help. When I first started my job in the computer lab, I was a smoker; I used run into an issue dealing with the large Novell network I supported, step out for a smoke, and come back and fix it immediately. Because I was young and stupid, I thought that the nicotine was somehow stimulating my brain and giving me the power to solve the problem. In my latter years (I stopped smoking in 1995), I realized that it had nothing to do with smoking and everything to do with being willing to walk away from a problem for a while. In those days, Google didn't exist, and so I really didn't have much recourse but to figure out problems on my own. In today's world, there is no excuse not to use a tool like Google before you do anything else. If there is an error in a log, google it! If something weird happened while you were checking out of the local grocery store, google it! If you can't find a solution to a problem in your project, google it! Chances are that whatever you are experiencing, someone else has already been there and done that and wrote an article or created a video on how to get around it so that others who follow them don't have to suffer like they did. I don't care if you google it, call a friend, consult tea leaves or—*gasp!*—take a trip to the public library to fix your problem—you are still the same hero to me. In fact, your willingness to reach out for answers instead of feeding your ego by trying to fix it yourself makes you an even bigger hero!

### Collaboration

Collaboration is the second most important ingredient to having an innovative culture. I have been in environments where departments were encouraged to be competitive with each other, and I discovered that this is counterproductive. The competition did the opposite of fostering collaboration, instead encouraging secrecy, judgment, and for those that were perceived as "losers" in the competition, dejection. Cooperation is also an enemy of collaboration because it creates a quid pro quo environment. When people participate in cooperatives with others, they are cooperating to achieve their own personal goals as opposed to working collectively on a shared goal. Collaboration is the process of sharing the secrets to success, and replicating the best ideas and processes to every corner of the organization. Collaborative initiatives represent cross-department and cross-functional initiatives that will have dramatic impact on the entire organization. Collaboration sometimes needs to be forced to happen. A good manager will facilitate collaboration even if the managers aren't naturally collaborative by creating meetings to share ideas or digital workspaces where idea exchanges can happen easily.

An important part of fostering collaboration is being careful about praising specific people or departments for successes. For example, if a manager praises a department that has some success in a collaborative environment without acknowledging the other contributors to the success they run the risk of offending the other groups who as result will return to being parochial with their information and ideas. In these cases, it is better to acknowledge the success itself rather than the individual departments. The success should be attributed to the entire organization. This is a not an "everyone gets a trophy" moment but a realization that in a true collaborative culture, any success is a culturally connected event that involves the entire organization. This is especially true of a digital environment where it is likely that the improved service involved multiple departments in the organization.

Another important aspect of collaboration is to avoid hierarchy for the sake of hierarchy. This means that members of departments should feel free to communicate with others in the organization without fear of retribution from management. This is a challenge because many managers treat their successes as a personal win as opposed to a team win. Managers who feel this way will often want to take credit for these successes. They feel as though if the communication about the successful project doesn't come from directly them, then it is not valid and they didn't get the credit for their leadership in the project. It's important that leaders don't personalize their projects to the extent that they feel attached to them and cannot be objective about their value. When leaders insist on reviewing all intradepartment communication, it creates a bottleneck in the organization, where ideas and vital information get stuck in limbo while they wait to be vetted by a member of management before they can be released to the organization. This doesn't mean that management shouldn't be informed about collaboration sessions. After all you cannot have half the call center down in the collections department learning how to deal with a foreclosed mortgage loan; you also cannot have three of five tellers desert their stations to go to another branch to share ideas without informing management. Collaboration should be sanctioned by management and planned for in the work schedule like any other activity. The key is that the staff should feel empowered to share these ideas and not feel afraid to ask for the time to present to others or to learn from others.

### Communications

As I mentioned before, communication is a key element to culture. In 1993, IBM's incoming CEO Lou Gerstner encouraged any employee to communicate with him via email. He soon discovered that many projects that were listed as "on time" by his senior staff were stuck according to employees working on the project. The key to this approach is how Lou responded when this happened. He could've forward the email to the employee's manager with a simple "What's going on here, I thought you said this was on time?" but given Lou's stated approach of creating a team inside of IBM I find it difficult to believe that he would throw an employee under the bus. It is more likely that he handled this situation with finesse that kept the employee safe from retribution but also gave the manager a way to deal with the concerns and the miscommunication. I also doubt he took each employee's email missive at face value; in fact he spent the first few months visiting the far corners of IBM, and I am sure that he sought out those that emailed him to understand the problems. He turned email into a super communication platform that encouraged candor and cut through the hierarchy of the organization.[2]

In today's world, we have more tools for collaboration than we have ever had before. Email was the beginning, but now we have chat products like Slack or Microsoft Teams. Products like these organize chats into channels. Each channel can be relevant to disciplines in your organization. Here is an example Slack setup for a bank.

Channels such as Lending, or Call Center, can serve as a central communications repository that allows questions and answers to be captured in the open for others to see. The tool also allows other participants to search each channel for key words or key phrases. So if staff members had a question about procedures with a reverse mortgage, they could simply put the term in the search field and review any communications that specialists and experts had with other members of the organization in the past. This could either result in the employee getting the answer they need, or at least identifying someone to ask the question of that would likely have the answer given their past interactions. These collaborative tools have become the most important tools for fintechs. These tools are particularly effective in geographically diverse environments. As you might imagine, a tool like this would foster communication and collaboration, and because management could review it, it could serve as a valuable source of information to determine on which processes, channels, or services staff needs more training. A tool like this also sends a message to the staff that communication is encouraged, the simplicity of the tool lets the staff no that there are no barriers to professional communication with other departments to improve performance. It is far easier to deal with conflict or failure when there is an established relationship.

In the past, I worked with a team on a Customer Event management tool that solved a simple problem. If someone called into our organization and said, "I never received the PIN for my credit card," the customer service representative would tell the customer that the representative was resending it (at this time, we could only mail them; things have changed). If the customer for some reason didn't receive the PIN for a second time and called back in, it was not likely that the customer would get the same person, and because there wasn't a system in place for the new customer service representative to review the last interaction, the customer was forced to tell the entire story again. Of course, this is frustrating to customers and doesn't inspire any confidence that their problem will be solved the second time.

The system that was designed to solve the problem would allow the CSR to record any interactions that weren't resolved on the call so that if the customer called in again the next CSR would instantly have access to the open issue and could start the conversation by asking, "Hello Mr. Best, before we get started, did you get your new PIN in the mail?" As you might imagine, this conversation is far easier for the CSR than if the customer has to repeat the story. One interesting decision the institution made while designing this solution is that all outstanding issues had to be followed up on by the CSR who recorded the event. If the employee didn't update the ticket based on the prescribed deadline (for instance, four days for the snail mail of the PIN), the ticket would be reported to the manager; if the manager didn't do something, it went to a VP, and so forth and so on until it reached the CEO. Since the staff knew that this was the process, they were very careful to update their tickets. This accomplished two goals. First, it sent a strong message that this organization cared deeply about service, so much so that unanswered messages would be escalated all the way to the CEO. The second message was that being proactive, as opposed to reactive, was expected of the staff.

This single decision changed the culture of the organization such that other parts of the organization began to adopt the same philosophy; even non-customer-facing departments would follow the paradigm to deal with other departments (whom they considered their customers). This also allowed the organization to easily identify processes that commonly resulted in a delays and work on either speeding up these processes or reengineering them to be a self-service process. CSRs—who realized that this system was improving their throughput and reducing awkward and angry calls by allowing them to be perceived as "in the know" about customer problems—embraced this concept and instantly had ideas to improve it and how to use it for other things and because it was developed in house these ideas were collected and implemented in future sprints under the continuous improvement process.

Communication is a little like security. I don't think you can spend enough on communication in an organization. When the flight you're on is turbulent, you will see the flight attendants using the plane phones to communicate with the pilot and the rest of the crew. They communicate and react quickly to sudden and unpredictable changes in their environment. If the FI is to survive the turbulent times ahead for financial institutions, a strong communication platform that the staff understands and isn't afraid to use is the key to finding smooth air.

### Rewards and Evaluations

Do your rewards and evaluations line up with your culture? If you have a team culture but your evaluations are based on individual performance, it sends mixed messages to the staff. Incentivizing staff needs to be based on your cultural goals. If you are promoting a collaborative culture that involves cross-functional teams, then the evaluation should include sections that reward those who engage in collaborative functions and provide coaching and training for those who are not being collaborative or at least supporting collaboration. Rewards and evaluations are an important aspect of your culture, as they will dictate the behaviors of the staff. Like it or not, your staff members are all human, and all of them are pre-programmed to view monetary rewards, praise, and promotions as indicators that they are succeeding within the organization. If these elements are not aligned with the culture of the organization, the employees will naturally do that which increases their status, monetary position, or position in the company, as opposed to collaborative initiatives that do not provide the employee with what they perceive as a clear career boost in the form of promotions or raises.

## Achievement versus Alignment

I have a friend who runs a large company, and she likes to emphasize that achievement is not always alignment. I find in financial institutions that many people struggle with this concept, especially when it comes to budget season and project management. How are you incentivizing the completion of projects? If it's based on quantity, then you may have a big issue. When you reward quantity, managers tend to pad the projects with achievable things, which is great, except when these things are not aligned with your strategy. This is a cultural thing as well: if we reward any achievement regardless of whether it was aligned with the goals of the organization (which is also human nature), then we are sending the wrong message in terms of alignment. When projects are reviewed in the PMO, it is important that the process includes a way to measure each project as it relates to the stated goals of the organization. Often, when you sift through the requests, you are forced to prioritize mandatory regulatory updates against new technology projects and balance each of those types of project with the various security "have to do it or we will be hacked" projects. The pressure to continually update the digital assets of the organization and to innovate to keep up with the competitors starts to feel like two hands around your neck. The fact is that there is too little budget, too little resources, and too many projects to do.

It's time to readdress our budgeting process and implement projects that meet our growth goals, save money, and/or create revenue to offset your expenses. Each regulatory expense or revenue neutral project should be balanced with a revenue-producing project (to feed your strategy and invest in the future). It's kind of like planting a tree every time you cut one down. It's good for the environment and for your soul. Much like our rewards and evaluation programs, our project list should reflect the strategy and culture of the organization. The project list will influence your culture greatly. The priority of the projects sends a message to the staff as to what is a priority within the organization. All too often, our project distributions come out looking something like this:

| | |
|---|---|
| 80% | Keep the lights on: Includes regulatory and other non-negotiable projects |
| 10% | New features or new products |
| 5% | Process improvement |
| 5% | Replacing products |
| 0% | Innovation |

This formula often results in an organization getting stuck in a rut, since new features and services are not getting as much attention as operations. What is needed is a more balanced approach to the project categories. Consider the following approach:

| | |
|---|---|
| 60% | Keep the lights on |
| 15% | New features/products |
| 10% | Process improvement |
| 5% | Replacing products |
| 10% | Innovation |

This approach provides more balance across the categories while still acknowledging the disproportionate need for maintenance resources. It also better positions your organization to realize improved productivity, efficiency, strategic alignment, and revenue by more fully addressing these critical areas. I would also encourage organizations to *do less* in terms of project work, prioritizing quality over quantity for the next few years. Use the reclaimed time to work with consulting groups to retrain your organization in a new method of project management and implementation called agile. Organizations that embrace and master cross-functional agility will be better prepared to tackle even the most complex digital projects of the future. It's easier to train a group in new processes and procedures right now than in the crucible of a major technology expansion such as AI or analytics under duress from the market. Take the time to train and train with professionals to shorten your ramp up cycle. The issue isn't solely about budget dollars—even if funding were unlimited, there are only so many initiatives that can be realistically tackled at one time, not to mentioned a limited supply of skilled FTE with the knowledge base necessary to tackle these projects.

As I stated before, cultural muscle memory is the key to understanding your real cultural. What is your staff's default position in any given situation? In other words, how the staff reacts to adverse situations and their willingness to share their ideas is the true measure of culture.

---

**Chapter Review**

- Culture often travels from the top down. The further people are from the C-suite, the weaker the message.

- Culture can evolve as the organization matures. During times of crisis, the culture is often either validated or in some cases it is forced to change. It can also be difficult to scale.

- An organization's failure tolerability index (FTI) is an important indicator of how well a company can adapt, innovate, and fail—all important measures of the strength and efficacy of culture.

- Communication, collaboration, and rewards are the three most critical ingredients of culture.

## NOTES

1. Richard Farson and Ralph Keyes, "The Failure-Tolerant Leader," *Harvard Business Review* (August 2002), https://hbr.org/2002/08/the-failure-tolerant-leader.
2. Steve Lohr, "Welcome to I.B.M., Boss; Now, Check Your E-Mail," *New York Times* (April 10, 1993), http://www.nytimes.com/1993/04/10/business/welcome-to-ibm-boss-now-check-your-e-mail.html?mcubz=0.

# CHAPTER 12

# Culture and Technology

Awe

## A Tale of Two Cultures

Many years ago, when I was growing up in Germany, my mom would take me to a McDonald's as a special treat. It was one of the few American franchises you could find in Germany at the time, and it felt like home when we would go. My loving mother would purchase a hamburger for me and we would sit down at the table. Then, she would unwrap the burger for me, take off the top of the bun, and proceed to scrape off the onions, then put the burger back together.

As you know by now, I am a very lazy person, and I didn't think my mother should have to scrape off the onions, so I asked her, "Mom, couldn't we just say, '*Keine Zwiebel, bitte*'?" That roughly translates to "No onions, please," in English. I had been learning German in the school I was attending and one of our first vocabulary lists contained all the vegetables. She replied, "I wish I could, but they won't do that." In those days, McDonald's wouldn't take a special order. Today you could order a cheeseburger with a chicken patty on it with extra cheese, two pickles, and light onions, and the cashier or drive-through person wouldn't even bat an eye. It's likely that this order wouldn't even be the most difficult one they had to take that day. However, 30 or 40 years ago, you got what you got and you didn't complain. Things were about to change though: A royal competitor in the fast-food market noticed that people weren't happy about McDonald's rigidness.

In 1974, Burger King ran television commercials in which employees sang, "Hold the pickles, hold the lettuce. Special orders don't upset us. All we ask is that you let us serve it your way!" Burger King was capitalizing on the fact that McDonald's refused to do special orders. Someone in the Burger King leadership knew that tastes varied and that it was inevitable that fast food would have to become customizable. This concept directly conflicted with the McDonald's philosophy of efficiency and speed.

Mac and Dick McDonald originally conceived the idea for fast food after noticing that hamburgers were the best-selling item on their menu. Because of this, they redesigned their restaurant to deliver a simple menu of three or four items very quickly. This was a revelation in the restaurant industry at a time when most restaurants had 25 or more items on their menu and catered to a local clientele. The brothers obsessed over each item in the kitchen and, more importantly, over each step of the process of making their food. The key to fast and consistent food delivery in the eyes of the brothers was a rigid, repeatable one-size-fits-all process that would be adhered to by every one of their franchises. For years, McDonald's resisted the change, believing that Burger King would fail under the weight of the custom orders. They thought that Burger King's service would be slower and that there weren't that many people who wanted to customize their food, so McDonald's sat back to see what would happen. After all, McDonald's wasn't exactly going bankrupt. In the end, though, McDonald's retooled its processes to accept customized orders—something learned from the upstart competitors—and continued to thrive.

Financial institutions are doing the same thing to customers when it comes to digital products. Today's digital financial applications aren't very flexible in terms of how they present the information and what they allow customers to do with their data. Typically, these applications show balances and manage loans and credit cards. They might even offer a few configurable options. Some financial institutions have even created a customizable landing page that allows the customer to pick modules to display, so they do not have to click through menus to see alerts or bill pay. However, by and large, the experience of the application is consistently the same, even when you customize the content. A consumer can't download their bill-pay payees or ACH payees, or upload information. These systems are the equivalent of my hamburger with onions. If you want to do something with your financial information other than what the FI is presenting you would need to download it and make it happen yourself. (In some cases even downloading it is not possible.)

The truth of the matter is that retail digital products and services are quickly becoming very personal to consumers, and finance products are among the most personal services to consumers. Consumers expect to be able to customize everything in their digital world; they want to change their backgrounds, organize their apps, pick their ring tones, and dress up their electronics with fancy coverings that fit their personality and lifestyle. Digital is not a one-size-fits-all proposition for the people of Earth. Each of them thinks very differently about their finances, and each of them has very different goals for the banking platform. Sadly, financial institutions spend a lot of time and money trying to be all things to all people, only to fail miserably. This is evidenced by the overwhelmingly negative reviews of most banking applications on iTunes and Google Play. Even when they manage to make one group happy, they wind up upsetting a whole different group of people. So what is the answer? How can banks get to a flexible version of banking that meets the needs of different customers? How can they retool their kitchens to allow a customized order, so to speak?

## A Case for Flexibility

### Public Service Directive 2

To understand the future, sometimes it's helpful to get out of your familiar environment and learn what's going on elsewhere in the world of banking. Take, for instance, PSD2 or Public Service Directive 2 that is currently being implemented in the European Union and the United Kingdom by the year 2018. This regulation says that financial institutions must open their systems via application programming interfaces or web services so that third-party entities can verify payment and account information directly with the financial institution.

Forcing financial institutions to open up their systems has created a whole new level of innovation. I recently attended a leading international banking technology providers annual customer conference, and I was blown away by the number of technologies that were either enabled by the upcoming PSD2 change or provided more than the PSD2 change required. It seems that European banks have identified that this is a "go big or go home" situation, meaning that if you provide the minimum requirement access to satisfy the regulatory need you run the risk of being disintermediated. The answer to this danger is to "go big" and provide more than PSD2 requires and move your business towards an API-driven micro services environment. The idea is that a more agile micro services environment will allow fintech providers to become collaborators and not enemies by allowing financial institutions to quickly provide access to their data sources so that fintech providers can leverage their systems and the FI's customers.

OK, I hear you saying, yep but I don't care what is going on in Europe. To that I say, discount what is happening elsewhere in the banking world at your own peril. Many experts feel like the coming PSD2 regulation will also create a push in the United States to adopt a similar regulation, and even if they don't, other experts believe that in order to do business globally, US banks will need to at least create gateways that can communicate with PSD2-compliant banks as the EU banks begin to push all integration through these platforms and expect to be able to access something similar at a US bank.

Let's rewind all the way to the beginning: How will this impact the hamburger onion problem? If you think of the bank as a restaurant and all of its offerings as entrées, then the ingredients would be things like ACH, WIRE transfers, Billpay and other ubiquitous services that are used in multiple offerings. An API like PSD2 would allow the following solutions.

1. A customer could theoretically access these PSD2 interfaces themselves directly and create their own financial front end with everything exactly how they want it to be. It's the equivalent of getting the burger plain and putting the condiments on yourself.

2. A fintech provider could access the API and create a custom burger for the customer. This burger wouldn't make sense for the financial institution to provide because of scale, but the fintech provider would be happy to service these niche customers.

In both cases, the financial institution still maintains its deposit accounts, maintains it loans, and continues to service the accounts as well as bears the regulatory burden. In the second case, however there is a chance that the fintech provider could intervene in the relationship with the customer. This is a problem that will need to be solved by financial institutions, but it will likely not involve technology. It will likely be solved via contractual obligations when the API is first setup. The financial institution may insist on a "Powered by FI" brand or some other identifier that allows the customer to know that the underlying platform of the service is being provided by a trusted banking provider.

This, however, will require a culture shift within the organization. Sadly, many traditionalist and conservative bank leaders will not want to create a gateway to allow their services to be expanded upon. They will argue that this is the path to destructing the organization, not recognizing the need to adapt to the upcoming needs of consumers and the changing environment of banking. The path to convincing them is to provide data and seek understanding. Seeking clarity within the organization when it comes to opposing views of digital services is key to moving the organization digitally forward. This is, I strongly believe, because most if not all of their concerns are valid, collecting these issues and finding ways to mitigate them is the key to evolving the financial institution's digital approach. If you cannot mitigate them, then it is likely that the technology or service isn't quite ready for your organization.

McDonald's founders Dick and Mac McDonald were famous for their attention to detail and their processes. When Ray Kroc approached them to franchise their restaurant, they famously said that it couldn't be replicated. They worried that their name would be on something that they couldn't control the quality of (sound familiar?). Their processes were designed to deliver food fast, and because it had never been done before, people accepted the fact that to get it fast they wouldn't get to choose the ingredients or condiments that were on the burger. It made sense to people that if they wanted a burger instantly, they would have to be prepared to accept a burger that didn't exactly fit their tastes, or else choose from several burgers to get the one that was closest to what they wanted. Then technology and public tastes evolved and it suddenly became possible to "have it your way" and have it fast at the same time. Burger King challenged the conventional wisdom of the fast-food industry, specifically the notion that expedited service meant conformity and a rigid process, and as a result for a period of

*(continued)*

(*Continued*)

time they dominated the market. More importantly, Burger King forced McDonald's to change. This is the same challenge that financial institutions are facing now. The conventional wisdom that banking is something done at a bank, by a banker, is rapidly changing, and to survive, banks must begin to think differently about their interactions with customers.

## Having It Your Way—BYOP

I have been thinking a lot lately about what the new model for digital banking will look like and how to overcome the onions problem. Recently, I have discovered some concepts for digital banking that seem to resonate with the audiences I have tested them on. I call the concept BYOP or Bring Your Own Platform. In the current digital banking models, there is a tendency to ignore outside services that have become ubiquitous to digital customers such as email systems, task management solutions, and cloud storage platforms. Instead, FIs force their customers to manually enter information into their task management, or manually download digital statements and store them in the cloud. Digital platform providers choose to spend time and money recreating these systems inside their platforms, usually in the name of security or perceived convenience but with less than stellar results. The quasi email, messaging system in most digital banking platforms are no match for Outlook or Gmail. Task management tools such as Billpay or ACH are also no match for the current crop of task management tools. I believe new digital financial systems will be a series of integrations with platforms such as the Google suite or Microsoft suite. Here are some examples.

If digital services could integrate with Outlook or Gmail then payees could be imported or exported on the fly. Instead of typing in payee information, the contact feature of the email system would facilitate the payment. The interaction would look something like the following: User gets an email bill from a utility provider, and instead of logging into home banking or the utility providers site to pay the bill, the user finds the contact in his contacts folder, opens it, and clicks the payments tab. The payments tab has a dropdown menu that allows payment via Venmo, PayPal, ACH, or credit card. Each payment option would be facilitated by a payment provider that interacts with the Google or Microsoft platform. In this new model, it will be critical to keep the payees information up to date, so rather than pay for a bill payment service the end user would find more value in a service that kept their contacts up to date.

The same approach could be taken with task management. If you are a task management freak like I am (I have tried every productivity application that I can find), then having an integration with your digital banking solution and your task management software would be very valuable. Instead of sending email reminders for loan payments, the FI could create a task in the end users task management software of choice that reminds them when to pay their mortgage. The task manager software could also be used to facilitate recurring transfers. This is another example of a weakness in the current digital platforms. Each platform has a concept of recurring transfers but it usually lacks the options that heavy finance users would want to have such as more variety for transfer intervals than the standard weekly, biweekly options that are found in most digital banking systems. Using your own personal task manager such as Trello or Wunderlist to trigger automatic payments or transfers would allow the end user to exert far more granular control than the FI could ever hope to create. This is because the FI isn't trying to replace Outlook or Gmail, instead they have opted for a "one sizes fits all" approach. However, they cannot match the vast resources of either Google or Microsoft in this platform space. Having a programmable task feature would open the door to other kinds of automation and allow the user better control over their finances. This would also cut down on the support needed to maintain the redundant and subpar task and mail systems that are boiled into digital systems.

In the BYOP world banking statements would no longer take up space at the FI, users could instead opt to store their statements in their preferred digital storage platform. E-statements could automatically be delivered in a secure fashion to cloud-based storage platforms such as Dropbox, Google Drive, or OneDrive to customers who opted into the service. Many of the major storage providers will index documents and their content so it can be instantly searched.

This would provide a huge improvement over the current solutions that are provided by FIs today. For instance if you had all of your statements stored in a folder called "statements" and you wanted to find every transaction that you paid to your homeowners' association (HOA), you could easily select the folder and type the HOAs name into the search box. The operating system would return all the statements with a transaction that matches the search criteria.

Financial account alerts could be channeled to a single digital endpoint and then sorted in the same way Gmail allows you to write rules to sort your incoming email. Alerts that meet a certain criteria could be sent directly to an accountant, or alerts that need immediate attention could be routed to the TV or Amazon Echo in attempt to get the customer's attention. Utilizing this method for alerts would reduce the amount of personal information that an FI needs to store and put the control in the hand of the end user. Savvy users might write rules that would respond to alerts with action, such as setting up an automatic task to transfer money if an NSF alert is received via email.

This new digital banking paradigm relies integrating features and services from platforms that users are already accustomed to using in their everyday lives. The BYOP approach would reduce the amount of money necessary to support digital services by removing features as well as improve aspects of the service by creating new features. It's as though you bring your own ingredients for the McDonald's cooking staff to use, but they would add the meat and take care of the preparation.

Great work! Now you are starting to remove the onions from the burger by providing data when and how they want it. There is still a lot left to be done to transform the culture of your organization to support this—after all, Burger King didn't transform all of its kitchens in its stores to support the new "Have it your way" ordering overnight. It took time, but with effort, you can get there. In the meantime, it is time to start learning what your members really want from your digital platforms by engaging them with digital marketing, tracking their behaviors via your new API and routes as they use your various digital channels, and reacting to their feedback and behaviors by soliciting them with offers and other pertinent information—all of which will be far easier now that you have implemented the FI platform.

## Chapter Review

- Today's digital financial applications aren't very flexible in terms of how they present the information and what they allow customers to do with their data. Typically, these applications show balances and manage loans, and credit cards.

- Customization is one of the key attributes that consumers expect from digital products and services.

CHAPTER

# 13

# The Long View

**It came from the 4th floor, and it only wanted to help.**

It is not the strongest of the species that survives, or the most intelligent that survives. It is the one that is most adaptable to change.

*–Charles Darwin*

**M**any organizations find it daunting to keep up with digital changes. This chapter aims to provide some perspective on the incremental changes your organization can make to prepare for threats and take advantage of upcoming trends. Before doing this, it's important to understand the threats and opportunities that exist.

## The Problem: Banking and Financial Competitors

For many years, banks and credit unions have considered the behemoth banks to be their biggest competitors. Names like JPMorgan Chase and USAA come to mind right away. Both of those players, JPMorgan Chase in particular, are very large organizations that have a lot of money and resources to invest in digital technology. USAA is well known for delivering all services via technology, and they rank #34 in banks. USAA has 28,000+ employees and JPMorgan Chase 258,965 employees globally at the end of 2012. When people hear those familiar names, they think about their products and, especially, the breadth of services they offer. Most importantly, we think about the amount of resources they have to throw at various projects.

There's no doubt about it; big banks are tough competition, but local banks and credit unions are facing another problem as well. Other players are coming into our space. I don't mean other banks or credit unions. I mean entirely new types of financial organizations. For instance, Venmo, a person-to-person payment service owned by PayPal, which continues to infringe on traditional banking, has become known as the new $20 bill. As a matter of fact, I recently read an article with the title "Is PayPal the New MasterCard or Visa?"

When these new *nonbanks* move into this space, they don't have to jump through the same hoops that smaller, traditional financial institutions need to. Additionally, they are not under the same regulatory scrutiny. It is important to understand what these new competitors are doing. Every one of them looks at a small section of what you do and digitizes it to the best of their ability.

One example of this is Kabbage. Kabbage (www.kabbage.com) is a company that took advantage of the fact that most small business loans are incredibly difficult to get. The application and approval process takes a very long time and, as a business owner myself, I can tell you, it's not easy. However, Kabbage promises that within 24 hours of filling out their forms, you can have up to a $100,000 line of credit. This beats every institution that I'm aware of in the market right now. Also consider Intuit's Rocket Mortgage product. If you have ever watched a TV or glanced at one for more than 30 seconds, you likely have seen a commercial for this product. The product points out the complexity and length of time it takes to conduct a mortgage transaction with other institutions and simplifies the process. This simplification is built on digital interactions and digitizing paperwork and workflow. The end result is a mortgage application that can be completed quickly and is processed within minutes not days.

So, what does that mean? It means that many banks are being taken apart one little piece at a time. Brett King, author of *Breaking Banks*, described it as "death by 4,000 cuts."[1] It's the struggle for adoption of new financial technologies and how we have lagged behind in the United States.

How do we keep up? Well, one plan of action is to keep a close eye on the European Union (EU). In Europe you see mass innovation in the financial space: the revised Payment Services Directive (PSD2) and the General Data Protection Regulation (GDPR) are two EU regulations that work to guide and accelerate the adoption of new technology. Even when the United Kingdom leaves the EU, it will still share a common banking system.

## Threats: The *–tions*

Let's take a minute and talk about the threats that we face. I like to call these the –TIONS (pronounced *shuns*) because they all end in –sion or –tion.

### Interchange Compression

The first of the –TIONS is *interchange compression*. Notice that I did not say "interchange disappearance" or "interchange goes away." This phenomenon is compression, and we will continue to see it. For example, we are seeing the rise of the merchant wallet, an app-based payment method that links to a customer's credit card or bank account. In less than a year, Dunkin' Donuts, Taco Bell, and Chick-fil-A all debuted merchant wallets, and these services have been gaining adoption.

There are many reasons why merchants want you to use their app:

- They want you to have the best experience possible. When you use something like Apple Pay, you bypass loyalty points, in-app ordering, and other exclusive features. A specialized wallet app dedicated to their brand vastly expands their control of the experience.
- Single-sale revenue growth: Taco Bell claims that it sees 20 percent higher purchase totals from merchant wallet purchases.
- The application fosters engagement—having the app on your phone is kind of like having a magnet for that merchant on your refrigerator. Whenever you open your phone and flip through the screens, you will see the app. Especially services like "order ahead" and "repeat last order."
- They also collect data from the applications:
  o Location-based data: Have you been close to one of their stores?
  o Market segmentation data based on device
  o Instant user feedback
- Stored value transactions: Starbucks has proven that consumers will put money in a stored value account associated with their brands. Stored value means that the money they transfer to Starbucks is no longer in your checking account.

With this in mind, say you're a loyal customer of Dunkin' Donuts. You roll through its drive-through every day and you use your credit card (issued by a local bank or credit union) to buy your morning coffee. Every once in a while you buy a dozen donuts to share at the office. One day, you're passing through the drive-thru and you notice that Dunkin' Donuts has an app. You also see that you can get free coffee and donut discounts by purchasing with their app. What do you do? Obviously, you download the app. Logic would dictate that you would enter information for the same credit card that you've been handing to the cashier every day. However, many people don't do this. Most people have what they consider to be a *digital card* that they use for apps and online purchases. Usually, it's issued by one of the big players: Chase, Citi, Capital One, you get the idea.

I have a theory as to why that is. Many years ago, when the internet first came on the scene, it was a dark, scary place to do business. Fearing fraud, most of the small credit unions and banks counseled their customers and members to *not* store their credit card numbers online. The big players didn't echo that message. As a result, they got a foothold on that beachhead and secured *top-of-app* status. Lately the big players have been taking it another level. American Express has added incentives for their customers if they use their Amex cards as their payment for Uber. This trend will continue; meanwhile, our smaller financial institutions don't even notice these losses.

If not addressed, these small defections from either the credit card or debit card portfolio will add up to larger losses. For many years the financial industry has talked about being *top of wallet.* Now it's time to become *top of app.* Later in the technology section we'll talk about the tools that you need to succeed at being *top of app.*

A local grocery store puts out an app that allows customers to pay with a stored card. Imagine a consumer with a family of four spends about $360 at the store every two weeks—and each time uses a debit card issued by their credit union. If this consumer gets the grocer's app and, instead of entering her trusty credit union card, inputs the number of a big player card, you're now out $720 a month worth of interchange.

More importantly, we've got to replace interchange. This leads me to the next –TION: cannibalization.

### Cannibalization

We're seeing cannibalization, but we're not doing anything about it. For many years, PayPal has pushed its customers to create what it calls a *bank draft account,* which is really an ACH account. On average, ACH transactions cost most financial institutions $0.26 while creating no revenue. Many retailers offer their customers a ACH option to pay. Amazon is a great example of a retailer that has this option.

> **PRO TIP**
>
> Analyze your ACH for these sorts of transactions and track the expense and loss from not using your credit or debit cards. Incent these members to use your cards for transactions from these merchants.

Are we cannibalizing our own business? Are we making it too easy for our customers to use services that do not benefit the bank and therefore benefit the customers? Is it too easy to use ACH to move money out of the financial institution into bill pay services like Mint Bills. Will we eventually have to charge for ACH? (More on this later.)

### Digitization

Digitization is the process of reengineering processes, increasing communication, and reducing effort for both the consumer and the staff member by using state-of-the-art technologies like smartphone applications, data analytics, and enhanced workflow processing. When these technologies are used together, it shortens transaction times and reduces complexity for the consumers.

Companies like Kabbage and Intuit are leading the way in digitization. These companies take advantage of the fact that traditional banking processes are so cumbersome and take so long. They are working through these processes using experienced digital designers to create fluid workflows that are very easy and quick to get through. As a result, places like the Lending Club and Intuit's Rocket Mortgage are seeing spikes in their services because people are looking for simplicity, speed, efficiency, and service. Many think it's about having these services online or in an application on your phone. It would be a mistake to think that digitization is only about digitizing the application process. One of the main features of the Rocket Mortgage application is a chat helper on every page. If you linger on a page or stop moving your mouse for a while, you can be sure the Rocket Mortgage application is going to pop up with a chat asking, "Are you having an issue? Can we help you?"

The digitization process covers origination AND transaction completion. It's not about digitizing a single part of the process; it's about being digital from beginning to end, including out to the fringe players like title companies and car dealerships. Think about what it would look like if Apple sold you a house. What would its version of the transaction look like? That's what digitization is.

The world of marketing has changed considerably. New marketing paradigms like inbound marketing and data-driven marketing have pushed companies like Amazon and Zappos, and yet, we have not seen mass adoption of these new marketing techniques in the banking market. New approaches like inbound marketing and sites like HubSpot are revolutionizing the online sales process. The digitization of the marketing process is very prevalent; however, most banking sites have not employed any of these technologies.

### Mobilization

The next of the –TION is mobilization. Many of us have direct experience with this. At this point, it's table stakes for banks and credit unions to have a mobile app, but few smaller firms are looking beyond that. For example, what's going to happen when people start using wearable en masse? It is just a matter of time before augmented reality makes it way into our everyday lives via glasses or implants. Mobilization involves providing your entire digital offering in a mobile platform. This has been very challenging for many banking organizations who have struggled to provide all services in all channels. You can find complaints in all of the major mobile application stores about financial services applications that fail to provide access to real time credit card balances or allow a mortgage payment. The challenge with mobilization is that many financial institutions didn't anticipate the mobile shift, and as a result, their systems were not designed to support a mobile architecture. This leads to the missing feature symptoms described above.

Many financial institutions are trying to synchronize their mobile offerings with their online web-based offerings and as a result are falling behind in implementing the latest technologies.

### Disintermediation

Disintermediation is the last of the –TIONS. There's never been a greater time for disruptors to get between you and your customer. It happens all of the time with organizations like Mint or Envelopes. These apps and sites get the customer to enter a user name and password, and all of a sudden, your clients spend all of their time on that site instead of on yours. As a result, you lose marketing share and eyeballs.

## The Reality of Change

These are all real threats that we face, so we must change our path quickly. Despite being predicted many, many times, the big disruption wave hasn't hit yet. CUs and banks are still strong. However, the biggest catalyst for change is always a catastrophe. A serious threat leads to action, taking risks, and leaving comfort zones. How will financial institutions face these threats and adapt to the coming change?

Here's one of the reasons why fintech has become such a big threat. In 2000, according to CB Insights Upfront Ventures, it cost at least $5 million to launch a startup. You had to buy software, licenses, and firewalls. You had to hire engineers to run things. You had to have your own data center and so much other infrastructure to get off the ground that for most entrepreneurs it was out of the question to engage the financial services world.

Now take a look at financial startup costs in 2005. By then, it was only half a million dollars. We saw the rise of open source. Technology also came into play for horizontal scaling, which was the ability to scale out as opposed to having to buy bigger machines. You could now just add more, cheaper machines. Five hundred thousand is still a lot of money, but it's a tenth of what it took just five years earlier.

Now fast forward to 2009. The price tag has fallen to $50,000. Thanks to cloud services, all of a sudden a data center wasn't necessary. A startup could pay for only the processing that it used. This ushered in a whole new era. Suddenly, a startup could buy a small office somewhere. It didn't need a costly tier-four data center with signal coming in from two different directions and fire suppression and air conditioning. Now, the startup could just focus on what it did best: the business, the programming, and the creation of new things.

Fast forward yet again to 2011. Now anyone can start a startup for a mere $5,000. Why? First, you can see the introduction of open APIs. You can use all these products—Twilio, Office365, Salesforce, and other software as a service (SaaS). You don't have to rebuild the foundation when you start a new business, and if you don't like the existing footprint, you can change that easily. You get to create your own experience within these platforms.

This advancement enables the ability to globalize your workforce. You can be sitting in Colorado Springs and you can have people working for you in India or Los Angeles. I found my own assistant on a site called Upwork.com. I sorted through the marketplace and I found someone who wanted to work. We have met in person only once in two years—and everything's run smoothly. These are the reasons why people are starting these platforms, and why disruption gets easier day by day.

---

This raises an important question: Are you a technology company that delivers financial services or are you a financial services company that delivers via technology?

One of the great examples of a technology company that delivers financial services is USAA. It is second to none in its digital and online platforms. They're incredibly innovative and they're clearly organized like a technology company. Umpqua is a great example of the second type of organization, a financial services company that delivers via technology. Umpqua is a fantastic bank in the Pacific Northwest.

When comparing USAA and Umpqua at face value, you'd say there's not much difference. It's not about what they deliver on the front end. As a matter of fact, both approaches are equally effective. However, after drilling down into their organizational structures and methods, you will notice major differences. At the core of this book is determining what it means to organize your institution into one of these two structures—and how to implement and break your digital gridlock regardless of whether you want to be a technology company or a financial services company.

## Changing Features or Services

Here's the difference between the two: Imagine these as two sides of a block (Figure 13.1). It's when you live in the middle that the problem

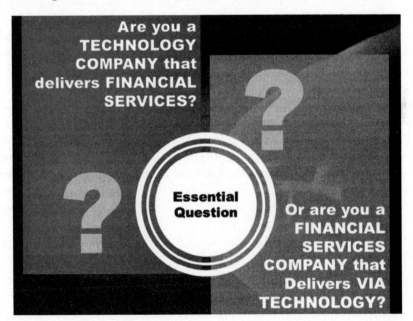

Figure 13.1    What type of organization are you?

presents itself. It's when you're not really a technology company and you're only kind of a financial services company, you're living in the middle. Living in the middle is akin to not knowing who you are as an organization; it causes confusion and fosters distrust. Read on to learn how this happens.

Let me explain how you wake up one day and find yourself in the middle. Let's pretend you're the CEO of Ahead of the Curve Bank (ACB). Ahead of the Curve Bank is a $10 billion organization with 50 branches and is well-known in the community for great service. Now, Ahead of the Curve Bank is very dependent on its technology providers. It has chosen to purchase turnkey solutions from its banking technology provider. For the purposes of our discussion, let's call that big provider BigTek. BigTek is a very big technology provider that provides pretty much every product you could ever want if you're running a financial institution. It provides your core platform, which processes your general ledgers, your debit, and your credit services. It provides you home banking, a mobile platform, and a bill pay platform. In theory, all of these services are integrated because they come from the same company, meaning that they all function together in a holistic way that is seamless to your customers.

One day, as CEO of Ahead of the Curve Bank, your chief retail officer comes into your office, and he is livid. He's banging on your desk, saying, "Look, we can't work with BigTek's bill pay platform any more. We're falling behind. The competitors in the area are overtaking us." He reminds you that it's an important product and was earmarked by the board as the centerpiece of the institution's growth plan. He says to you, "We need to look at something else!" You respond, "Well, tell me why we should move."

For the next hour, he makes a compelling argument to move to a new platform. He points out the more enticing features in your competitors' platforms and has customer feedback from iTunes and Google Play that Ahead of the Curve customers are clamoring for these features. You agree that it would be wise to explore other bill pay products in the market.

One of my rules of thumb is: *If you're going to move between products or platforms, particularly if it's for features, those features had better be 50 percent better that what you have today and your organization should realize at least a 50 percent lift in the use of services the product provides.*

### Cost

Cost is the first reason why banks switch services or products. Many organizations believe they're paying too much for service based on industry comparisons. Most vendors I know would much rather work with you on cost than to lose you as a customer because it's very difficult to get a new customer. Unless your organization or the vendor is being unreasonable, the cost issue can usually be negotiated.

### Service

Service is the second reason why banks switch products or services. Perhaps the service you are receiving from the vendor is bad or inconsistent. Maybe the product was unavailable to your customers for a whole week in the past quarter. Platform stability is a common complaint of platform services like bill pay. Unless your requests are unreasonable or the vendor is incompetent, most vendors will work very hard to solve your problem because it is likely a problem for the rest of their customers. However, if they do have some sort of systemic problem, then yes, the stability of the service would be a good reason to leave.

### Security

Are there security issues with the vendor you are working with? Has it suffered a breach? That is another reason to move as well, and a very good reason. Security will be covered in depth later in this book, but for now, if your vendor or provider has had a security breach that has put your organization at risk of losing your reputation, then leaving that vendor is most definitely an option.

### Features

Finally, features are a huge reason why banks make a change. While there could be many reasons to move between platforms or between services, the first reason is usually going to be features. Features are important because they often represent the sizzle that customers are looking for in a product and can often be a reason for a customer to move from one financial institution to another. Most products are about 85 percent the same and 15 percent different. Take bill pay as an example. All bill-paying platforms have payees, payments, and recurring payments as feature table stakes. These features are 85 percent of the stock features that make up a good bill pay platform. They are all pretty much the same between all other providers of this service. However, when we look at the different players out there, each one of those players may have some unique features that may fit the culture of your banks customers or have a benefit to your geographic area or be appealing to a particular demographic that your organization serves. Perhaps, for example, you have a large military group that really values the ability to utilize remote bill pay. This ability is the 15 percent of features that is different between each vendor offering and is what usually drives organizations to move from one product to another.

In this story, the CRO's most compelling point was the lack of features in the BigTek bill pay platform. However it must be noted that BigTek has a big investment in the bill pay that the organization is using. They have spent money integrating into their home banking and mobile platform, as well as channels like voice and Alexa. (More on that later. Chat is the new browser!)

## How Solutions Can Fail

Now you're in the position to try to take the bill pay product from another company, we'll call them BankMax, and implement their bill pay product inside of BigTek's home banking and mobile platform. First, you have to ask yourself this question: What is in it for BigTek to allow BankMax's bill pay to function as well as their bill pay inside of their platform? Why would they allow a competitor to have as good or better implementation inside their platform? Yet, I know so many institutions that either have convinced themselves or been convinced by one or the other vendor, that, yes, they can integrate these two products seamlessly and successfully. The common dynamic is usually that the old vendor is hesitant about the change and whether or not it will be successful, and the new vendor is excited and confident that it can integrate their product successfully into other vendors' platform. When it comes down to it, you need BigTek's resources to fully implement and integrate BankMax's product, and it's not in BigTek's best interest to do a great job of implementing and integrating a competitor's product. What does that mean? It means you're now going to have to go and find someone or some entity to help you do integration. There are things that BankMax can't do because it needs access to the BigTek platform at a level that BigTek isn't willing to provide a competitor, and now your organization and ultimately your customers are caught in the middle.

What do you do? Well, the good news is that your CTO seems confident that he can solve this for the organization. In fact, the CTO knows a programmer from a previous job that he is confident can handle this integration. To be fair, the approach does seem to solve the problem. BigTek won't let BankMax fully integrate the product, but BigTek will allow your organization, as a customer (for a price, of course), to use its services to create your own integration. Begrudgingly, you (ACB CEO) approve a new full-time employee (FTE) and bring on a programmer that specializes in digital platform integration. That doesn't mean the organization didn't have programmers in the past. However, in the past, most financial institutions' programmers are programmers who have been dealing with balancing general ledgers or writing logic inside of spreadsheets or programming switches for debit/credit in the ISO 8583 standard. Most of the programmers we have in the financial services space are not disciplined digital platform integration programmers who are used to dealing with the rigors of creating or integrating online services. Integrating online services demands special skills with regard to digital security and platform ubiquity. What this ultimately means is that your organization wants its products and services to be secure and work on an IPhone as well as it works on an Android. This sort of work is not trivial—or cheap.

So, you bring this person in and he does a fantastic job of integrating the new bill pay. He still runs into roadblocks, but ultimately, the implementation turns out to be a success. Your team now gets the bill pay platform into production. Because it's the first implementation of this new platform, the new version just gets you back to parity. What I mean by parity is that you finally get BankMax's bill pay product implemented and all the organization has achieved is to have the exact same features as the previous bill pay platform from BigTek. As a result, the customers don't see any benefit from the upgrade but they have noticed the service degradation during the transition between the old and the new platform and complained in the iTunes and Google Play comments section. Since none of the new features the chief retail officer really wanted are in there, there isn't a perceivable business lift. On the bright side, the organization has been promised that, now that the hard part of integration is out of the way, the rest of the features for the new BankMax bill pay platform will be available to your customers in a matter of months.

Meanwhile back at the ranch, the organization's staff suddenly discovers this programmer is a powerful individual who is capable of many amazing miracles, and because he doesn't have the protection of a true digital governance policy, he is besieged by other departments that want similar miracles performed for their digital products and services—and of course, he can't keep up. Boom, all of the sudden, this person is fixing your internet and solving random problems all around the institution. With no digital governance in place to set his priorities and with no plan for long-term growth and sustainability in this newly established programming area, you have inadvertently unleashed a digital kraken into your world.

In the meantime, another vice president convinces the organization to implement yet another new product from a vendor that is also a competitor with your main provider BigTek.

*A quick note: I'm not saying it's bad to go away from the BigTek model. Nor am I saying it's bad to use the BigTek model. The lesson here is that it's bad to just dip your toe in the water of technology without fully understanding the scope of what you're getting into, as Ahead of the Curve Bank did with the integration programmer.*

This is the path to the *middle*. The organization purchases the second competitor's product and the miracle programmer implements yet another new platform into BigTek. The programmer now has two platforms to support. This is an important point, because your organization has implemented the integration for these two new platforms, so your organization is now responsible for the support of the integrations, and since this wasn't factored into the work plans of the programmer on staff, the programmer is now faced with making a choice of implementing the second platform or installing the new features for new bill pay integration that he was originally brought in to do. Worse yet, it's been nine months (amazing how fast time goes by in the digital world), and the organization still hasn't implemented the next update of BankMax's bill pay platform, and as a result, the chief retail officer is blaming your information services group for being unresponsive and your CIO is reminding you that the second platform update is what is causing the hold up.

It's at this point in the story that our hero (you, the CEO) usually throws up his hands and says something to the following effect:

*"I give up. I bet my mailman or my meter reader doesn't have these problems; no one calls him at 3 a.m. about a bill pay platform"* – Actual quote from a CEO

Welcome to the middle of the road. Your organization is not really a technology company because a technology company would have the following attributes:

- A true code review process, or at least a company to do this
- SDLC (System Development Life Cycle) Program
- Project managers who have experience with deploying and integrating digital software
- A team of programmers that would include architects, database developers, user experience specialist, and quality assurance engineers
- A platform to store and secure the code that is written by the programming team
- A system to track defects of the code that is written by the programmers
- A digital governance charter that outlines what the digital services are for the organization and captures and records technical debt
- A digital governance group that meets regularly to review the current digital offerings as it relates to the overall business strategy of the organization

When an organization chooses the technology company approach, it then focuses on best-of-breed platforms, top-of-line user experience, and omnichannel approaches. The technology company is NOT dependent on BigTek and has chosen to control its own digital destiny.

The organization is also not operating as a pure financial services company, either. The financial services organization wouldn't leave the BigTek model when faced with the bill pay platform decision. Instead, this organization would be focused on good pricing, sales, and service. In the organization's digital governance policy, there would be a provision that states that, as much as possible, all services and features will be provided by BigTek and its partners, and instead of buying a competitor's platform, the financial services organization would work hard to participate in the technology decision processes of BigTek by either serving on its advisory board or in some other capacity. These roles would allow the organization to influence the feature set of the platform so that the features that their customers want to have would be top of the list for the platform's next update. Failing that, the institution would partner with BigTek and pay it or an approved BigTek partner directly for the new features if necessary so as to guarantee ongoing support and growth in its platform of choice.

But when you live in the middle, you're neither. As a result, it makes it very difficult to proceed. You are trapped between two worlds. It's hard to spend the money necessary to create the technology company environment without a guaranteed return on investment and equally hard to be completely dependent on a partner for your digital services.

The one thing that I hope you walk away from this book understanding, and the most important thing to know in order to break digital gridlock, is that digital is not a product, it's a discipline. It doesn't matter which kind of financial company you want to be—in both cases, your digital services will require leadership and discipline if you are to succeed.

Let me explain what I mean. Every bank or credit union I work with has an accounting department. Now, if I watched enough educational YouTube videos on accounting and got good at QuickBooks, would you let me be your accountant? Probably not. Accountants bring knowledge and experience to the organization that is very important. The skills that accounting professionals provide to the organization go far beyond what any software can provide and are invaluable. The value of what they provide is so important to the everyday operation of the organization that they have their own department in almost every company, regardless of whether it's a financial company, a health care provider, or some other industry. In the end, it's not just about me knowing how to operate QuickBooks. It's about me understanding the rules and discipline behind accounting processes.

Sadly, most banks and credit unions have been buying a home banking or mobile platform and calling this their digital offering without regard to the discipline that it takes to create a good digital journey for your customers. Digital is not any single product or platform, it's a complex combination of platform integration, user experience, security, and stability. It takes discipline and experience to safely manage an environment that is as complex as even the most generic bank or credit union's home banking or mobile platform. This is not something to throw at your average IT department or put under your average CIO. I'm not even sure it's something you want to put under your CTO. Not to put the CIO or the CTO down, but they have other very important things to worry about, like your phones, your computers, your network, and your infrastructure.

Digital services need 24/7 focus, and not just of the technical kind; the discipline of digital includes reviewing how members are using services, reviewing security logs, and aligning the platform with the business plans of the institutions and constantly evolving your services and features. After all, most digital banking platforms serve many more members in a day than any one branch does in a week. Ultimately, the care and feeding for a digital platform is difficult and demands a myriad of skill. Digital is a unique and diverse collection of services with special needs, and it demands to be respected as a powerful entity within your organization.

So which type of organization are you? A technology company that provides financial services, or a financial services company that provides via technology? In the middle? Which one do you want to be? The key is to learn to adapt to the continuously changing digital environment and where to focus your finite and valuable resources.

Respecting your digital platform and understanding that it is a discipline are the first key adaptations you will need to make so that you can break the digital gridlock in your organization.

---

### Chapter Review

- Competition from big banks and new, digital upstarts will be one of the biggest strategic challenges in the financial industry.
- To stop strategic gridlock, an organization should ask the essential question: Are you a technology company that delivers financial services or a financial services company that delivers via technology?

*(continued)*

*(Continued)*

- Digital is not any single product or platform; it's a complex combination of platform integration, user experience, security, and stability. It takes discipline and experience to safely manage an environment that is as complex as even the most generic bank or credit union's home banking or mobile platform.

## NOTE

1. https://www.linkedin.com/pulse/death-4000-cuts-chat-brett-king -john-best.

CHAPTER

# 14

# Digital Governance

Let me start this section by saying I am not a big believer in creating governance for the sake of saying we have it. I believe one of the great enemies of an innovative and productive culture can be too much governance. That said, I do believe that the right amount of governance done for the right reasons can be very effective and improve every aspect of your organization.

To begin with, let's cover a couple of kinds of governance that people often quote in books like these. ITIL, which is an acronym for Information Technology Infrastructure Library, is a detailed set of regulations or guidances for services such as ACH or Billpay, which are referred to ITSM or Information Technology Services. These are designed to align these services with the business objectives. It's full of checklists, best practices, tasks, and procedures that are not organization specific. It has its roots in BS (British Standard) 150000. It was eventually replaced by ISO 20000, which is an update to the ITIL standard that was revised in 2011. It is a valuable tool for an organization, especially if you are exceedingly large, and by large I mean that your IT department is over 1000 people. If you are reading this and your organization is at this level, then this is a good standard for you to look at—and chances are, if you are that large you already have something like this in place. However, if you are an organization that is more medium sized, then trying to implement something like this is like using a sledgehammer to pound in a penny nail. There are great things in it, but it has a lot of bloat that is specifically in place to deal with large organizations. This is likely not their official position and I am not an ITIL-certified professional, but these are my thoughts after being asked to consider several different ways to implement governance in medium-sized financial institutions. So bottom line, ITIL is great, and parts of it are very useful.

The second one that I am often asked about is called COBIT (Control Objectives for Information and Related Technologies). COBIT was created by ISACA (Information Systems Audit and Control Association), and like ITIL is a practical collection of procedures, tasks, checklists, and other processes that are designed to ensure best practices in IT (think security or storing data properly), formally document business requirements, and map them to procedures and processes, measure performance, and document how all systems interact. In my experience, this framework also provided good tools and things we could use to improve organizations. I still feel that implementing this in a small organization would also be overkill, but there are elements of it that could really help an organization in a growth stage.

The final approach I have considered is the plan, build, and operate framework. McKinsey (www.mckinsey.com) envisioned the plan, build, and run, and groups I have worked with in the past have enhanced this framework by adding security as a fourth major tenet of the approach. Traditional tower-based or segmented approaches to governing organizational infrastructure and services have reached their limits, and in the increasingly digital future, it is necessary to have an agile approach to governance.

So what to do? Let's start by taking a quick quiz to determine what you have in place already:

1. We have a group of people who meet regularly to discuss digital services that is made up of middle management and key system experts. (YES/NO)
2. We have a services catalog that I can refer to that helps me to determine how systems interact with each other and who to call in the event of a problem. (YES/NO)
3. When we have a new project, it is a reviewed by the group mentioned in question number 1. (YES/NO)
4. We have regular audits of digital services. (YES/NO)
5. We have regular stand-up meetings to review upcoming digital services and offerings. (YES/NO)

Chances are, you were able to answer "YES" to many of these things, but in the back of your mind you were thinking, "well, we meet on these things, but it's not formally organized, or it's not regularly." In any case, almost every organization could use some help in these areas. If you have a group that is meeting, but you haven't formalized its charter, then now is the time. Another one of my beliefs is that names are important. When I am brainstorming an idea with my team, I like to name it very early, even if the name we come up with isn't the eventual name of the product, group, or service. It's good to label it early on so that people can easily identify the concept during conversations.

The same is true of governance groups—labeling your groups helps teams to understand their purpose and communicates to others the objectives of the group. The digital governance group is just that—a group that is responsible for governing the digital services that your organization provides to its consumers and its staff. Your CDO or closest facsimile should be the chair of this group. The group should have a core and include leadership from each of the major divisions, but also should be flexible to expand to others when necessary and shrink when necessary. The priority of the group is to document your organization's services and create a services catalog.

What I am about to take you through is what I usually recommend to organizations just starting to implement governance in their organization. It creates natural processes and encourages open and candid communications regarding digital services within the organization. It represents the parts of ITIL, COBITS, and McKinsey "plan, build, operate" paradigms that I believe are valuable, but it excludes some of the more tedious processes that tend to slow down organizations and are perceived by the staff as pointless red tape. This approach should be considered a starting point for governance, and as the organization matures, these processes should be evaluated and reviewed, and organizations can adopt more of the guidelines and practices outlined in the methodologies described above as necessary.

A services catalog is a common element among these approaches and an important tool for the organization that wishes to transition to digital services. The services catalog is a list of services that the organization provides to either customers or staff. The list includes who in the organization is ultimately responsible for the service, exactly what the service does, the service level agreements, service dependencies, emergency contacts, service escalation points, and much more. On the website you will find a sample services catalog. Have you ever been using your home banking or mobile application and discovered something wasn't working—for instance, bill payment? So you call your CTO and he checks it out from his side and says, "Well, it appears to be working for me" (this is what I call the *mechanic effect*—the car won't make the funny noise in the presence of the mechanic), after a bit you discover that it only doesn't work in the mobile application, and after a few hours of research, it is determined that there is a dependency within mobile that allows bill pay to work that isn't present in the home banking (or web) platform.

Having a services catalog would expedite finding these problems by providing a list of dependencies for anyone to check and determine the problem, or possibly this service would've been identified by the digital governance committee as critical and as a result it would be monitored or even duplicated in an effort to build resilience into the infrastructure. Unfortunately, this scenario is very common in the world of financial institutions. It is a reactive approach to redundancy, only adjusting for adversity in the face of a problem as opposed to planning for failures and building redundancies ahead of time. In the postmortem, you discover that the bill-paying platform is full of redundancies but this single point of failure wasn't identified, as it was part of the mobile application and wasn't considered in the design phase because mobile was added after home banking. This is exactly what a digital governance committee or group would be tasked with resolving. The governance committee would've been involved in the mobile implementation, and during the project the services catalog would've been updated and it would have included the dependencies of the services and services and features that were aggregated through this channel.

The digital governance group ideally should meet once a month, but also should be flexible and meet when necessary during important stages of projects or in an emergency situation (like a security breach or outage). The responsibilities of the digital governance committee are discussed in the following section.

## Review Proposed Products and Integration

Any product or feature that is being proposed for the organization needs to be vetted by this group. The group should look at whether the product or feature can be integrated, what it will take to support it, and what is the top-line revenue. Does it need to be reviewed by the data governance group? What are the SLAs? What is the risk if the product is breached or it is out of service for a significant amount of time?

### Change Control

Change control should be reviewed in the monthly meeting by the team. The team should review changes and make sure that all protocols are followed, including rollback plans. Changes and change approvals should be recorded so that if a change has a systemic effect, the logs will show when the problem started. An example might be a change that is made to the login process on the mobile application. After this the team might see that the failed logins have been rising, upon further examination the failed logins started to rise after the date of the login process change. When this is discovered the committee may insist that the change be rolled back by following the procedures set forth in the rollback plan for the change. High-risk changes should be identified and the committee should question all facets of the systems involved, including whether backups are working, whether or not a penetration test has been performed, and when necessary the committee can recommend stress testing.

### Review Security

Results of all security tests should be reviewed by the committee to determine if the tests are still effective and whether or not the testing procedures need to be changed. Digital security is the most important aspect of a digital transformation. It is where the trust between your organization and the consumer lies, and this relationship must be treated with the utmost care. A single breach or a public incident can erode the trust of even the organization's most ardent supporters. I have always followed a philosophy that you can never have enough security. In that regard, I have always advocated for exceeding any security regulations rather than just meeting them. This will be discussed in more detail in the security sections in chapter 7 and 8.

### Accountability

The committee will share accountability with the service owners, which is an important aspect of the committee. Often in organizations where accountability for digital systems is centralized to IT, other departments tend to turn their back or place blame when systems fail or a system update causes errors. Since the committee is made up of leadership across the organization, there is no excuse for a lack of communication regarding digital services. This is why it is so important to have diversity on the digital governance committee.

### Business Continuity

As financial institutions become increasingly dependent on digital services, it is vitally important that all systems in the portfolio have a business continuity plan and that these plans are regularly tested. I often find that organizations are behind on their business continuity testing or their testing doesn't include newer systems that have become critical components in the organization's infrastructure. My favorite example of a business continuity system that doesn't get tested enough is backups. In Ed Catmull's book *Creativity Inc.*, he tells the story of how someone accidentally erased the entire file system for *Toy Story 2*. The person was upset but knew that they regularly backed up these files, so they resigned themselves to reloading the backups. Sadly, they learned that the backups had stopped working more than a year before. This loss would've put the movie two years behind schedule. The movie was saved by the fact that someone had copied the entire movie to his local system to work from home. In the financial world, a local copy of a database or file system on an employee's laptop would be expressly prohibited.

I believe in backup fire drills. It's a good idea to have a schedule of backups to be restored. This way every backup is tested within six-month intervals. This should also include failover systems, if you have an active/backup system then I would recommend failing over to the backup system and running on it for a period of time, then failing back. Another aspect of the team is to make sure you can go back to normal operations once the systems are restored. At one of my jobs we offered BCP services within our data center. One of our clients declared a disaster and failed over to the systems they housed at our shop. During this time our operations people took over the job of caring for the system and running the nightly financial processes. A few weeks went by, and I asked our data center manager if they had restored their systems (as it turned out the disaster was declared due to bad memory in their mainframe) and he responded they are still trying to figure out how to fail back to their normal operations. It is a mistake to think that IT can handle this all by themselves, BCP is the responsibility of the entire organization and the Digital Governance committee is great place for the team to come together and acknowledge these responsibilities as a group.

### Schedule Approval

From time to time, there will be collisions in the organization between two scheduled tasks. Perhaps there is a need to perform an upgrade on the ATM fleet, and the vendor has given a deadline to do this on a certain date, but that date is also being used to update another system. It is always best practice to avoid two major changes or updates on the same date. The committee should vet these changes ahead of time and make a decision based on the risk, cost, and urgency of the updates.

### Build versus Buy

Building software internally versus buying it from a vendor is undoubtedly one of the most important decisions that the committee will make. The committee should also be intimately involved with the development group. Many times, a group will decide that they need to work with IT to build a product or service to satisfy a need within the organization. Building software needs to be carefully considered, especially if the organization hasn't ever built software before. I have seen many organizations build a great service or product without considering the long-term care and feeding of the product, and as a result, over time the product or service isn't viewed as a valuable. If the care and feeding of the product had been considered in the planning stages of the product this degradation could've been avoided, or perhaps due to the cost of care and feeding, the organization may have chosen to buy a product rather than build it. It is also important to distinguish between building and integrating. Integration is far different than building an entire product. For instance, let's say the team has decided on a new feature or service, and this service needs to be installed throughout the organization. The service needs to be delivered via the branch, home banking, and mobile. The team may decide that integrating this service into the delivery channels by using internal resources is the best path. Even integrations need to have an evaluation done on the long-term care and feeding of the integration. If the home banking provider or the mobile provider makes changes, then there is a high likelihood that the integration will need to be tested after to make sure that the changes haven't broken any part of the integration. Here is an interesting build example from my past. At one of my jobs, we had an issue with address synchronization. When a customer would call in and change an address, the customer service representatives of the organization had to update the address in three different systems. This problem was brought to the committee and a search was started to find a solution to update addresses across several systems. One of the requirements was to use the NCOA (national change of address) service to check the addresses before updating the systems. After an exhaustive search, no product that fit the specific requirements of the organization could be found. It was decided that a solution would be built in-house. A simple website was built that the entire organization could use to update addresses. The addresses would be checked in real time against the NCOA service and then the website would update all of the necessary systems in real time. Over the years, the software had to be updated, more features were added, and as far as I know, to this day it is still in use. The factors that lead to the build decision were that the system would bring a lot of value to the organization by reducing errors and speeding up a process that was taking over five minutes per request, that there wasn't something on the market that would satisfy the requirements of the organization, and finally, that the scope of the build was within the organization's capabilities.

### Final Approval on Recommended Vendors

When the decision has been made to implement a new feature or service and a new vendor or system will be implemented as a result, the committee must have final say on the vendors. This is extremely important because only the committee can properly weigh technology versus features in a platform. Time and time again I have reviewed institutions where a service or feature is not present in their digital offerings because of a decision to purchase a product with a limited ability to be integrated. When the decision is left to departments or groups that are not thinking of the solution from a digital perspective, they will often choose a solution for features over the ability to be integrated. Older systems tend to have more features because of their maturity; however, it is often very hard for these systems to be retrofitted with the latest technology that allows for integration into newer systems such as mobile platforms.

If this process is run through the committee, then there is a chance for each of these aspects to be reviewed, and a balance can be struck with regards to features versus ability to integrate the service into the organization's digital ecosystem. This is also a chance to make sure that the service's underlying platforms fit in with the rest of the organization's infrastructure. For instance, if your internal expertise is in Microsoft software and the preferred service runs on a Linux platform, then a decision must be made whether to acquire the appropriate resources to support the service, which would mean additional cost or keep searching for a service that runs on the organization's preferred platform to take advantage of the in-house expertise. No matter how good the system is, if it can't be maintained properly, then it will ultimately be a failure in the eyes of the end users.

As you can see, this group is very important and provides a valuable service in the form of check and balances for an organization going through digital transformation. The group should not be determining business strategy, but rather, enforcing it by aligning the digital services and processes with the strategies of the organization.

## Data Governance

In the evolving digital world, an organization's ability to transform data into information will be the difference between surviving and disappearing. So if data is money, then it too must be governed and curated. Although this might seem like something the digital governance committee would handle, it's a completely different discipline that involves understanding regulatory and privacy laws around data and should be given its own group.

Here is why you need a data governance committee. Imagine that one day your team purchases a new service that is using social media to help determine creditworthiness. The team does the right thing and puts the system through the newly created digital governance committee and follows the process. However, during the discovery process it is missed that the system is capturing and storing social security numbers—more importantly, these numbers are being stored in clear text. As luck would have it, this system is compromised by hackers, and as a result, your customer's social security numbers are now being sold on the dark web. Customers notice a trend and the breach is tracked back to your organization. This creates a reputation issue that cannot be easily resolved.

Another example would be if a new system had data that was duplicated in other systems, or conflicted with your system of record. *The system of record is the authority or source of truth in your data ecosystem*—in other words, if you had a conflict between two pieces of data, the system of record would be the one you trust. It ties all the other systems in your ecosystem together (see the center of the mind map illustration below). Having data duplicated on external systems is costly and inefficient; it also can lead to errors in processing. The data governance group is responsible for identifying, classifying, and organizing data within your organization. The data governance group will determine if data are duplicative or must be treated specially, such as personal data. This group will also be responsible for determining data quality. As each new system is implemented in the organization, more and more data are being introduced, and if there isn't governance to make sure the new data sources are accounted for then your organization could wind up playing cleanup for years or, even worse, leaking data without even knowing it.

The data governance group should be chaired by your CAO (chief analytics officer) or a reasonable facsimile. The group should include subject matter experts from each department. It is important that group is made up of people who can work together to make decisions and have the expertise to identify the data in your organization and what that information means to other processes. In every department, there is a "go-to person" for reports—you know the one: she or he is frequently mentioned in meetings when someone on the team asks for data. These are the people that you want on your data governance committee.

For instance, let's say your group implements a new lending system and as a result, several reports need to be changed because the current source that the data is drawn from will be going away. It might seem like a simple solution, just retool the report to get the data from the new source, but this would only work if the data between the two systems exactly match. What if the new system has new features that split up payments or allow partial payments? Then the due date or the balance could be affected. This would mean that the reports would have to be retooled to support the data. However, without oversight from a group like the data governance committee, these issues could easily be overlooked, and either the reports would be wrong until someone noticed or the problem would surface during the project, and since it was unaccounted for in the project plan, it could increase the cost or extend the project timelines. There are many nuances to data governance, and it is a necessary ongoing process for your organization.

As we move into a future that will include artificial intelligence and business intelligence, data will be the fuel that drives these important services. A data governance committee should start with finding all the organization's data and reviewing it. This may take some time, and it may be worthwhile to hire an organization who specializes in mapping data. The initial data map will become the baseline for your organization. This map will be invaluable to your organization going forward. The second step for the committee is to review the security of the data discovered during phase I. Do all the data storage and transmission paradigms meet compliance regulatory standards? If not, what is the plan to get the data in to compliance? At the same time, the committee will be developing policies and standards to be applied to any new product or services and added to the master data dictionary. As mentioned above, this will reduce future problems and make implementations go smoother.

Figure 14.1 describes the continuous cycle that the data governance group will engage in. Because of the amount of data that we are continually collecting, this cycle will be important to your future. The data mapping cycle is the process of understanding the location of data in your organization, and what its relationship is to the rest of the data ecosystem. It will involve creating a document that is like the services catalog. Each data element is cataloged, with its attributes noted. Table 14.1 represents the most common data elements that are captured during the data mapping phase.

In Figure 14.2 one could drill down into each of the systems and see the data associated with them. The data then could be tracked back to processes, services, features, and projects within the organization. As you might imagine, having such a tool will be invaluable in the future.

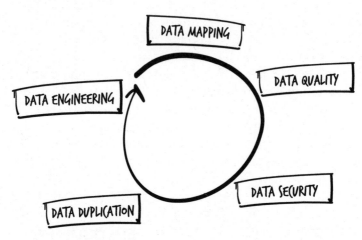

Figure 14.1    Data governance cycle

Table 14.1    Data-mapping key concepts

| Attribute | Definition |
|---|---|
| Data type | Is the information a number, string, or computation? |
| Data permanence | Will data be provided in real time or be updated by another system using an offline process? |
| Data retention | How long should the data be kept before being destroyed or moved to an offline archive? |
| Data security | Should the data be encrypted, and if so, what regulations, such as PCI or Sarbanes–Oxley, apply to the data? |
| Data controls | Who has the authority to look at the data? |
| Data management | Who is accountable for the data? |
| Metadata | Will other data be used to describe or derive the data? |
| Data relationships | Are the data elements duplicated or mapped to elsewhere in the system? |

### Data Quality

Data quality is the process of evaluating each data element to determine whether it is viable for reports and analytical functions. Data points are checked against norms within the industry to see if any fall out of bounds. For example, how many times have you eyeballed a spreadsheet or report and saw something that seemed off? The number was too large, or too small. Usually, a report error like the one mentioned above is related to a data quality issue. The data that the report was derived from was flawed in some way. Testing data against norms is a valuable process to determining if you have processing issues or other errors causing inconsistences in your organization.

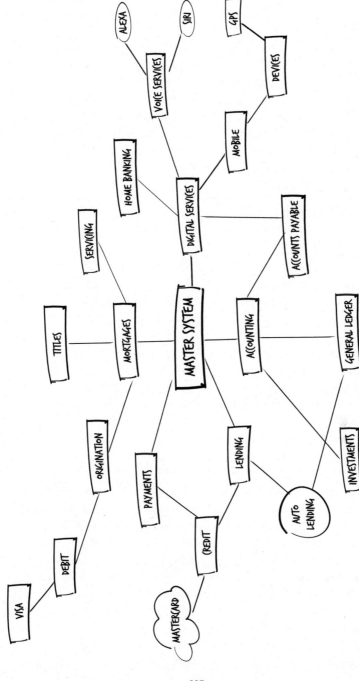

**Figure 14.2  Basic data map: High-level overview**

237

### Data Security

Data security is the act of evaluating data against the organization's policies and procedures as well as regulatory policies to determine if the data is being appropriately stored, handled, and transmitted. This is critical in a world where there are new breaches and cyber threats every day. Usually, the hacker will obtain access to a database by elevating the privileges of a hacked user or exploiting a known flaw in the software that allows them to get the database but if the data are encrypted, this makes their job that much harder, because now they must decrypt the data before they can use it. Encryption is going to be one of the most important services in your organization soon.

### Data Duplication

Data is often duplicated in systems, usually for the purposes of convenience. For instance, it is easier to copy the credit score data into a field on the central system so that the customer service representatives have access to it, rather than build a interface into your lending platform. This convenience can often cause problems in an organization. While the purpose of the duplicated data was to give customer service representatives the ability to share the score with the customers, sometimes a new process might find the data and use it for something else. This is bad approach if you are not aware of the source of the data.

In this scenario, let's say the lending system credit score data gets updated once a week but the scores on the central system are only updated once a month. There is a chance that the data that the new process is using will be stale. Instead the process should use the data from the lending platform to make sure it has the most current data. Therefore, it is important to understand and document duplicated data elements in the system. Another common scenario is that a new system or process has a placeholder for data also stored on the central system and again, rather than create a costly integration (usually because without a data governance group in place, these issues are identified after the fact and the cost of this process was not considered in the budgeting phase) someone will come up with the clever idea of writing a job to update these fields from the central system. Again, this can be a ticking time bomb. It is important that the end users of this data understand where the source is and what the update frequencies are.

### Data Engineering

Data engineering is the act of determining the attributes of the processes to either extract, update, delete, or archive the data throughout the ecosystem. How often should data be updated, are there circumstances when the data should be purged? Is data transient? Should data be cleared on a regular basis? If the data will be encrypted, how are the keys stored, and how strong should the encryption be? You might think that's a stupid question—why not just use the strongest encryption always? But if you took that approach, you could slow down your entire platform or worse yet, bloat your processing and power bills because the high-level encryption causes extra CPU and power consumption. These are all factors to be considered when working through data engineering; this is especially important when introducing a new product, feature, service, or project that will bring foreign data elements into play.

Once data mapping is complete, the data policies are in place, and remediations are in progress for current data issues, it's time for the real magic to happen. While all this activity is valuable on its own, the real value is when you begin to put your data to work. Now you can start to shift your organization toward a data-driven results paradigm. Any new project, any new service, or undertaking can benefit from using your CAO to validate the assumptions associated with each undertaking. For instance, when we market without data-driven decisions, we make assumptions based on our intuitions about the community or segments of the population we serve.

Good marketers are reasonably successful at making these assumptions, but what if you could make your marketing plan 50 percent better by using your data? Consider recent Finnovate winners AlphaRank (www.alpharank.com). AlphaRank provides a service that allows you to identify the influencers in your population of customers, and it has been proven that marketing these influencers directly will dramatically increase adoption of any product or service. As expected, before you can engage a company like AlphaRank, you must be able to collect your data, anonymize it, and send it to their team in a safe manner. If you have ever been involved in an effort like this, you know what a trial it can often be to get the necessary data from your organization. It often requires a cross section of the entire organization and a full-on project plan. This process is often costly and time consuming. Another byproduct of data governance is that it will become much easier to identify the success metrics for each product, project, or service that your organization engages in, and by monitoring these metrics the organization can determine when to give up or when to dig in, or perhaps how to pivot to create success. Data is fuel that will drive your organization forward.

Data also drives innovation. I will cover this further in the innovation chapter but data is the most important ingredient to drive innovation within your organization. Innovation by its very nature is risky, but no one knows how risky. Data can help you drive your innovation by helping to validate your assumptions.

When I was starting BIG in 2014, I had an idea for a product. I was in a big meeting at a credit union in one of my first speaking gigs. It was a meeting with all the management staff of the organization, and they were all sitting around big round tables listening to me talk. I was talking about mobile wallets and it occurred to me I could do a quick straw poll with the audience I had to validate something that had been on my mind. My idea was that non-name-brand banks and financial institutions didn't have a huge penetration into the emerging digital lifestyle applications like Netflix, Hulu, Amazon, and iTunes. So, I asked the group a quick question. I asked everyone who had a Netflix account to raise their hands. I wasn't sure what to expect. My gut told me that this should be a large number but I wasn't expecting the reality, as almost the entire room raised their hands. I quickly said "Put your hands down," and then I said the following: "Please raise your hand if you have THIS financial institution's (the one you work at) debit or credit card in your Netflix account to pay for the service." Again, I wasn't sure what to expect, I had a theory, but it had all come down to this moment. Less than five hands went up in response to my query. I was blown away. These were managers of this financial organization and if they didn't have their workplace's tender in these accounts, how could they expect the customers to do the same? I repeated the process for iTunes, Amazon, and Hulu with the same results. After this, I worked with 10 medium-sized financial institutions to run reports to see if my straw poll could be validated with larger numbers.

This process wasn't easy for a lot of the institutions I worked with. Creating these reports proved to be difficult, which is why I am recommending that all organizations start a data governance committee as soon as possible. In this instance, I had an idea for an innovation that would increase penetration into these accounts that became SetitCredit.com, but before I embarked on this journey, I validated all my assumptions with real data. This is how data can support innovation in your organization.

---

**Summary Points**

- Data = money.
- If you don't have a data governance committee, get one started today.
- Mapping your data is the first and most important step.
- Data can be used to validate your assumptions for new services, products, and projects, but you only trust it if you have your data clean and organized.
- Many future services will depend on your ability to send and receive data in a rapid and efficient manner.
- Data will drive innovation BECAUSE having good data enables you to measure risk.

---

CHAPTER

# 15

# Using Data Analytics

I am sorry sir your card declined. Do you have another way to pay?

So now that we understand what data analytics is and why it's important and what we need to survive, let's talk about some simple use cases to get you started.

Before we go there, I think it's important to understand "the why" of our members. Not too long ago, I was watching a TED Talk by

Simon Sinek. He was talking about understanding the why of what you do and he describes a golden circle. In the center of the circle is the word "why." The next ring of the circle has "how." And the final ring says "what." Sinek talks about how most people communicate from the outside in. They'll start with the what, tell you the how, and then get to the more fuzzy why. Then, he gave an example of what would happen if Apple were to communicate this way. Apple would start with the what: "We sell great computers." Then, they'd move onto the how: "We use only the best parts and are really careful to make them user friendly so people want to buy them." But the why is where things get murky in this process.

Sinek says he's noticed that really effective communicators and really effective companies start with the *why* and work from there to the what. In the case of Apple, the why would be: "We think differently at Apple." Then, the how would be tied to *how* they think differently. Perhaps the response would be: "We challenge the status quo. We use only the best parts. We have the idea that our software has to be intricately connected to our hardware." And the what is: "We make people want to buy a computer." As you can see, inverting the circle changes the whole conversation. That makes me think what our members and customers get out of bed in the morning. There are a few things that you can do to focus on the why—and they all come down to analytics.

## Look Ahead

In 2008, the world crumbled around the financial institution I was working for. It was a horrible time. We lost lots of money and we began to realize that our collections department was going to have to grow. Our leadership at the time, who was absolutely brilliant, had the foresight to go out and bring in 80 collectors, increasing the collector staff about 16 times. As you might imagine, this was a shock to the system.

In 2008, the mortgage bubble finally popped when people discovered that homes weren't worth whatever they had paid for them at the market peak. There was moral corruption in the system, people were packaging bad loans with good loans and selling them out, and everything finally burst. People were losing their homes and their jobs.

Well, one of the things that we were trying to understand at the time was how to get ahead of people who were losing their loans or were not paying their loans. How do we determine that someone is in a bad financial position before it happens? And finally, one day, I came up with a simple solution.

Most people prefer to use direct deposit for their paychecks. I don't know about you, but I haven't cashed a check at a bank in a long, long, long time. So when that direct deposit comes in, it's usually going to be deposited into the place where a person also has loans, because then it's easier to make those payments.

In 2008, direct deposit rates started to drop, and I began to wonder why. I thought, "If someone's direct deposit stops, it's likely, in this particular environment, that they have lost their job." There are other reasons, but this is a good one for us to start with. This is important information for the bank to have. It is one of the indicators that I added to our list of data analytics to be able to identify and help customers who need it. And if you think about it, it's a great opportunity to make a phone call.

Imagine how that call would go. Bear in mind that there are other reasons direct deposit might stop, so it's important to approach this tactfully and respectfully. At the bank I worked at, employees said something like this: "Hello, Mr. or Mrs. Consumer, I noticed that we're no longer receiving your direct deposit and we were concerned that either there was an error or perhaps that you have found another financial institution, and we wanted to see if there was anything we could make things right." If this person has lost his or her job, you'll probably get a vague response, something like, "Well, I'm no longer with that job." It's possible that the person might be getting a new job, in which case you have the opportunity to solicit their direct deposit so you could make it easy for them, send them a direct deposit form, or send it directly to their employer.

It could also be that this person has lost a job and doesn't have a plan for a new job yet. You might look at the loans and say, "You know, we have a program called Skip a Payment that allows you to skip a loan payment. We will reorganize the loan or we'll recalculate it, reset the rate, and give you some time so you can get through this." When a bank calls in the midst of a stressful time and says, "I'm here to help you," customers will remember it for the rest of their lives.

We've covered two reasons why customers might stop direct deposit: (1) a job loss, or (2) a job change. There are other reasons, such as that they are moving to a different bank. That could be a sign that they will be moving other accounts as well. That's also worth a phone call, because it's worth understanding why they're leaving and maybe even recovering the business. If a bank doesn't recognize this trend and act on it, the customers will be proven right.

Here's a fourth one, one that's not commonly considered. What if a horrible tragedy has occurred and the customer is deceased? That's also worth a call, to help the surviving family get the finances in order.

Finally, the fifth reason why a direct deposit might stop: human or technical error. What if the person at payroll at the customer's job forgot to process the payment? What if something went wrong with an employer's payroll processing system? What if the incorrect hours were logged? What if there was an error at the bank that prevented the account from being credited? It would be fantastic to get a call from the financial institution that said, "I notice your direct deposit didn't hit this month or this week and it usually does." And when an organization does, it can help its clients.

No matter the reason, if a direct deposit stops, it's worth a call to the customer. This is such a simple thing to track. It's easy predictive analytics because the outcomes are so easy to understand. I can predict that if someone's direct deposit stops, one of these five things has probably happened.

To do this, someone working on strategy and data analytics has to say, "Hey, I need to identify all the direct deposit accounts," and then the bank begins to track them. The names that are identified should go on an outbound list for your call center along with an outline of how to approach the conversation. This little thing could be the difference between maintaining a loyal customer and losing a loyal customer. So there's one simple thing that banks can implement—when they know the why.

## Credit Card Usage

Credit card usage by vendor can also be incredibly useful for actionable data analysis. I'm fond of asking banking and credit union CEOs, "If I were using your financial institution's credit card or debit card to buy all of my airline tickets, and all of a sudden I stopped, would anyone from your institution call me?" The answer is almost always no. No one would call; no one would even notice. This sort of income, which we call *interchange*, is very valuable to financial institutions. This is just one piece of data that is tied to a larger data-analysis strategy that tracks customer trends and behavior. When steady customer behavior falls off, banks have an opportunity to find out why and make some changes.

Tracking travel is very easy because the consumers actually tell their banks when they're going places because they want their credit cards to work at their destination. When they're leaving the country or traveling out of state, they tend to let financial institutions know because our neural networking, otherwise known as artificial intelligence fraud algorithms, will prevent their credit cards from working if they are doing something that is out of the normal behavior of them, which would include traveling to a foreign country. Why wouldn't FIs also track what customers use their cards for when they travel and encourage them to use their bank cards? Provide them with personalized rewards.

This is another simple use of analytics. But more importantly, it is a chance to pick up the phone and talk to this person. I'm betting that, more often than not, banks would hear that this particular consumer has decided to use an airline credit card or some other rewards-based card that gives them a perceived value that, in their mind, is better than the FI card they were previously using. However, usually these cards come with fees and a higher interest rate. If you were to just do the math and say, "That's great that you've got a new card that gives you two free bags and extra miles. But the $400 a year fee combined with the higher interest rate, will cost you more than our card, which has a 10 percent interest rate. With the money you save, you could buy another three plane tickets." Unfortunately, most banks don't have a way tell these stories—and as a result, they let the business escape. Data analytics lets banks identify these customers and keep their business.

General tracking of credit card usage by vendor can also be useful. It can help a bank pinpoint vendors that everyone in an organization or demographic relies on. For example, Amazon, iTunes, and Netflix are hugely popular retail and services sites that are pervasive in almost every demographic. It doesn't take heavy-duty data analysis to identify these organizations and determine the penetration by measuring how many of your FI's cards are being used by these retailers. The next time you are at one of those big meetings where all the managers are sitting around circular tables, stand up and ask everyone in the room who has an Amazon account to raise their hands.

Based on my experience, that at least 90 percent of the room will raise their hands. Then ask them to raise their hands again if they have a credit card or debit card from the institution that employs them in the Amazon account as a form of payment. Unless you work at one of the major players (e.g., Chase, Citibank, Capital One, Bank of America), it's likely that only a small percentage of your own staff are using your credit cards in these digital providers. The question to ask is, "Why?" Are they motivated by rewards points? Are they motivated by security? Are they reacting out of habit because they started using this card for online purchases a long time ago and now it's just muscle memory? If so, we have to understand the why to break the habit or find the right motivation. It's always important to track down the why.

Recently, my team and I were working on statistical analysis of purchases from a credit union, when we discovered a cache of $40 transactions from Netflix. These transactions fell out of our analysis as outliers. After all, how would one even incur a $40 charge from Netflix? The usual charge is around $12. I could understand one or two such charges out of a few thousand transactions, but this file had hundreds.

After reviewing the file with the credit union, we determined that it was fraud. I started to wonder what other outlier transactions from subscription services we could find by using a simple routine to track charges that should be consistent. My list included Spotify, Apple Music, Hulu, DirectTV, and many others. Tracking and understanding outliers will be a new feature for financial institutions in the future. In the same way that neural networking is used to stop credit fraud by watching for transactions that don't match your patterns, new techniques using the same technology will be used to determine if customers are at risk of defaulting on a loan or are currently involved in a crime, or are in the midst of a divorce. The outlier approach is another simple win that could be implemented at any financial institution to reduce fraud and provide a service to their customers.

## Usage Monitoring

Not long ago, I enrolled for an account on a website of a web-based productivity tool. Let's call it Happy Go Lucky. I was visiting the site pretty regularly for a while, and then one day I finished the project and didn't really have a need to continue to go there anymore. About a month went by, and I got an email from Happy Go Lucky, and it said, "Dear John, we miss you. When are you coming back?" And I thought, "Aw, they miss me." Then I realized that the folks who run this website have realized that my usage had dropped off.

I frequently asked CEOs and CTOs if they monitor usage of the digital channels, and if someone stops using it, whether they contact their customers to determine why they stopped using the site. The message shouldn't be cheesy or out of sync with your bank's messaging, but it should encourage them to come back or, more importantly, to try to find out the why of why they stopped visiting. After all, if we can't figure that out, then we're in bigger trouble than we thought.

These are great use cases for analytics. Don't be intimidated; data analytics can be an easy way for you to start looking at your data and maybe even seeing some direct outcomes from putting these easy use cases into use. People don't realize how simple it is to make a phone call to just ask a question to understand the behavior of other people.

The key to understanding why is to be willing to challenge the conventional wisdom of the industry and your organization. There are so many common tropes in the financial industry, but data analytics can let you know how many of these are true. Think of these assumptions:

- Billpay is a sticky feature.
- Digital customers are cheaper than branch customers.
- Mobile members are made up of mostly millennials.
- Only 25 percent of your consumers use a branch.
- Customers that have more than two products are a better credit risk.

Each of these cases involves understanding a customer's *why*. *Why* is billpay a sticky feature? Is it because customers have a difficult time getting the data back out once they spend time setting up their payees? This reason is actually a risk because it is only a matter of time before someone (a browser plugin, maybe) devises a way to automatically populate payee information. Understanding the why would allow a financial institution to pivot to a more beneficial scenario for the customer, such as implementing a rewards system for using the service or allowing customers to export and import their payees as contacts similar to a mail client like Outlook or Gmail.

## Digital "Why" 101

Here are some common things I look for when examining an organizations digital data:

- More than 15 percent of the population of digital users being subjected to multifactor authentication. If more than 15 percent of your customer base must answer additional questions to access digital services, one of two things is wrong.
  - Your multifactor authentication is not working correctly. Here is a good example: I often access sites that have a click box on that says, "Don't ask me for the code again for 30 days when I use this computer." I click the box, and yet these sites still ask me for the code on the next time I log in. Since I have a background in coding online services, I know I am not clearing my cookies, changing my IP, or any other part of my digital footprint that would break the way a click box like that works. On many sites it simply doesn't work, and this is very frustrating for customers. It is important that the security for your site works as advertised, because if it doesn't, customers will lose trust in the services behind the login.
  - There is a possibility you are under attack. There is a chance that your organization is being slowly trolled by cybercriminals testing the limits of your security services. These are usually easy to spot in the data. However, without a trend to follow, its hard to spot these sorts of things in the sea of data that a typical digital service provides.
- Less than a third of digital base is using mobile. If your digital mobile users are under a third of your total digital membership (the digital membership consists of customers that have actively used your digital services in the last three months),

then something is wrong with your mobile application. Here are some common things I find:

- o Customers cannot log in. Many organizations gave up access to their credentials to their home banking provider, and as a result had to create new credentials for the mobile application. This is unacceptable to customers in 2017, and many will not try very hard to get into your mobile application.

- o Your mobile application is missing a critical feature that customers expect. For example you cannot pay a mortgage, or see your commercial accounts. Credit card accounts are not visible or you cannot pay an auto loan on the mobile application. A lack of utility in the mobile application can spell certain death for the mobile platform in the organization as it is hard to recover from a perceived lack of services.

- o You have horrible reviews on iTunes and in Google play. I have seen this many times. Organizations don't monitor their reviews in these services and as a result they have a horrible reputation. Customers do look at the feedback from others, they decide if the application is worth loading based on the amount and quality of the feedback. Many organizations are reputationally damaged by one bad version of the mobile application in the application stores and never recover. The key to recovering is to work with your customers to have them review the applications. Honest reviews are important. I am not saying to "buy" or "encourage" good reviews, but try to get your customers to tell you how they feel about the application. When you discover there is bad feedback address it immediately.

- Online ACH debits are more than twice as large as the ACH credits. This is definitely a sign of fraud and should be looked into immediately. Any form of transfer that allows funds to be moved out of the accounts should be reviewed regularly.

- o On more than a few occasions I have discovered ACH fraud that goes back months. This is because the criminals have targeted the accounts of the elderly who perhaps are not watching their money as closely as others or lack the technical capability to set up alerts or check online. The fraudsters often socially engineer their way into these accounts, and as a result, they are able to sneak money out of accounts and into ACH mule accounts without garnering any attention from organizations security systems.

- Digital active users are less than a third of the total customers. This is a big red flag because it either means that age demographic of the customer is so high that digital services are not enticing to them or that the digital services are subpar and as a result aren't being used. Worse yet, the digital services are fine but not being marketed correctly.

So these are simple why tools and criteria that you can implement at your financial institution. One, track your direct deposit. If it stops, find out why. Two, track people's usages of your credit cards in major vendor sites like Netflix, Amazon, and airline sites. Watch for trends and watch for drop-offs. If it stops for some reason, contact them. Find out the why. Watch for drop-off trends and digital channels, particularly ones that you want your consumers to use, like home banking and mobile. If there are drop-offs, track down those members and ask them why, because at the end of the day when we learn the why, then we can deal with the how and the what.

## Digital Marketing

The time is coming when financial institutions will no longer be able to rely on the marketing techniques they have used in the past. Most financial institutions are still stuck in the digital dark ages when it comes to marketing. They rely on print media, billboards, signage at their branches, and digital banners in their digital channels.

When the digital channels evolve to be more personalized platforms, customers are going to be able to control their advertising and most will likely opt out of marketing all together. Your digital transformation strategy should include radically rethinking your marketing strategies to take advantage of your new digital platforms.

The first marketing technique that needs to be mastered is inbound marketing. Inbound marketing is a marketing method that attracts customers to your products and services by providing rich content that pertains to your products and services. Financial institutions have been doing this for some time. For example, I can remember helping to set up seminars at Suncoast Credit Union on getting a mortgage or planning for retirement. Print media with articles relating to financial health were sent to the customers on a regular basis. The idea is to provide valuable content that doesn't overtly sell your products or services, but rather, educates a customer about the various aspects of a product service. The goal has always been to become the customer's trusted advisor for financial services, and as such, the first place they will turn to when they need financial help or new products.

In the digital age, this process has evolved from sending marketing to someone's house to emailing a customer targeted articles that are relevant to where they are in their financial life. The key to accomplishing this task is executing on the data analytics section of this book. Data analytics will reveal your customers' specific needs and allow you to engage them with topics that will cut through the inbox clutter and spam and grab their attention. The content for these articles can come in many forms. For instance, if you are rolling out a new product feature, it may be useful to create a video that demonstrates the feature. If you are seeking to grow your investment portfolio, your investment team might do a podcast or blog about investments. In Kirk Drake's book *CU 2.0*, he describes a marketing message as asking more questions than telling someone what to do. He states:

> It's not enough to say, we have free checking accounts! The message needs to simultaneously educate and advocate. Asking a question is more powerful here: "Do you need a free checking account?"

If the consumer bites and follows the topic, instead of finding a product description page with the features in bullet points, the consumer would find a well-written article on the value of a new free checking account without overtly selling the financial institution's product. The article would also be written in such a way that it would be picked up by search engines such as Google and Bing. This would also bring new traffic from internet searches, and the traffic would be people looking for information about free checking accounts. If your article is useful to them, they will be back for other financial information. In this way, you can attract new customers. You may choose to write more than one article on the topic with different perspectives or details. Each article can be used to collect data from the readers and determine which articles' message resonates with customers.

Today, your organization can hold webinars with hundreds of attendees. You can use webinar tools to provide free content and financial advice. The webinars can also be recorded and then reused as content on your YouTube or Vimeo channel. If a picture is worth a thousand words, a video must be worth millions. I have watched my millennial son and his friends look for instructional YouTube videos for everything from fixing their cars to how to finish a level in a video game. A quick search for the word "mortgage" in YouTube brings back 1,790,000 results. While there are many videos on how to get a mortgage, very few are professionally done by a financial institution. A complex process like a mortgage is exactly the kind of topic that a customer would like to see simplified.

Inbound marketing also includes using technology to track your progress across all of your channels. One of the most prolific tools in the marketing space is a product called HubSpot. In fact, HubSpot's CEO, Brian Halligan, coined the term *inbound marketing* to describe what his company does. Inbound marketing is about your ability to harness your data and use it to determine who your customers are individually and using the information to provide them valuable information.

Get outside of your four walls. As mentioned before, I foresee a day when your customers may not need to visit your home banking, website, or mobile banking platform to get their balances or history. When this happens, it will impact the banner-based digital marketing that FIs have depended on for so long. New marketing techniques will need to be employed that include email, social media, and targeted website marketing. Your organization will need to partner, hire, or learn the ability to market in the same ways the big players do like Google, Amazon, and Apple. I can almost hear the groaning from here about this. I realize that you believe that what the big players do is out of your reach, but I have learned from running my own business that these tools are well within reach of the average financial institution. In the past, the large search engines would give more weight to larger content providers; however, the new search engine algorithms give more weight to content that is regionally related, meaning that if your organization can write articles that include relevant financial points about the local community, then your articles can appear above the major banks' articles. If you need help to determine what to write about, I have a simple solution:

Step 1: Find a millennial. They are easy to find—look at the local hipster cafe, coffee shop, or local restaurant (not a chain).

Step 2: Ask him or her to tell you what he/she knows about buying a house.

Chances are, this person will have more questions than answers.

Step 3: Write down all of his/her questions (make sure you capture all of the details).

Step 4: Have your staff, or hire someone to, write articles that answer these questions.

Step 5: Pick another topic such as checking accounts, or credit cards, and go back to step 1.

In this way you will become an educator, and all people (even nonmillennials) value educators. If you can become an educator, then you become an advisor.

Now that you have some great content, it's time to get the word out. Tools like HubSpot or Marketo can help you create a plan to deliver these articles to the right people, at the right time and on the right channel. There is an art to when to send out a tweet, post, or email and it is not a one-size-fits-all approach. Once you get to this level, it's time to stop marketing to the composite member persona that you have been using for all of these years. The composite customer persona represents a homogenized profile of all your customers. This approach is no longer effective because the average person is smart enough to see through an email subject, tweet, or Facebook post that has been homogenized. It's the difference between sending out an email with the subject line: "Save money by transferring your balance to our lower Credit Card," and sending out an email with the subject line that says, "Learn how you can save $1,398 a year by transferring the balance of your Citi credit card to our new low-rate credit card." The specificity of the second subject line makes it far more likely to be opened by the intended recipient. The key here is that the subject line has to be true, and to do this you will need to leverage data about your customers. The good news is that we have the technology to individualize offers in the manner I have described above; it's a matter of working with your data governance committee to get access to the credit reports of your membership. Each customer must be individualized and the marketing must be tailored to the customer's specific needs.

Even if after you manage to customize your marketing and start sending customers specific content, you may find that they still are not opening your email. The new tools for email and other channels such as a social media allow us to see who is opening our mail or reading the articles. When you discover customers that are not responding to your marketing, it's time engage "Plan B," as in A/B testing.

A/B testing or split testing is the process of creating two different versions of your content for marketing campaigns. The marketing audience is then split in two, and each group is sent a different version of the content. Each version of the content can be monitored to determine which one is more successful in terms of getting customers' attention. The better of the two is then used for a future marketing campaign. Many organizations will use A/B testing in succession to dial in their marketing message and make sure it is resonating with everyone. Others will use the process to overcome users who are not responding to the individualized content.

The content you are providing should have a place for people to comment on the articles. This is critical because it will allow your customers to provide feedback about your content, and as an added bonus, it can improve your search engine placement. However, you must also be ready to receive negative content in these forums. It is very possible that a frustrated customer may choose to use a comment section of a piece of content that might be related to the service or product that they had a bad experience with to voice their frustrations with the financial institution. The first instinct of most organizations is to delete content such as this. I would argue that, unless the content is vulgar or inappropriate in some way, it is a bad idea to delete this content. It would be far better to address the problem right there in the public arena. If customers believe the forum is being moderated or censored, they will not trust the legitimate recommendations and praise that are also often offered in the comments. The same is true of social media feeds, iTunes application reviews, and other public digital forums where customers can publicly display their discontent with your organization. What's better than a happy customer? An unhappy customer that has been converted to a happy customer, right in front of your very eyes.

Another key to success in digital marketing is overcoming some of the cultural issues that have kept your organization from doing digital marketing in the past. In the new world you must be ready to market in what some FIs and their boards would consider questionable places such as Reddit, Twitch.tv, Facebook, Google, and community blogs. This allows your organization to be seen in common places that customers have come to expect to see advertising. It's no different than having a billboard along a major highway.

Another key component is to make sure the marketing messages are consistent across every channel. Wherever the customer chooses to engage the organization, he or she should see or hear the same message. Also if the customer opts out of an offer in one channel, this should carry over to all channels.

So what happens after customers read an article or several articles? Then it is time to convert them from students to business prospects. This can be done in many different ways—for instance, you can engage the customer in a chat right on the website screen, you can also display a banner for your product on the content page, and finally, you can do something insanely crazy. You could (and this seems weird) call the member by cell, Skype, or regular phone line. That's right, you could engage the outbound mode of your call center, create a queue of opportunities, and when the call center representatives have free time, they can use the time to make outbound scripted sales calls to prospects. These conversations are very different than a cold sales call. This is because you know, based on the customers' online behaviors, that they have an interest in the product or service you are trying to offer them. The conversation is usually far easier than a normal sales call.

Another evolving digital marketing method is to write an e-book about a subject. The e-book is usually longer than an article and is done in a format that provides quick value to the reader. The e-book offer is presented in trade for the user's email address or other contact information. Once the users provide their email address, the system can start to target market them with products that will be of interest to them.

Another note: No one wants your calendars, foam fingers, and refrigerator magnets. In fact, most stainless-steel refrigerator front doors are not magnetic anymore. Here are some better items to put your logo on and give to your customers: USB sticks (at least 8 GB), USB chargers (these are gold), USB hubs, screen cleaners, and smartphone credit card holders. If your marketing is going to be digital, your marketing materials should be digital as well.

Developing a digital marketing strategy will be critical to your digital transformation. Using digital marketing to educate your customers and your prospects on your digital services is a perfect match.

## Chapter Review

- In the digital era, strategy must be supported by data analytics.

- Data analytics allows financial institutions to predict which consumers are risky. It can also help banks detect changes in consumer behavior and circumstances, allowing them to make an important connection that will help both the business and the individual.

- Data analytics can help financial institutions uncover the reasons behind customer behavior.

- Your strategy must include marketing strategies that take advantage of new digital platforms.

# CHAPTER 16

# Big Data and the Zombie Apocalypse

**Using data to reload!**

Y ou are probably wondering what big data has to do with a zombie apocalypse. While I was thinking about the rules of an apocalyptic world, I realized that I follow the same thought process I use to think about what the rules are going to be for the new digital world, particularly in banking. I have said before I am not going to do a book where I try to scare you into doing digital; in fact, what I am trying to

259

do is help to understand how to go digital, and part of it is going to be spending some time going over what data analytics really is.

I am going to recap: If you don't remember why we are going to have an apocalyptic world, let me refer you back to Chapter 13, which discusses the *TIONS*—interchange compression, cannibalization, digitization, mobilization, and disintermediation. We also talk a little bit about payments and how interchange is not disappearing and is not going away, but it is suffering from price compression, and we're going to see more price compression as time goes on. Alternative payments are going to be cheaper, and that means that as things move to ACH, and we see different models for payments, that's going to cut into our revenue. Lending is going to change. FICO won't be enough. We're going to see higher loan fraud from auto loan fraud rings—more bankruptcy changes, right? Student loans are in the crosshairs with that, as well, as we're continuing to see the CFPB hand out damage awards. Now, the CFPB may not exist in its current state, given the administration that's in power right now; however, over time I do believe that we'll continue to see more scrutiny in the banking space.

In this new, apocalyptic world, how do we survive? I started thinking about it in terms of how characters in zombie movies and TV shows survive. First, they're often transient. This is similar to how we're going to have to learn how to be more transient—more *mobile*—particularly with our data and our services. This is where the cloud comes in.

In the zombie apocalyptic world, you also have to make a little go a long way. I like to think of what a world of scarcity means in banking terms. In a world where scarcity becomes the new law, banks are not going to be able to count on catching an elephant, one big client that will provide a windfall. Banks that do manage to catch an elephant will have to figure out how to store it for the future so it will last. More importantly, you are going to have to figure out how to survive on rabbits, and it's going to take a lot more of them to sustain the bank.

Another thing to keep in mind is that in the world of the apocalypse, the law is not a primary factor in society. The old rules just don't apply anymore, particularly the rules about being nice to each other and playing fair. Banks will have to fight for their turf, and that's something that we have great difficulty with in this particular industry. We're going to have to learn to really make cases for ourselves in the light of regulation to make sure that we don't lose ground to fintechs and other folks.

## Apocalyptic Risk

We need to identify risk quickly. It's important to note the difference between *identifying* risk and *avoiding* risk at all costs. It's OK to have risk. It will never be possible to avoid risk; that's an impossibility. However, if financial institutions can identify risk quickly and react, they will have the ability to survive. As discussed later in this chapter, data are critical for identifying risk and deciding how to respond.

My father was a military man. He liked to say high speed, low drag. That means he liked to move fast and jettison anything that held him back. In this world, opportunity is going to move fast, and what was here today might not be here tomorrow. For example, I know many financial institutions that have a team that's set up so that when a person calls and says, "I would like a 10-day payoff on my auto loan," they'll call that person back. Sometimes it takes them an hour, though. In today's world, an hour is too long. By then, your customer has probably completed the loan, been put through the process, and they are driving off in their car. Meanwhile, your loan has been paid off, and your customer has a loan with the car company or someone else. We have to learn to react faster, and we have to learn to get rid of the things that are dragging us down.

In the process, we also have to learn to travel light, which is not a common practice in our industry. We live in a world where, if you've got a channel, we don't deprecate channels. We don't get rid of things. Drive-throughs, teller lines, ATMs, voice-response units, home banking—we still have all of it, and have no plans to phase anything out. We are now adding mobile, and piling on. The problem is that more channels require more resources. Without focus and planning, this will be unsustainable—and data will show us the way.

## Staffing in an Apocalypse

If you think about the future in apocalyptic terms, you also need to consider the people who work in your organization. There are likely a lot of people who were helpful in the past but are not cut out for the future. To pick up our zombie analogy, what skills does a florist have that can be useful in the new and frightening world? Flower arranging won't matter at all, but perhaps she will know about edible plants that you can collect in the wild. Perhaps, her skills won't have to do with her previous career at all. Maybe the florist is really most valuable because she knows how to drive a stick shift or do tae kwon do. I consider moms to be pretty valuable, versatile employees. They are a little scary and they are also very resourceful, so I'm always looking for mothers to join my team.

Around my house, we have a saying: we're always talking about whether or not you want to be on our team. When the zombie apocalypse comes, we try to decide who we want our team, and who are the people we want around that we would be able to survive with. What I would ask you is to look around and decide, who's on my team? You might be surprised at the different people that are around in your organization that can be helpful in this new world.

Just to give you some examples of new titles that you might see, a chief analytic officer. We discussed this in Chapter 10. This is someone who's going to oversee this group. Statistical and optimization engineers—people who are optimizing algorithms to get the most out of them and doing statistical analysis to make sure that they're correct. Data scientists—There's a stat that says that there are only 13,000 qualified data scientists in the entire United States. How are we going to be able to bring those folks in and get them to work with us? Behaviorists—I read a great article about how folks in the digital world now are looking for philosophers and people with philosophy degrees, because understanding people's behavior is far more about understanding their philosophies and understanding their habits than it is about technical expertise. User experience specialists—people who can translate oddball data into changes to your digital front end that create opportunity for you. And then you are going to need a whole project management group filled with scrum masters and project managers and QA and all of these things, and it just seems enormous. What will you do? Well, here's the good news, you don't have to have all these things at once, but you do need to understand what these people do. You do need to understand what these roles are so you can grow into it.

Having these positions filled with the appropriate people will keep financial institutions in a good position for the future. In terms of resources—human and other—organizations will need to be well stocked. In the financial world, being well stocked requires people who have data and know how to use it. And, believe it or not, financial institutions are very well stocked with data. It's the people who already understand it that are very valuable. These are the people who know how to use analytics and machine learning to increase their marketing. That's going to be a huge opportunity. It's great that we have data and know what to do with it; it's great that we're willing to share it, but we're going to have to have some insights. This goes back to philosophy, poli-sci (political science)—those types of degrees where people can look at a string of data and make an assumption or an intelligent guess based on the human mind.

People who can collaborate will also be vital to organizational success. In the banking world, we're going to have to collaborate some, whether it be with other fintechs, which I think is probably likely, or whether it be with other like-minded financial institutions, we're going to have to be able to collaborate.

It might seem contradictory, but these collaborators will also need to know how to fight. In this world, if you don't know how to fight and if you haven't taken a punch recently, you're not going to be useful. After all, we cannot run away from risk, nor can we plan around risk. What we can do is plan for risk and how to respond to it. We have to be willing to fight for our ideas. We have to be willing to fight for our consumers and customers, and more importantly, we have to be willing to fight for our ideals. If we stick to those, we have an opportunity to win.

We also have to be willing to break the status quo. If you look at the main technology players, you look for example at AirBnB, arguably one of the largest hotel chains on the planet without actually ever building a room anywhere, you look at Uber, you look at Lyft, the sharing economy is a great example of breaking the status quo. What are the banking status quos, the clichés that our industry must break to bring people to us?

How will analytics help? If we really look at it, analytics has the power to bring us new engagements, to help us max out profitability, create cost-effective services, find new sources of income, help us to deepen our relationships, create digital relationships and, more importantly, help us to understand the habits, the trends, and the needs of our consumers.

Where will we find people who are a good fit for what we do? If you're a commercial bank, where will you find entrepreneurial people who want to use your services? Analytics can help with that. Analytics can help you by finding opportunities in streams of data that you did not know were there. Maxing out profitability—we talked about this before. We can't just drag an elephant back from the jungle, take one bite, and then throw it away. We're going to have to figure out how to use all of the elephant, and what that means in bank-speak is, we've got to do our best to engage our members and get them using all of our products and services.

## Creating Value

Now I'm going to dispel a myth right now. I'm going to call it the myth of the *primary financial institution*. I've heard the PFI so many times that it makes me want to cry. That is not a reality. No one is going to bank with just one place. I do not believe that that's the case anymore, and if you want to be nostalgic and look back, you can certainly can find a time when it was like that, but in the new world, people are to have more than one financial institution to back them up. They're going to have a credit card from one place, an auto loan somewhere else, and a mortgage at a third. What you can do is look to be three out of maybe four other viable products in their wallet. You could be their auto loan, you could be their checking account, you could be their CD or their investment services, but you might not be their mortgage, and that's okay. What you can't be is just their checking account, particularly at the rates they have today. We have to find a way to drive up that profitability. We have to find a way to make the right offer at the right time to the right person for the right place for the right amount. That's what analytics will bring to you.

We also have to create cost-effective services. How do we determine what we're going to provide consumers? Well, we can no longer just put our finger in the air and let the wind blow by and try to decide the direction that customers are going. We are going to be using algorithms. We are going to be using data to look for data-driven results. To do that, we're going to use our history, we are going to use other people's history, and this is where collaboration can come into play. You might want to share your data with others to pull together to make some determinations of the future.

Can you provide valuable insights to your customers? If you can do this, you can create new sources of income. Would it be useful to them to know if they go to Chili's one more time, they are not going to be able to pay their mortgage? Sure, and you can do this, and that's some of the opportunity that analytics is going to bring, not to mention the ability to dig through streams of data and learning from what that data says, what people need. This leads to deeper relationships with customers. Social media is another critical source of data that can support deeper relationships. For example, do you know your customers' Twitter and Facebook profiles? What do they reveal? Have customers ever mentioned or contacted your organization online? Are these folks influencers in your world? Are they evangelizing your organization, or are they detractors? Data analytics will help determine what place data holds in our world.

Digital relationships are vital to an organization's future success. I know that sounds weird to say *digital* and *relationship* together, but the reality is you can have digital relationships by creating a meaningful connection with your consumer. That can happen over a mobile device or over a website. You don't have to see customers once a week in the branch like in the old days; you can see them online instead. You can relate your brand to them, and you can understand their needs, their wants, who they are, and who they are digitally. You can understand what services they use. Is there a difference between a person who is enrolled in Netflix versus a person who uses Hulu? Is there a difference between a person who uses Apple products versus someone who uses Microsoft products? You bet there is, but it is up to you to discover the context and what it means to you and your organization.

## Digital Insight and Intuition

When we talk about insights, we usually mean intuition that you might have about a piece of data or something that's going.

How do people look at data analytics? Who will benefit, and who will be threatened? There's a great Pew research chart that states that global banks are going to benefit the most from analytics and data.[1] Information is really valuable when you have a lot of it, and this is going to take me back to the collaborative portion of this. Our medium-sized or small-sized banks may not have enough data in order to make the intuitions or the insights that they need. They will have to collaborate with others to make sure that they have enough variety in order to make insights into what they're looking for. We'll talk about volume, velocity, and variety here shortly, and what that means.

When we look down at community banks, credit unions, regional banks, they have the most to lose from analytics, and I like to think of it like this, when FIs who are armed with analytics show up and compete against local FIs, they're going to know more about their customers and more about their business than most other organizations. This will result in a cowboys and Indians situation. When the cowboys showed up with guns and sadly the Indians had bows and arrows, and we all know how that went. Adapting to the coming data-driven retail environment will be an important skill that FIs must master if they are to survive in a fintech-dominated banking environment.

### Data Is Valuable

Your first action item is this: stock up. Just like you would do in the zombie apocalypse, find a backpack and start stocking up on what you can find. Take an assessment of what you have. Did you know that as financial institutions, we're sitting on some of the most valuable and sought-after data in the world? We can tell you what home someone has. We can tell you what credit cards they like to use. We can tell you what they buy. We can tell you when they buy it. We can tell you if there is a trend to how they buy it. We can use our mobile apps to tell you where they bought it. We can tell you by what kind of phone they use. We can give you their credit reports. We can tell you what bills they pay on a regular basis with bill pay, and in some cases, for those of us that have a budgeting software or a personal financial management platform, we can even tell them what other financial institutions they have. This information is so incredibly valuable yet so unorganized from financial institutions. So, step one is to have someone take stock of your data.

Not only that, but are you deleting your data? Are you deleting the logs from your website on a regular basis? Are you deleting your mobile statistics on a regular basis? You might just be throwing away money. You need to stop deleting now and plan on hoarding. Hoarding is what we do when things get scarce, and in the new world, things are going to be scarce. So, sit down and decide with your team what data you have, and then find out how everything is connected. What's the process if you want a 360 view of one of your customers? Think about what's required if you want to say, "Tell me everyone who bought something from Home Depot in the last three months." Or, "Tell me everyone who lives in the vicinity of this store." You have to be able to do that. The challenge is, can you relate the two pieces of data? Can you say, "Show me everyone who has a home loan with us and who has a Netflix account on our credit card?" That's when things get fun. That's when the trends pop out, and that's when the opportunities happen. So, stock up. Those who are well stocked are going to do very well, and you need to know how well your team knows your own data.

Let's talk about some of the things that are a drag. These are the things I hear when I talk to smaller financial institutions that have attempted to do something with data analytics. The first one is, we have too much data and no one knows where everything is. Data analytics is done department by department. I've watched organizations putting together their reporting for the regulatory environment and it gets passed around from department to department, where a person in mortgages adds their portion of the report and someone in the call center adds their data and so forth and so on, until finally there's a report put together, and the reality is that no one person knows where everything is, and in reality and totality, we are not even sure that anyone knows where everything is. This is an important issue, and it's a big part of the drag, right? You sit down to go do something, only find out that you are not organized and you don't have the data you need, and nothing is more demoralizing than having a good idea and not having data to back it up.

The second thing that I see a lot that drags organizations down in the data analytics space is, they feel like they don't have enough processing power. You want to say to them, "Hey, why aren't you analyzing your bill pay data?" Or, "Why aren't you analyzing these various aspects of the data?" And they say, "Well, we'd like to, but last time we ran that job it took us three months or two months or it never finished or it took a whole day." In a world of quantum computing, or a world of distributed processing, we should not have that issue.

What can we do to deal with that? One, we can collaborate. Two, that's where the cloud could come in—you could buy a really large machine and only use it for a few minutes or however long it takes to run the data and then shut it down. There's a lot of ways to get around processing power in today's world. The key is that we have to want to do it and we have to look for those opportunities rather than just sort of admit defeat when we run into these problems. Another comment I hear is, "You know, we had a guy and he was great, but he left and now we can't find someone else." The reality is that there is a true shortage of people who have the skills to do it; however, if look at your situation I think you will find that you don't need a full-time data scientist. Outsourcing these positions can pay great dividends. You can easily make a business case around having several data scientists on consulting teams who are able to take your loan projections or perhaps your delinquency projections, bring those down and increase your loans and pay for these engagements in a short amount of time.

Finally, analytics is viewed as a single product by management and not a capability or strategic partnership. That's a huge challenge, and I mention this in the digital space as well when I said digital is not a product, it's a discipline. Well, in a similar mindset analytics, it's not a product, it's a discipline. If you think about it, if someone was really good at QuickBooks, we wouldn't call them our CFO. We can't just buy QuickBooks and check off the accounting function of our organization. We have a CFO, we have trained accountants and CPAs. We rely on these trained professionals in our banking organizations to deal with the complexities of bank account rules. Why would we think analytics is any different? Analytics is a discipline, and it deserves a seat at the table where decisions are made. It is important to understand that in the future, analytics will be involved in every aspect of the financial business. If you open a new branch, you are going to want to understand the demographics of the area that the branch will serve, you are going to want to understand the foot traffic and what people might abandon a branch that they were using to go to the new branch. This is a job for analytics, and they should be involved from the start of the project. If you are designing a new financial mobile application, you're going to want to understand why the people would use it, who to market the application to, and what services the users will expect. Process engineering is also a good place to engage the analytics team. They can help determine what data to collect, how often to collect it, and how long to retain it. I think you can see the pattern here; analytics should be involved in every decision, every new project, and every process.

More importantly, it could be that your analytics group is a strategic partnership headed by someone in your organization who either understands analytics or has expressed an interest in understanding how to manage it. Ideally this person should be an executive with staff that has been involved with the reporting and with a seat of the table where decisions are made. This person might also look for an intern or a junior data analyst to help him interact with the consultants. Finding a consulting partner is a great way to learn what your organization needs in terms of analytics. It may be sometime before the organization is ready to create a full-time analytics group.

## Data Is a Discipline

If we are going to survive in this world, we have to understand that analytics is not a product, it's a discipline. Our ability as an organization to execute on analytics is paramount to our survival in this new world.

Let's look at some examples. Let's look at Google. Google processes 3.5 billion requests a day. It is currently building data centers all around the world. It is anticipating an exabyte a day. That's an insane amount of data. Eric Berlow, TED speaker at our latest Analytics and Financial Innovation (AXFI) Conference, was asked what he thinks is behind the analytics boom. Most people think increased processing power and more sophisticated algorithms are behind it. Berlow thinks that it's the volume and the vast amount of data that we have access to now that companies like Google or Amazon or Facebook or Microsoft or Apple are collecting on a daily basis about us, and all of that data means that you can mine it and you can look through and learn things about the data—you can find opportunities within the data.

Facebook collects 500 terabytes of data daily, including 2.5 billion pieces of content, 2.7 billion likes, and 300 million photos. And it has admitted to storing 100 petabytes of photos and video—as of 2012. Amazon draws data from 152 million customers, and if you don't think that it is running systems and things through its AI, you are crazy. These companies are learning from reviews, feedback, what you looked at, and what you clicked on.

I have a favorite story about Amazon. I was riding into work one day and, as a huge Van Halen fan, I decided I wanted to listen to an interview with David Lee Roth by Howard Stern. When I tuned in, there was an on-air testimonial for a product called a Squatty Potty. My curiosity got the best of me, and when I got to work I googled "Squatty Potty" and I clicked on the Amazon link that came up. I learned that Squatty Potty is a tool to allow you to go to the bathroom easier. It's like a footrest you put in front of the toilet bowl. The Amazon page had a drawing of a person sitting on a toilet and using the Squatty Potty. You may have noticed that the things you view on Amazon have a way of popping up in ads on other websites. That's called a super cookie. Well, that image of a person on the toilet followed me around for days, and I could not get it to stop. Now, that said, it's an effective way of doing sales, but in my case, during presentations to hundreds of people, I would pull up some site to illustrate something and there would be that man on the toilet, which was more than a little embarrassing.

This is a great point, and I can already hear you saying this: John, we've been thinking about this, and our board is just not comfortable with using data like this. There's a fear they were invading people's privacy, there's a fear that we'll become like big brother. Recently there's been a lot of stories in the news regarding privacy issues. Edward Snowden, arguably the biggest story about privacy in years, exposed the government's ability to digitally spy on the citizens of the United States in the name of protecting the homeland. Right or wrong, he exposed the government's incredible reach in to our daily lives by using our cell phones and online habits to track people of interest.

Another recent case of privacy involved the terrorist attack in San Bernardino in February of 2016. Investigators collected one of the terrorist's cell phones, which happened to be an Apple iPhone. The iPhone was protected by a passcode that the FBI couldn't break without risking erasing the phone and losing its contents. The FBI then contacted Apple in an effort to gain access to the phone by requesting that apple create a special back door. Apple declined due to a policy to never undermine its own security measures. Most financial institutions regularly work with the authorities to deliver data when requested via subpoena; however, in the future I expect financial institutions to institute similar encryption techniques that may put FIs in the same position as Apple was with the San Bernardino case. Google and Facebook are in lawsuits worldwide, and, of course, one of the most documented and famous data overreaches occurred at the retailer Target.

Target is one of the biggest users of analytics. I recently read Charles Duhigg's book *The Power of Habit*, where he describes the now infamous Target incident in detail and gives a behind-the-scenes look at Target's extensive analytics department. Target discovered that by analyzing the buying habits of its customers, it could make predictions about their future needs. For example, the analyst at Target found a link between customers who purchase large quantities of lotions, or certain kinds of vitamins, and pregnancy. Target then compared these results to its baby registry to determine the accuracy of the model. Using the baby registry as its guide, they identified common buying trends that allowed them to accurately predict if someone was pregnant and even how far along in their pregnancy the customer was. It turns out that pregnant women are highly sought after by retail stores because statistically, wherever the mother buys her baby supplies like diapers and bottles is where she's going to buy other things like groceries, because it's convenient. New moms value time (and possibly sleep) above all, and because of this, they tend to prefer one-stop shopping.

Target sent an advertising flyer filled with coupons for baby clothes, cribs, and other baby needs to a young lady who had bought some of these items and fit their model. Unfortunately, this young lady was a teenager who was still in high school at the time, and her father took offense to the overt target marketing and complained to the store that Target was encouraging his teenage daughter to get pregnant—only to find out later that Target's model was right and his daughter's baby was due in August. Target discovered that sending ads that are filled with a particular type of item clued people in that their shopping habits were being monitored, and it also discovered (thanks to the very upset father) that people don't like it when they feel like they are being manipulated into buying things. Target changed its advertising so that alongside the targeted items (such as the baby supplies), the ads included other unrelated items such as TVs or lawnmowers. This approach allowed it to target market customers without alerting them to the fact that their purchase data had been analyzed to create the flyer.

Target has a lot of data about its customers but that pales in comparison to the quantity and quality of data that a financial organization has about its customers. I have talked to many executives at financial institutions who are very concerned about mining their data and using it to advertise to their customers, for fear of creating a situation similar to the Target incident.

Here is my theory on the privacy issue for financial institutions: Do anything you want to do with data in the banking space as long as it works in favor of the consumer and you're transparent about what you doing. If you're honest, up front, and you are doing something to help somebody save money, make money, or make good financial decisions, then do whatever you want. Financial institutions must resist the urge to use the vast amount of data that they have to manipulate their customers. As organizations become more proficient with their data, the lines between being creepy and doing the right thing will get increasingly difficult to discern.

In Europe, they are particularly sensitive to privacy issues and have passed laws that are designed to protect people's online and digital privacy. The new law is called General Data Protection

Regulations (GDPR) and goes into effect May 25, 2018. The law has two main pillars, Right to be Forgotten and Informed Consent.

Let's start by dissecting the part of the law that states that everyone has the right to be forgotten. In Europe, once this is enacted, an individual will be able to contact Google and Facebook and request that they delete your search history and any other profile data that the company has stored about you. The law also states that multinational companies (such as Google and Facebook) will be treated as single entities. As of this year, many of the largest US multinational organizations are spending hundreds of millions of dollars to comply with the regulation. The regulation states that organizations that are not in compliance could incur fines of up to 20 million euros or 4 percent of global revenue (whichever is greater).

As of this writing, a major breach has happened at Equifax, a provider of credit services with millions of accounts and access to very private data. Had this happened after the GDPR deadline, Equifax would have had to pay 4 percent of its global revenue (more than $3 billion), or $120 million in fines. Remember that if you house any data from a citizen of a EU country, then GDPR theoretically would apply to you.

Informed consent means that we cannot put 50 pages of a EULA, which stands for End User License Agreement, and have a button or checkbox that states "I agree I have read and understand the EULA." GDPR states that an organization must be able to clearly communicate in simple terms to customers what they are agreeing to. Many people discover their data on the internet and later realize that a EULA for a piece of software they installed included a provision that allowed that company to mine their personal data. A company called PC Pit Stop decided to test to see if anyone was actually reading its EULAs and included a provision that promised financial consideration for anyone who emailed an address in the disclosure. It took four months before someone read that part of the EULA and sent the email (that person got $1,000), proving that no one really reads the EULAs. Informed consent provides protections from users against organizations inundating users with large documents that they know no one has the time to read. It also clearly states that the EULA should not contain other provisions that don't specifically pertain to the software or data processing that the EULA is intended to cover, and if they do, they must be clearly spelled out to the end users in such a manner that they can clearly see that the request is out of scope for this particular EULA. This means that there cannot be any loopholes in the EULA that, say, allow the company to sell data about how you interact with its service to a third-party, especially if that provider doesn't have a clear connection to the product or service that EULA covers.

The good news is that financial institutions have plenty of data, we have access to the right people, we have good intentions, and for most of us, laws like GDPR don't affect us. We can use our data to drive results and we can use our data on behalf of those that we serve—as a matter of fact, most of them are expecting it. Speaking of expecting, let's dive into the different kinds of analytics.

## Types of Analytics

Let's talk a little bit about what data analytics is and what the tools of the trade are so that when you're starting to access people, software, and tools, you have some idea of what the lingo means. The first thing to understand is the types of data analytics. There are three types of analytics that most people talk about. The first one is descriptive. Descriptive analytics tells us what happened and not what will happen. It's historical data. A great example would be a branch report. Please tell me all the people who came into the branch and used the teller line last Friday. Tell me all the people that used the drive through; tell me all the people that used the ATM. Because these are all things that happened in the past, they are considered descriptive analytics. Reports described something that happened. I find that most organizations are already proficient at this sort of analytics; many have been relying on historical reports their entire career and still use descriptive analytics for decision making. People who make decisions on descriptive analytics are usually looking for trends to decision on. Consider a branch manager reviewing stats from the previous year. She might take note of the fact that in the winter around the holidays the branches are far busier, and as a result would adjust her staffing accordingly. She hopes that the trends she is seeing hold. While this approach has been used for many years, it doesn't account for changes in the environment that might affect the amount of foot traffic that the branch will get. For instance maybe there will be construction in or around the branch that prevents people from getting to the branch and as a result drives down the amount of customers.

That leads us to predictive analytics. Predictive analytics is the art of taking historical data, adding other data, and intuitions, and coming up with future trends. While we can certainly forecast what might happen based on the past, when we add new information to the data set we increase our chances of finding new opportunities. One example of new data is doing comparisons with other channels such as the ATM or home banking to increase the validity of the results and find additional trends. This is where most organizations are trying to get to—they are trying to go from descriptive to predictive, especially in light of new regulation. A great example of predictive analytics can be found in the ABA's change to the Current Expected Credit Loss (CECL), which replaces the current "incurred loss" model with an "expected loss" model. The *incurred loss* is largely based off of historical data and trends and has its roots in descriptive analytics. This is in stark contrast to the new "expected loss," which describes an event that happens in the future. The new rules require financial institutions to essentially "predict" risk in their portfolios between 2020 and 2021, depending on whether your organization is considered a public business entity (PBE).

The final category is prescriptive analytics. Prescriptive analytics is about scenario planning. It gives you actionable data, data that you can use to make decisions when choosing between two scenarios. Prescriptive analytics can also be used to mitigate potential future risks For example, if there is a concern of a bubble in mortgages or a future drop in the market, a prescriptive analytics model can be fed the different parameters of the market and it will provide many decision options to address that risk. All of this sounds great, right? It's exactly what a financial institution needs! So how do I make it happen? Well, the reason I put this one last is because it's very difficult to achieve without mastering descriptive and predictive analytics first.

Prescriptive analytics will be the catalyst for implementing machine learning or artificial intelligence. For instance, let's say we were trying to determine which customers are planning on buying a car in the next six months. How would we go about determining this? The current way is to combine historical data on customer behavior and compare it to a baseline of customers and their behavior in the six months before they made a decision to buy a car. With this model, you would get good feedback, but it would rely on human observations, which can sometimes be blind to trends that aren't obvious.

A prescriptive analytics model could also employ artificial intelligence to process the inputs. The human model would look at all the people who have bought a car recently, and then we would comb through their actions in the months before they bought the car and try to use human intelligence to determine what the common trends are. When utilizing artificial intelligence in your model instead of relying on human intuition to discover common trends, you feed it a massive list of people that did buy a car. You feed it as much other information as you have on hand that relates, for instance branch visits, website information, purchase history, and anything else you have lying around, and you let it find the trends. As it gives feedback, you may have to weed out false positives or train it, but eventually it will learn, and as you get more people that buy cars, you keep feeding it these opportunities, and you'll also get a baseline. Then you give it your target list of people that didn't buy cars. The artificial intelligence will then use the classifier it created from the baseline to identify the people who are likely to buy a car in the next six months based on matching behavior.

The more you feed the model, the more it will learn what the prerequisites are. It will begin to discern what the forward-thinking trends are, and most importantly, what the leading indicators are for people who are going to buy a car. It could be that they are expecting a baby (maybe partner with Target?) and they're going to need a minivan. It could also be that someone has spent a lot of time in the car section of your website, which would be obvious, but there might be unobvious things—things that only a computer could find, such as a high amount of payments to an auto repair shop in their purchase history. The only process that could possibly see these trends, because the human mind is not capable of comprehending or perceiving this data, will be artificial intelligence. These sorts of analyses are going to be game changers for financial services in the future.

Let's talk about the terms of the trade. Here are some simple terms. You are going to hear some weird stuff, and it's probably good that you at least know what these things are. The first one you hear a lot is called *Hadoop*. It's an open source large data set manipulator, and has become pretty popular for folks who are trying to crunch large amounts of data and look for trends. It has a cute little elephant for a logo, and if you've run into it you would know. The next one is just a letter of the alphabet, which is *R*.

It's yet another open source tool; however, its intended purpose is to provide statistical analyses and data visualization—if, for example, you wanted to do a 3D plot map on a site to determine which of your members are more likely to go to a certain branch or adopt a certain product based on geography. Finally (and this is kind of an overarching term covering a lot of different products), is *machine learning*, also referred to as *cognitive analysis*. It's currently the most popular course at Stanford, and ultimately, it is another name for AI. As we get bigger and bigger and bigger data sets, machine learning is designed to discover trends and point out behaviors that will lead to opportunities that a human would never find. Each of these tools has specific purposes and builds on the three disciplines of analytics that we have been discussing in this chapter: descriptive, predictive, and prescriptive.

Now, let's talk about the data itself, and what are the tools that you need to have to be successful at data analytics. We like to think of them as the three Vs. The first one is volume. The more volume you have, the more likely your organization will come up with outcomes that will be viable. If you don't have a large data set, then it's possible that your outcomes will be tainted by a lack of scale. In other words, if you want to find out a trend about apples, you are going to need more than 10 apples to determine a trend. You are going to need to look at thousands, maybe hundreds of thousands, of apples before you can really make a factual statement about apples. That's volume.

The next one is variety, and that's the diversity of your data. If all you have is apples and you are trying to trend fruit, then you would be missing oranges and bananas and all the other types of fruit that could affect your trend. Having a variety of data is very powerful. The more data variety you have, the more likely you are to determine trends, to detect anomalies, as well as make accurate predictions. If you were looking at a group of customers and you only included data from one zip code in your data set, your outcomes could be wrong due to the regional behaviors of a particular group. Variety fully plays into that.

The final one is velocity. Velocity of data is fast becoming the most important aspect of analytics. Data over five hours old is useless. Case in point: Earlier we talked about someone who called her FI about a loan payoff. When the financial institution called back to say, "Hey, what are you doing? Are you buying a car? We want to help you!" the customer responded, "Oh, I already bought a new car." Like life in the zombie apocalypse, things move fast, and because the response speed of the FI had not caught up with the speed of making a loan at a dealership the FI lost a customer and a loan. If you're working off a data set that was most recently updated last quarter, it's possible that the situations that you are including such as credit card balances, assets, or financial positions have changed. Not only that, it's even more likely that the environment that facilitated the outcomes you are using in your dataset have changed as well. For this reason, we will see a shift to real time data, or close to it, being used in future analytic models to avoid making offers or assumptions from stale data.

Again, to recap, that's volume, variety, and velocity.

Closing out, what are our opportunities here? We are going to have to become digital services slayers. We're going to need to create digital streams that allow FIs to take the digital services that are bringing us so much data and make use of it to improve our customers' financial health. Notice that I didn't say to manipulate people, that's not what we're talking about. We're going to need AI (see Chapter 4). We're going to have to have the ability to determine, as I mentioned before, the difference in behaviors between someone who owns an Apple iPhone and someone who owns an Android mobile phone. What are their wants, what are their needs, how do they make their living, and what do their life choices say about them and their character? After all, most of determining loan risk is about assessing character.

Finally, we're going to have to monetize our own data. I know this is again an anathema to our industry, but people are already doing it. If you think about Mint, if you think about Yodlee, if you think about all the products that log in and screen scrape through our platform and then pull our data out, others are already monetizing our consumer's data, and the customers are opting in and allowing these third parties to do it. Monetizing data may mean working with digital marketers to advertise cars in our home banking or mobile products, or market local retailers services that are trusted to the customers.

In summary, here are the key points to stay alive in a zombie apocalypse:

- *Be mobile.* Don't stay in any one place too long. Always be looking for the next safe harbor.

- *Stock up.* Make sure you are not deleting important data. Take stock of what you have. Start hoarding today!
- *Choose your teammates carefully.* Make sure that your culture will support a data-driven approach.
- *Data analytics is a discipline.* It is not a product.
- *Act quickly and decisively using data to validate your approach.* What was here a few minutes ago might be gone in the next five minutes. Windows are shrinking.
- *Learn how to use the tools of the trade.* If you can't shoot a gun, then just having one handy isn't going to protect you.
- *Determine your capabilities.* Know where your organization is operating based on the data analytics models: descriptive, predictive, and prescriptive.
- *Monetize your data.* If you don't, someone else will.

So that's how you survive the zombie apocalypse with data analytics.

---

### Chapter Review

- It's important to note the difference between *identifying* risk and *avoiding* risk. It will never be possible to avoid risk; however, if financial institutions can identify risk quickly and react, they will have the ability to survive.

- Financial institutions have access to some of the most valuable and sought-after data in the world. The industry needs to stockpile it and be able to quickly act on it, changing strategy when necessary.

- Financial institutions will be able to monetize these data by creating services that bring in new ways to use so much data to improve our customers' financial health.

---

## NOTE

1. Pew Research Center, https://www.pwc.com/gx/en/banking-capital-markets/banking-2020/assets/pwc-retail-banking-2020-evolution-or-revolution.pdf.

# Conclusion

Strategy: a plan of action or policy designed to achieve a major or overall goal.

If you have made it this far, congratulations: you have survived my onslaught of ideas, suggestions, and stories. You are probably excited about getting started but also overwhelmed and unsure where to begin. If you are C-level employee, then you might well have the power to make some of the changes suggested in this book, but if you are middle management, you may be facing a harder battle. Fear not! There is a way to get going for everyone, no matter what your level in the organization, and the first step is an easy one. If you look at the definition above, a strategy is always in service of a goal. So, your first step is to decide what your goal is?

In her book *Get your Sh!t together,* Sarah Knight describes a goal as a version of winning. She asks, what would it look like to really win in your life? I would translate this to "What does it look like for your <insert department, job, or organization here> to really win at digital? " The kind of win that would have you doing press releases, dancing in the streets, and planning celebrations with your staff. If you are in the lending area, maybe it's the two-page digital loan application. If you are in the call center, maybe it's leveraging artificial intelligence to answer 35 percent of the calls that come in. If you are the CEO, maybe it's a full digital platform that can be leveraged across the organization. If you are in HR, maybe it's a comprehensive workflow that includes onboarding and training all staff digitally. What would make your organization and its customers happy?

So here is a good place to stop and meditate a bit on this; it might take a few days to formulate your goal into concise sentence. Something like "It will only take our customers 5 minutes to get a loan," or, "No customer will wait for more than 30 seconds to speak to a representative," or "Our digital platform will allow continuity across every department." Whatever it is, write it down, and stare at it for a while. Once you have your goal, the harder part begins. It's time to develop a strategy around achieving your goal. Here are some questions that need to be answered.

1. What exactly is your goal? It's time to go from the sentence to the full description; be as specific and descriptive as possible.
2. How long will it take to reasonably achieve the goal?
3. Who will you need to make it happen?
4. Who will try to stop you and why?
5. How will you pay for the resources to make the goal happen?
6. Can the goal be broken into phases?
7. What is the value proposition of the goal to the organization?
8. How will this goal affect the culture of the organization?
9. Will the goal require hiring people?
10. Will the goal result in firing people?
11. How will you monitor your goal's progress?
12. What are your leading indicators?
13. What are your key performance indicators?
14. Is there data available to support your approach?
15. When happens when the goal is reached?

These are all critical questions that need to be answered so that you can develop a plan of attack or a strategy to deliver the goal. Your digital strategy is the beginning of your digital transformation. It doesn't have to be an all-encompassing strategy; it can be a smaller strategy if it is adopted by the right people. For instance, suppose the goal is to improve your wait time in the call center. You might be able to make this happen with a product or service that could extend to the rest of the organization, so you do want to make sure that you socialize your goals and get some understanding of its collateral effects on the organization. Therefore, it is necessary to fully define your goal. If your goal includes a new website with a flow, don't be afraid to grab a piece of paper and draw it. In fact there are many tools on the Web to allow you to easily mockup a digital process (for example, balsamiq.com, lucidchart.com, moqups.com, or wire-frame.cc, all of which have free tools). I can hear you saying that your I.T. department would never allow you to use these sites or download this software. OK, then go to your local library and do it there. You must want this—that's why it's your "dancing in the streets" goal.

Now that you have the first iteration of your strategy finished, it's time to get real with the goals. This book is broken down in to six distinct parts: Processes, Technology, Security, People, Culture, and Strategy. Each section has information on how these areas of your organization can either help or hinder your goal. Let's go through each section and use it as a guide for your strategy.

## Cultural Issues

How does your goal fit into the culture of the organization? For instance, if your goal is a sales goal and your organizational culture is based on service, then you may find that there will be resistance to implementing your processes or purchasing the necessary assets to achieve your goal. Identifying how your goal fits on the organizational culture is a critical step before presenting it.

Will your plan involve changing the culture, even if it is just your local department culture? For instance, let's say that you are plan-ning on creating a digital workflow that would improve your process for reporting lost or stolen cards, or how account closing is handled. Any change of process is going to affect your culture. It's impor-tant to understand that most financial organizations are not "change friendly," and as a result, the culture in it is entirety is very static. If you are going to introduce a change, you must think through how that change might impact the culture.

For example, any digital workflow that reduces manual work is likely to be viewed by staff as an attempt to reduce the number of employees by replacing them with automated processes. If your change will require you to add resources, employees may be worried about overhead in their department or competition for their jobs. The sad part is that almost any change will be viewed in negative light by some or all the organization. As someone who has introduced a fair amount of change at the organizations I have worked at, I can truthfully say that there is always a group of people who will find the negative in the planned change no matter how positive the outcome of the change.

In the examples above, how will you counter these concerns? For example, with the digital workflow that reduces manual work, what can you do with the recovered time? For instance, if the process you digitized used to take minutes and now takes less than 30 seconds, what can your employees or your teams do with the extra time? Could the time be used to increase engagement with the customers? Are there things that would be nice to do but you never had the manpower do to them? If you are going to add resources for your new process, how will you introduce this group into the culture? It's one thing to hire a new employee now and then, but it's a different game when you bring in 10 or more people at once.

Does your new idea or process run counter to the culture of your organization? If your organization is not a heavy sales organization and you are introducing a process where employees are expected to sell a product or upsell items, you may be in for a big surprise. If the culture of the organization will not support the idea, you will encounter strong headwinds. It's not impossible to introduce an idea that is counter to your culture; however, you must approach it in a much different way to accomplish your goals. One approach is to introduce the idea to influencers first.

Understanding who the influencers are in your organization or department will save you a lot of time when implementing a change. Instead of teaching the entire staff or department, start by chatting with your influencers, get their feedback, and determine their concerns. Getting them on board will go a long way to the success of your strategy.

## People Strategy

If there is one thing I have learned, its never to go into battle alone. If you are planning a new digital process or any kind of change, it's important to socialize the idea in smaller circles to get feedback. Rather than be blindsided by staff, its far better to get feedback from smaller groups and identify supporters along the way. The feedback allows you to develop counters to the issues that will be raised, and the supporters will be first adopters who can assure the rest of the group that the change isn't a bad thing.

The second question you need to answer is the WHO. Who are the people that you will need to accomplish your goal? On the website you will find a strategy startup guide that you can download and print.

It would be a good idea to download this guide and start filling in the answers to the questions. Please be specific with the who, if you can. If you write down "information technology," please specifically say who it is in IT that you will need to accomplish your goal.

Now that you have the who, it's time to determine the length of time it will take to accomplish the goal. One issue with determining the time frame is that you often don't control the resources that you will need to accomplish the goal. Don't worry about this for now; pretend you have unlimited resources, funds, and time to do it perfectly and outline what you need to get the job done.

## Process Changes

If your new idea is going to change processes that are outside of your control, then you must deal with this directly. I have a good story about this. One day I was working with one of my team members on a very early version of home banking. We were in the middle of implementing check images. Up until then, if you were reviewing your history online and you saw a check, you could only see the amount and check number. With the new technology, were able to allow the customer to click on a link and see the back and the front of the check, which included the memo field and the payee field. Being the nerds that we are, we thought this was the coolest thing ever (remember, this was in the late 1990s). The employee I was working with was also an expert in the platform that our teller and call center staff used to support customers when they call in. Together, we hatched an idea to make it so that the tellers could click on a link and see the check images as well. The employee I was working with went back to his office, and a hour or later came back to my office and showed me he had implemented this. We both thought it was pretty cool and thought nothing more of it. At the time, the organization had just installed a Citrix environment that allowed for all of the desktops in the organization to be virtualized. Little did I know that when the employee modified the software to pull the check images, he modified the main image that all of the tellers and customer service representatives used in the organization so other employees could see it as well. The employees came in the next morning to find that they could access checks from within their terminals (these were green screen terminals, so it was a pretty cool trick for back then). They noticed the link and clicked on it. This would've been fine, but the organization was being charged per check pull. Needless to say, it didn't take long for accounting to find me and ask why the check image cost was so high. In fact, the number was very high to my way of thinking. Since I had never informed anyone else in the organization that we had rolled this out, I had also upset many of the managers who were blindsided by questions from the staff about it. They asked me to turn it off, but I couldn't let go of why the number was so high. I could see people just playing around, but that should fade over time. I was concerned that maybe I had introduced a security issue. So I went to a branch that was nearby my house and visited the teller line, as this branch seemed to be among the biggest offenders. I asked if they had seen the feature and what they thought. I was blown away by their response. They said, "We love this feature! Instead of going and manually pulling a signature card when a customer wants to do a large transaction, we can just click and compare their signature to a few checks. It saves us tons of time." So this story had a happy ending, but had I followed a better process to inform the staff and socialize the idea, I could've avoided the animosity and trouble that I caused for other managers.

The important concept here is to try to account for the unintended consequences of a process change. In today's hyper-connected digital world, most processes will have unintended consequences. To the extent that you can identify them either by thinking them through, socializing the idea, or researching at other organizations, the collateral effects can often be avoided.

## Technology

Here are a few rules of thumb that I use for technology strategies.

Is the technology you are upgrading to or implementing at least 50 percent better than what you have today? As I mentioned in earlier chapters, most banking technology is 85 percent the same and 15 percent different. The key here is to make sure that the effort it will take to change or implement the platform is worth it. I have seen many organizations bounce back and forth between credit card platforms, lending origination, and servicing platforms, expecting dramatic change, only to find out that the platform isn't that much better than the platform that they replaced, and they find themselves years behind in their project plans due to the implementation of the new platform.

It's important to consider the amount of effort that it will take to implement whatever you are planning and weigh that against the benefit of the new software. I find that in most cases, rather than replacing a platform, it would be better to work with consultants or that company's professional services to extend the platform to accommodate feature gaps. While this approach cannot go on forever, it is useful to keep a platform in play until there is a transformation that makes it worth the work to do the conversion.

The digital governance group should also be engaged before starting the project. This group can make sure that your project is in alignment with the technology standards of the organization. They can also review your project schedule to make sure there are no collisions with major organizational technology plans. For example, if your project is a new lending process and the technology group is planning on upgrading the lending platform, then you may want to wait to start your project so that it doesn't interfere with the upgrade, or perhaps there is overlap with the new features the upgrade will provide and your project. The technology group will help you to identify these issues and align your project with their plans.

If your project requires additional technology resources to complete, then the digital governance group will help you understand the technology impact of your project. A good example of this would be if your chosen product provider only supports a Linux operating system and your organization is primarily a Windows organization. Then the digital governance committee might inform you that it does not have the expertise in house to support a Linux platform and will ask you to include the cost for a new FTE to support the platform. Another example is if your product is only supported in an SaaS model, and your organization has never implemented an SaaS product. The digital governance group will need to review or change its policy on delivery via SaaS platforms.

What are the data analytics implications of your project? Will your project provide new metrics or data that could be valuable in other parts of your organization? For example, if you are implementing an enterprisewide calendar system that allows customers to schedule appointments with your financial specialists from their cell phone, what kind of data can you collect from this new system, and how can it be used to benefit the organization? This is the purpose of engaging the data governance group before you start the project. This way, team members have a chance to identify any data that would be valuable to the organization and work with your technology provider to collect and store the data for future use.

## Security

This is most tricky part of the strategy section, because it involves being ready to abandon an idea if necessary. When working on a new idea or process, it is important to engage security with an open mind. Security personnel can make or break you. Security can either decide your idea is too risky and kill it or decide to help you. It most cases, your approach to the project will be the factor that determines how the security team or person will respond. Here are a couple of key items to consider when approaching security.

It is also recommended to perform your own risk assessment before you bring the project to security. Using the project risk assessment forms on the website, you can identify many of the business risks and security risks for the project before you approach the security group. This process also allows you to have some ideas for remediation of immediate issues before you approach security.

Try to get Security's blessing early in the project timeline, rather than waiting until the end. Security may have ideas to help with your project, but it may take time or resources on their side to help you get to the finish line. The sooner you get them involved, the more time they will have to implement changes, make purchases, or finish a task or project that may help your project. On the other hand, if there is a security problem or risk with your project that makes it either cost prohibitive or not feasible, it is better to know early on before you spend a lot of the rest of the staff's time.

It is also important to look at other similar-sized organizations that provide a similar feature. Often times, if you can point the security team at successful implementation of a product or process at another organization, they can work out how they did it and gain some perspective on your ideas.

Don't be afraid to do your own security research, if you know there is a questionable aspect of your idea. You can use this amazing website I discovered called "Google" to research the security concerns and come to the table with some concepts or solutions that others have used in the past. It's important to recognize that you are not a security professional and perhaps the solutions you are looking at are not feasible for your organization. However, most security professionals will respect your effort and appreciate the time you have put in to trying to help them along in the process. Security research is always valuable—even if it is off base it may help you to spawn new ideas or new ways of thinking about a problem.

The most important question you can ask yourself is, "How does my idea or goal fit into the overall organizational strategy?" If you are a CEO reading this book, chances are you get to set this strategy with your executive team and board and you are living out the strategy each day, but if you are part of the executive team, or middle management, then it's your job to identify every opportunity to support the strategy. It's important to recognize in your everyday work if your actions are in support of the organizations strategy, particularly in the digital space. If you find yourself reworking a process that you know ultimately will need to be digitized in the future, are you really supporting your organization's digital strategy or are you prolonging the inevitable? For each manager, implementing strategy will depend on the ability to balance the strengths of the manager's part of the organization against its weaknesses. Leaders who work hard to understand their organization's strategy will find that they can easily identify which projects they need to do and, more importantly, the projects they should not do. Strategy is the measuring stick we use to define what is in the scope and what isn't.

The goal is to achieve strategic clarity in your organization. If any member of your organization can clearly communicate the strategy of your company when called upon, and more importantly, can explain how they are personally executing on the strategy, no matter their position in the company, then congratulations! You have achieved a Zen-like clarity, and you should be proud. However if members of your organization complain that there is a lack of communication, or they feel like there are too many priorities, then it is likely that your message got lost along the way. Organizations that are caught in strategic paralysis often have a great business strategy on paper. But if the organization lacks the ability to communicate the strategy beyond the boardroom, and lacks the technology to continuously provide easy-to-understand updates on the key performance indicators to everyone in the organization, then they will find that their employees are often frustrated and confused as it relates to how they can participate in the company strategy.

Finally, what happens if you follow all the rules, you do everything that this books says to do, and you fail? Have you planned for failure? The first thing to do is to redefine failure—the word itself is misleading—did you really fail, or did you miss a goal? I like to reframe failure into two categories. The first category is *setbacks*. A setback means that you have encountered a problem that has forced you to rethink a portion of the project, or it has caused someone to start over in an area. Setbacks should be expected in any project. The good news about a setback is that you can recover from it.

The second category is *learning opportunities*. This is for a pure failure of a project—whatever you tried to do, it flat-out failed. These should be considered learning opportunities. Learning opportunities can be planned for ahead of time as well. Make sure that you identify the learning opportunities for each project you take on before you start the project. This is helpful to do beforehand because you can also include tasks such as documenting certain aspects of the project in detail in support of the learning objectives. This way, if the project should fail or be a setback, the learning opportunities that were identified as part of the project charter can be looked upon as a valuable asset of the project, as opposed to throwaway data.

When it all comes together, a goal that is executed within this framework can be extremely satisfying. Goals that are aligned with the strategy of the organization are important indicators to management that their strategy is being understood and executed on by the entire staff.

**Good luck on your digital transformation.**

# About the Companion Website

This book includes a companion website, which can be found at www.wiley.com/go/digitalgridlock. Enter the password: best876. This website includes the following documents:

Chapter 1:     Product Risk Review
Chapter 5:     API readiness report
Chapter 8:     Scenario worksheets
               DDoS worksheet
Chapter 10:    Job Description templates: CDO/CAO
Chapter 14:    Services catalog
Conclusion:    Strategy worksheet

# Index